THE DUKE OF EDINBURGH
AND
H THE DUKE OF CONNAUGHT
Birmingham.
AND
178, NEW BOND STREET
London.

Webley Solid Frame Cartridge Revolvers

RICs, MPs, and No. 5s

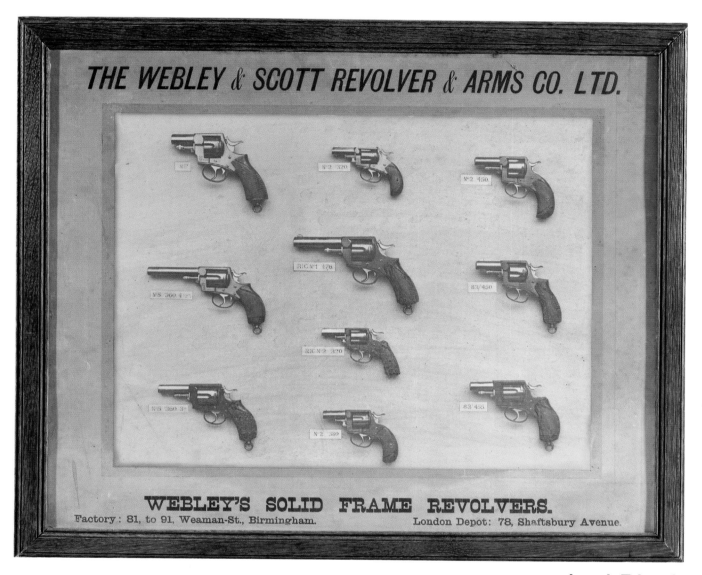

THE WEBLEY & SCOTT REVOLVER & ARMS CO. LTD.

WEBLEY'S SOLID FRAME REVOLVERS.

Factory: 81, to 91, Weaman-St., Birmingham.   London Depot: 78, Shaftsbury Avenue.

Joel Black

Joseph L. Davis

Roger G. Michaud

Schiffer Publishing Ltd

4880 Lower Valley Road, Atglen PA 19310

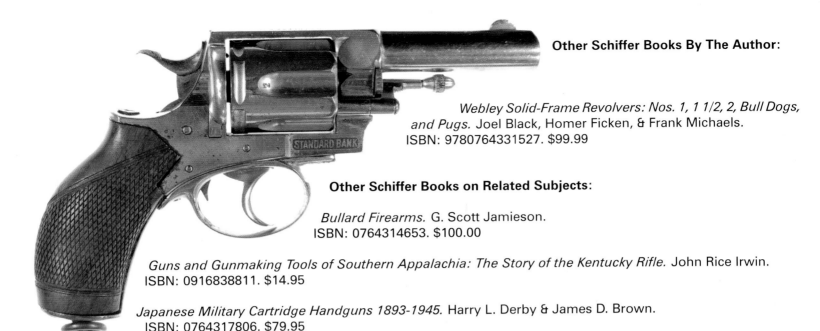

Title page: An 1897 Webley advertisement.
Used with permission of Hemann Historica Munich.
http://www.hermann-historica-ohg.de/gb/index.htm

Copyright © 2010 by
Joel Black, Joseph L. Davis, & Roger G. Michaud

Library of Congress Control Number: 2010933826

Designed by Stephanie Daugherty

Type set in Bernhard Modern BT/Zurich BT

ISBN: 978-0-7643-3553-2
Printed in China

Contents

Introduction

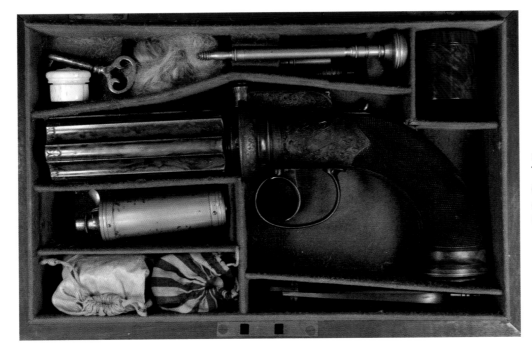

The "WD" mark on the rammer/mold encased with the beautiful Henry Tatham pepperbox pictured below is emblematic of the humble beginnings of what would become P. WEBLEY & SON.

John Gailey collection

In 1838 Phillip Webley married Caroline Davis, who, along with her mother Sarah, had been struggling to continue the business of her late father and well known Birmingham mould maker William Davis (WD). Phillip and Caroline eventually changed the name of the business to P. WEBLEY & SON. When Phillip's brother James Webley died in 1856, his business was incorporated into P. WEBLEY & SON. Like Samuel Colt and Oliver Winchester, Webley excelled at self-aggrandizement and hyperbole rather than firearm patent designs. The "WEBLEY'S PATENT" stamp applied during their early efforts was based on unimportant improvements to common Birmingham trade guns.

Webley Bentley. *Courtesy of Horst Held. http://www.horstheld.com/default.htm*

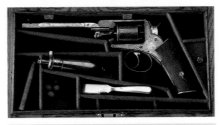

Webley Wedge

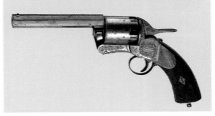

Webley Longspur. *Courtesy of http://www.hermann-historica-ohg.de/gb/index.htm*

Pre-RIC

This "category" of Webley has caused much confusion around naming the early solid frame models. The simple truth is despite the shameless puffery at which the Webley Company was master, until the sale of 1000 revolvers to the Royal Irish Constabulary in 1868 (see Appendix I), Webley was just another small shop in what was known as the "Birmingham Trade." So called "makers" would start out with a small number of malleable castings purchased from a foundry. Barrow boys were dispatched to a myriad of small shops in the Birmingham gun quarter to buy the requisite parts to produce a revolver. The shape of the frame of each week's output was determined by which foundry happened to have the best price at the time. The result is that these early Webley revolvers are found in many frame styles. Thus begins the problem of nomenclature. Webley, like Mauser, wanted to appear to be making a great number of firearms. To accomplish this, serial numbers with 5 or 6 digits would sometimes be affixed to revolvers that should not have needed more than 3 or 4. A worse problem occurred after their sale to the Royal Irish Constabulary. This bit of serendipity propelled Webley from the rank of a small shop to a lofty manufacturing company. The following 1874 newspaper description of Webley's revolver division wondrously describes the use of a milling machine combined with locating holes on the frames. At the time, Webley's Weaman Street factory was state of the art. Yet, modern eyes would consider it a mid-sized, out of date machine shop. In any case, the adoption of this specific frame style with lock and ejector fixed the look of .442 and larger Webley solid frame revolvers for the run of the contract and even longer. The problem for collectors is that this did nothing to establish a standard frame for either the .380 or .320 revolvers. These continued to be produced in both variety and quantity for a number of years before a final decision was made.

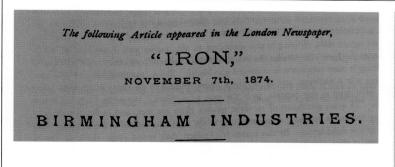

The following Article appeared in the London Newspaper,

"IRON,"

NOVEMBER 7th, 1874.

BIRMINGHAM INDUSTRIES.

This article appears in a Cornell Publishing reprint of an 1877 Webley catalog. *Used with permission of Abby Mouat: http://cornellpubs.com/index.htm*

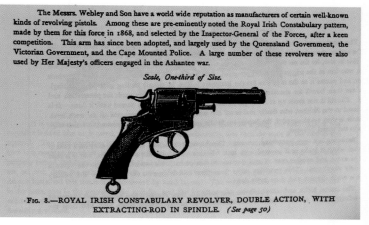

The Messrs. Webley and Son have a world wide reputation as manufacturers of certain well-known kinds of revolving pistols. Among these are pre-eminently noted the Royal Irish Constabulary pattern, made by them for this force in 1868, and selected by the Inspector-General of the Forces, after a keen competition. This arm has since been adopted, and largely used by the Queensland Government, the Victorian Government, and the Cape Mounted Police. A large number of these revolvers were also used by Her Majesty's officers engaged in the Ashantee war.

Scale, One-third of Size.

·FIG. 8.—ROYAL IRISH CONSTABULARY REVOLVER, DOUBLE ACTION, WITH EXTRACTING-ROD IN SPINDLE. *(See page 50)*

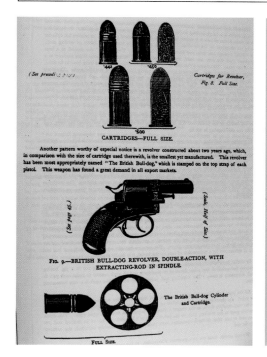

(See preceding page.)

CARTRIDGES—FULL SIZE.

Cartridges for Revolver, Fig. 8. Full Size.

Another pattern worthy of especial notice is a revolver constructed about two years ago, which, in comparison with the size of cartridge used therewith, is the smallest yet manufactured. This revolver has been most appropriately named "The British Bull-dog," which is stamped on the top strap of each pistol. This weapon has found a great demand in all export markets.

(See page 45.)   *(Scale, Half of Size.)*

FIG. 9.—BRITISH BULL-DOG REVOLVER, DOUBLE-ACTION, WITH EXTRACTING-ROD IN SPINDLE.

The British Bull-dog Cylinder and Cartridge.

FULL SIZE.

We will now initiate our readers into the mysteries of revolver making. You first see the pistol body, which is a rough-looking bit of maleable iron of the form and shape required. In the centre of each of these pieces of iron is a square hole, which is, after several processes, to receive the cylinder containing the chambers of the revolver. The first process is to force a long piece of cutting steel, called a "drift," through this hole, and thereby cut it into shape. Two "drifts," the second of a finer cutting power than the first, are used, and the force required to effect this sometimes amounts to a pressure of ten tons. This forms a "standard," to which all the other parts of the work have to be done, and it must be absolutely true. The next operation is a very beautiful bit of machine work. The piece of iron is put in a block the size of the drift-hole, and by moving it backwards and forwards the sides are planed or milled quite true. This machine also cuts out the recess by which the cartridge passes into the chambers. When one side has been milled it is reversed, in order to mill the other side. This beautiful machine is capable of the most delicate working; in proof of which we saw, on a piece of iron, the name of the workman, which he had cut out as an illustration of its power.

The milled body is next placed in a jig, in which all the action-holes are drilled; then the strap is made for the handle of the pistol, and it is next cut along the top of the strap and round the body, and the slot for the shield-spring is cut in.

In making the cylinder, a round bar of steel is cut into the required length, and a hole then drilled through the centre. This centre is the standard from which the rest of the work is done. The cylinder is next turned quite smooth, and to its exact guage. It is then placed in a chock, and the chambers are drilled. In the chuck are the divisions giving the number of chambers to be drilled in each cylinder, and as each chamber is made, the chuck and cylinder are turned to the next division, and is again drilled, and so on, until all are completed. The ease with which this drilling machine works is manifest from the fact that a six-chambered cylinder can be drilled in from five to seven minutes. The bolt holes are then cut, and then the ratchets, there being as many bolt-holes and ratchets as there are chambers in the cylinder.

This done, we go to barrel-making. A square bar of solid steel of the length of the barrel is placed in a chuck in a lathe, and is slowly drilled through. After drilling about three-eighths of an inch, the drill is drawn out, bringing with it the dirt and refuse. A barrel of four inches and a half in length can be bored in ten minutes. Soapsuds are used in this operation, which are in a bucket suspended over the lathe, and flowing down through a hose, continually runs on the drilling tool, and thus preventing it from getting too hot. When bored, the barrel is cut down for screwing, and the screw cut for jointing to the body. It is then cut into shape. Two nuts are fastened on the screw end, and it is laid in a pair of cutters and by a succession of cuts up the barrel, it is finally shaped.

By similar processes the hammer, sear, and trigger are made. Each being put in a jig, having the necessary holes drilled, the sides flattened or machined, and all work needful to make each part fit and work accurately is done. The rounding and pointing the nose of the cock is a very interesting operation.

All the parts being thus prepared, they are put together by the action-maker, and afterwards sent for proof. On returning, the pistol is taken to pieces, smoothed up, and sighted. These operations have to be very carefully done, as the utmost accuracy is required in making a good sight. This done, the revolver goes to the stocker, then to the polisher; after it is polished it has to be cleaned and put together, and at last, after all these operations have been skillfully and carefully executed, the revolver is ready for use.

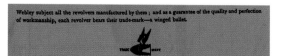

Webley subject all the revolvers manufactured by them; and as a guarantee of the quality and perfection of workmanship, each revolver bears their trade-mark—a winged bullet.

In some ways this circa 1870 prototype revolver in .442 with a swing out extracting mechanism is of no importance because it was never put into production. Being fully functional, it is hard to understand why the world had to wait eighteen years later for Colt and S&W to fashion a similar arm. It is suspected that the unresolved problem was a tendency for the rim of original Boxer cartridge cases to tear off, making simultaneous extraction impractical. What is important is this presents a roadmap of steps taken to make the Webley solid frame revolver. The encircled teat at the grip bottom is an artifact of the casting process used to form the rough frame. The holes have been drilled for all the screws, but those still stand proud of the frame. At the front of the barrel, the outside bevel has been cut, but the vestigial rib has not yet been filed away. The surface has been roughly milled flat. Neither the concave depression that allows a cartridge to be loaded into the cylinder nor the cut for a loading gate has yet been machined.

Nick Preston collection.

The file marks on the front of the crane are still very visible.

Despite its unfinished state, the revolver is fully functional. In addition, the barrel had been bored, but not rifled.

Webley Pre-RIC Dual Cylinder (Percussion/Cartridge Conversion)
SN 2521   .450CF, 6″ octagonal barrel, 6 shot, blued, one-piece checkered wood grip, the extra cylinder for cartridges is smooth and has front locking recesses, ball rammer on left side, and ejector on right side.
Retailer: P. WEBLEY & SON S^T. JAMES'S LONDON (engraved)

Note that the hammer is the standard, conical shaped rather than the flat sided shape normally found on conversion models. This is a very late example. *Joseph L. Davis collection*

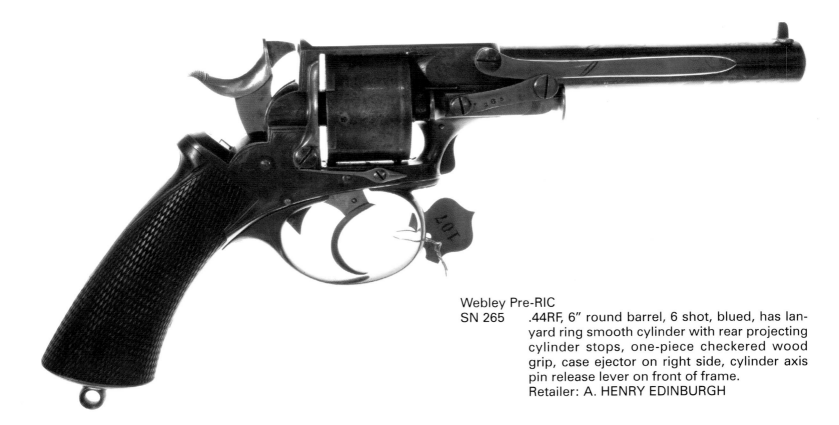

Webley Pre-RIC
SN 265   .44RF, 6" round barrel, 6 shot, blued, has lanyard ring smooth cylinder with rear projecting
cylinder stops, one-piece checkered wood
grip, case ejector on right side, cylinder axis
pin release lever on front of frame.
Retailer: A. HENRY EDINBURGH

*Frank & Jean Pycha
collection. (former W.C.
Dowell collection).*

8

Webley Pre-RIC
SN 1   .577 Boxer, 4" octagonal barrel, 6 shot, one-piece checkered wood grip, cylinder with flush rear face and recessed chambers, rear mounted cylinder friction spring is absent, Tranter sear on trigger, locking notches on Tranter/Braendlin patented cylinder backplate, push button cylinder pin retainer on left front of frame lacks a lanyard ring, loading gate, and ejector rod.
Retailer: P. WEBLEY & SON ST. JAMES'S LONDON

Courtesy of Robert J. Maze.

Courtesy of Ken Hallock.

This early revolver was assembled on a huge Webley frame with the backplate, cylinder, and lockwork all supplied by Tranter.

Webley Pre-RIC
NVSN   .44RF, 6 1/4" octagonal barrel, blue, 6 shot, smooth cylinder with front locking recesses, plunger ejector rod on right, checkered wood grip with diamond shaped escutcheons, push in curved spring holds cylinder axis pin in place, loading gate swings to rear from the bottom, lanyard loop on grip cap, "Longspur" style hammer. "WEBLEY'S PATENT" on top strap, no retailer name on gun

Roger Michaud collection

Webley Pre-RIC
NVSN .320RF, 4 1/2" barrel, 6 shot, blued smooth cylinder with rear locking projections, rearward opening loading gate, commercial London proofs ejector rod with flat faced head, cased with A.J. Cowan (in ink) and Church Lane (in pencil) marked on inner label.
RETAILER: J.BRADDELL & SON CASTLE PLACE, BELFAST

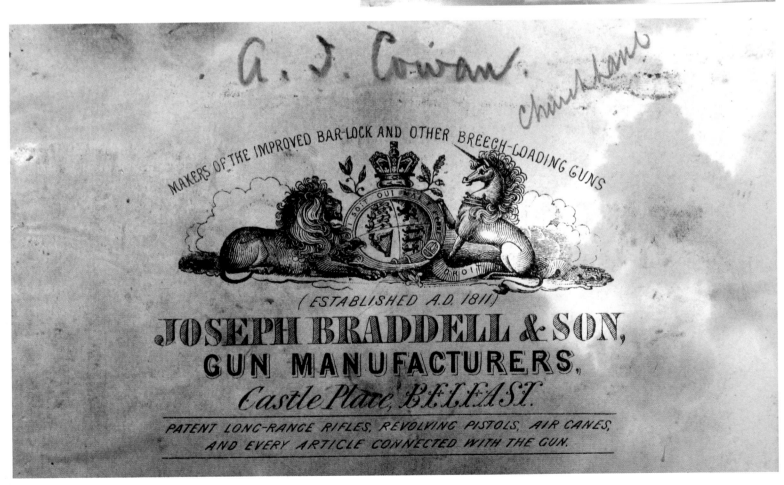

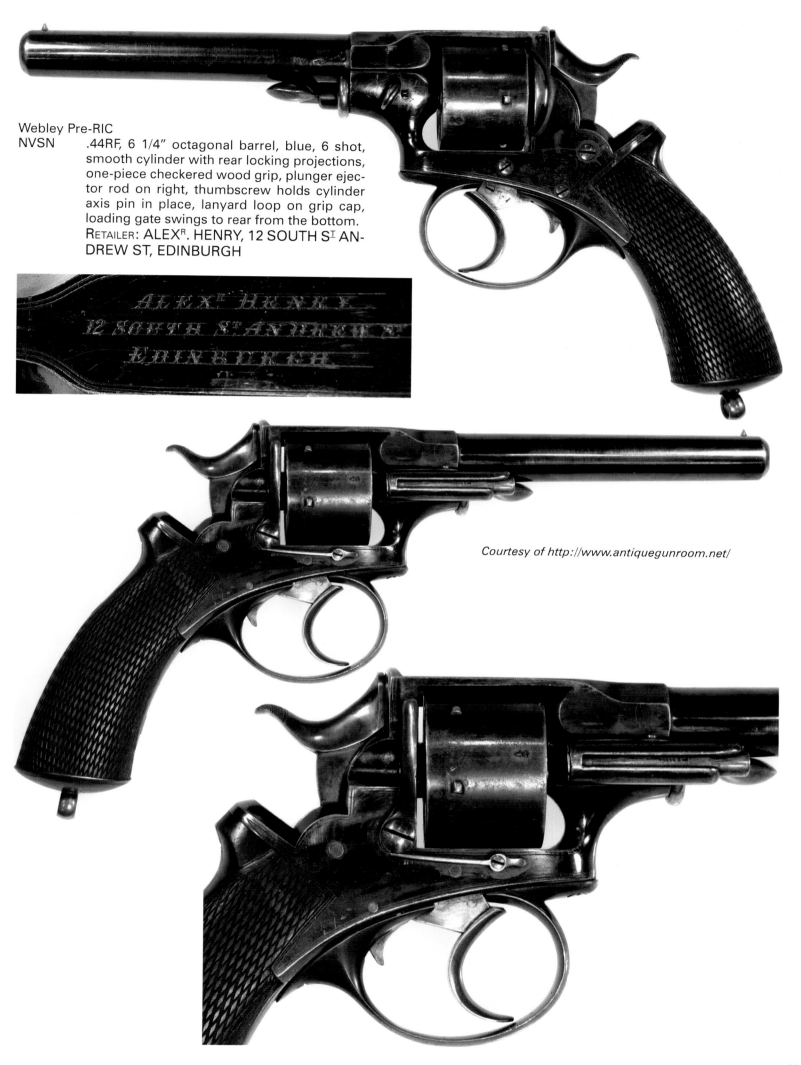

Webley Pre-RIC

NVSN .44RF, 6 1/4" octagonal barrel, blue, 6 shot, smooth cylinder with rear locking projections, one-piece checkered wood grip, plunger ejector rod on right, thumbscrew holds cylinder axis pin in place, lanyard loop on grip cap, loading gate swings to rear from the bottom. RETAILER: ALEX^R. HENRY, 12 SOUTH S^T ANDREW ST, EDINBURGH

Courtesy of http://www.antiquegunroom.net/

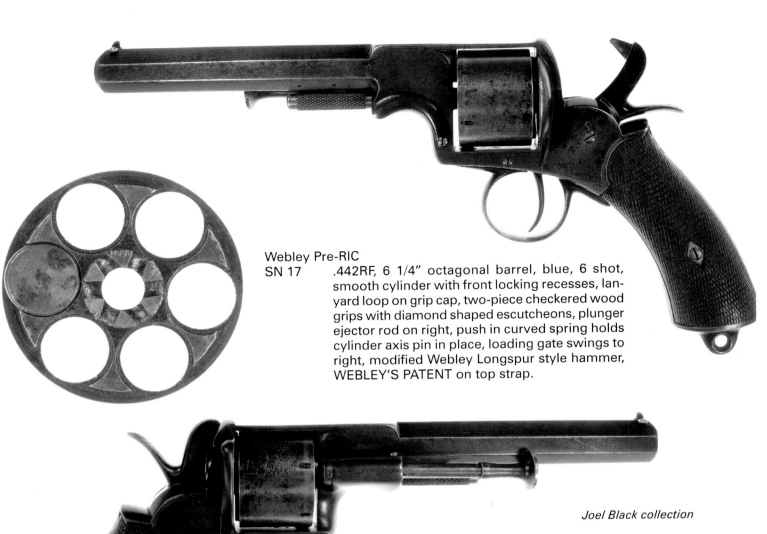

Webley Pre-RIC
SN 17   .442RF, 6 1/4" octagonal barrel, blue, 6 shot, smooth cylinder with front locking recesses, lanyard loop on grip cap, two-piece checkered wood grips with diamond shaped escutcheons, plunger ejector rod on right, push in curved spring holds cylinder axis pin in place, loading gate swings to right, modified Webley Longspur style hammer, WEBLEY'S PATENT on top strap.

Joel Black collection

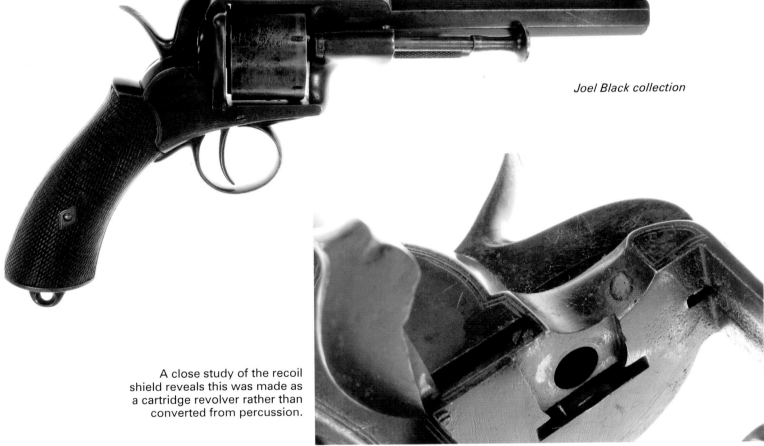

A close study of the recoil shield reveals this was made as a cartridge revolver rather than converted from percussion.

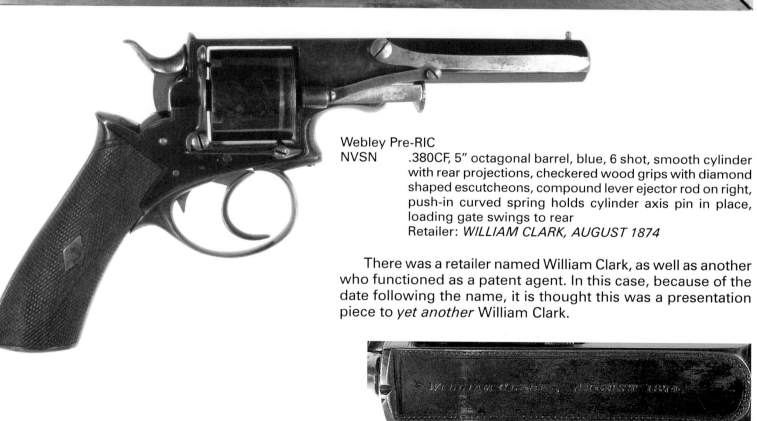

Webley Pre-RIC
NVSN   .380CF, 5" octagonal barrel, blue, 6 shot, smooth cylinder
          with rear projections, checkered wood grips with diamond
          shaped escutcheons, compound lever ejector rod on right,
          push-in curved spring holds cylinder axis pin in place,
          loading gate swings to rear
          Retailer: *WILLIAM CLARK, AUGUST 1874*

There was a retailer named William Clark, as well as another
who functioned as a patent agent. In this case, because of the
date following the name, it is thought this was a presentation
piece to *yet another* William Clark.

Greg Reddick collection

13

Webley Pre-RIC
SN 293   .442, 4 1/4" round barrel, 6 shot, smooth cylinder with rear projecting ratchet stops, friction brake mark around front circumference of cylinder, checkered wood grip with diamond shaped escutcheons, cylinder axis pin release lever on front of frame, ejector lever on right side of barrel, WEBLEY'S PATENT oval on left, rear opening loading gate, frame rounded at front.
Retailer: GEORGE GIBBS BRISTOL

Frank & Jean Pycha collection

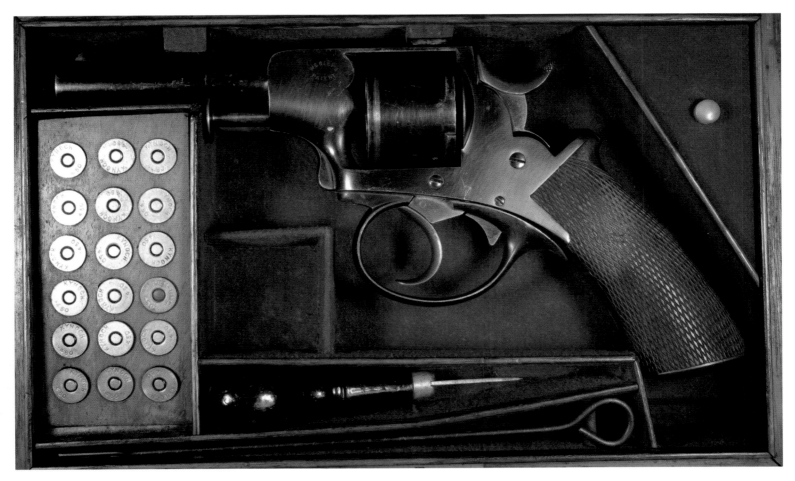

Webley Pre-RIC
SN 636 .442, 5" octagonal barrel, blue, 6 shot, smooth cylinder with rear projections, one-piece checkered wood grip with diamond shaped escutcheons, spring on left to set hammer at half cock, ejector rod in stock, thumb screw holds cylinder axis pin in place, loading gate swings to rear, W&S logo on both sides.
Retailer: J. BLANCH & SON. LONDON

Joseph L. Davis collection

The designation of this revolver as a Pre-RIC might cause confusion among readers who observed what appears to be this same frame in *Webley Solid Frame Revolvers, Nos. 1, 1 1/2, 2, Bull Dogs and Pugs* (Schiffer Books 2008 http://www.schifferbooks.com/). In that book, this style was designated as a Pre-No. 1 angular frame. That frame, while appearing the same as SN 636, was much smaller and evolved into angular frame revolvers marked "Webley No. 1" in .32 and .38 calibers.

While there were both .44 and .45 caliber guns marked "Webley No. 1 1/2," these were only made with a rounded frame. We have observed several large caliber angular frame revolvers, but it seems that Webley never stamped these with a model name.

Webley Pre-RIC
SN 4 .442CF, 5" octagonal barrel, 6 shot, solid frame revolver, barrel and grip are formed as one piece with the frame, checkered wood grip with diamond shaped escutcheons, smooth cylinder with projecting ratchets at rear, spring on left side sets the hammer at half cock, cylinder axis pin is held by thumb-screw on the left side, ejector rod housed in butt, loading gate swings rearward, winged bullet logo on left side of frame.
Retailer: LONDON ARMOURY Co. (JAS. KERR & Cos. SUCCESSORS) 54 KING WILLIAM S^T. LONDON

Roger G. Michaud collection

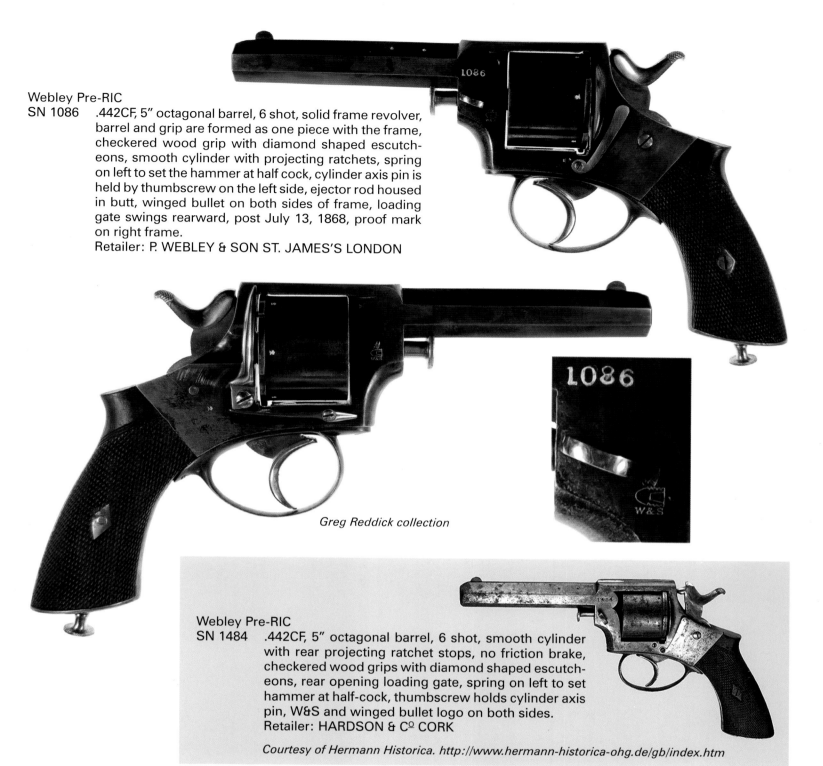

Webley Pre-RIC
SN 1086 .442CF, 5" octagonal barrel, 6 shot, solid frame revolver, barrel and grip are formed as one piece with the frame, checkered wood grip with diamond shaped escutcheons, smooth cylinder with projecting ratchets, spring on left to set the hammer at half cock, cylinder axis pin is held by thumbscrew on the left side, ejector rod housed in butt, winged bullet on both sides of frame, loading gate swings rearward, post July 13, 1868, proof mark on right frame.
Retailer: P. WEBLEY & SON ST. JAMES'S LONDON

Greg Reddick collection

Webley Pre-RIC
SN 1484 .442CF, 5" octagonal barrel, 6 shot, smooth cylinder with rear projecting ratchet stops, no friction brake, checkered wood grips with diamond shaped escutcheons, rear opening loading gate, spring on left to set hammer at half-cock, thumbscrew holds cylinder axis pin, W&S and winged bullet logo on both sides.
Retailer: HARDSON & C° CORK

Courtesy of Hermann Historica. http://www.hermann-historica-ohg.de/gb/index.htm

Webley Pre-RIC
SN 1749 .320, 2 3/4" octagonal barrel, 6 shot, smooth cylinder with rear projecting ratchet stops, no friction brake, checkered wood grips with diamond shaped escutcheons, rear opening loading gate, spring on left to set hammer at half cock, the cylinder axis pin is chipped at bottom, ejector rod in grip bottom, W&S and winged bullet logo on both sides.
Retailer: WILLIAMS & POWELL LIVERPOOL

Roger G. Michaud collection

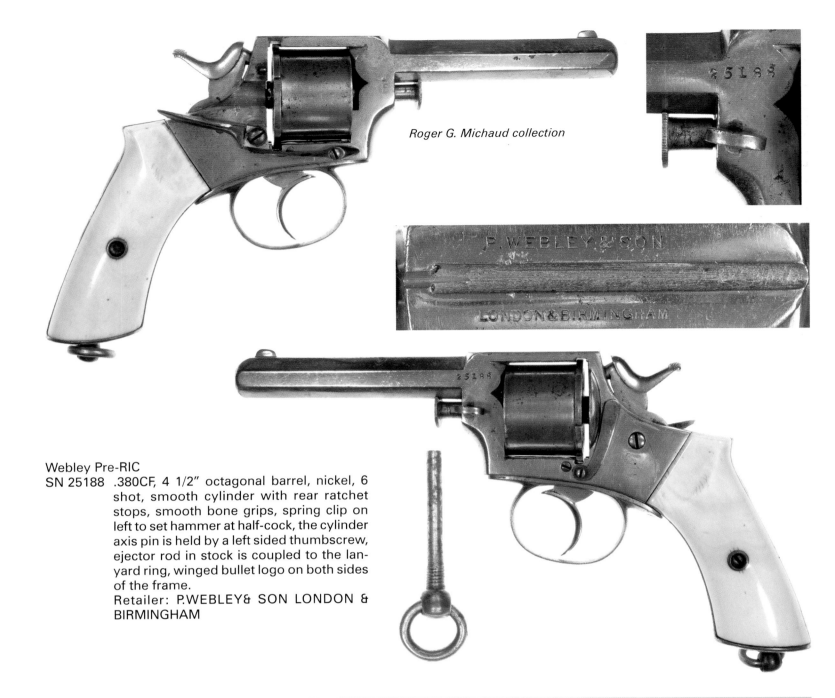

Roger G. Michaud collection

P. WEBLEY & SON

LONDON & BIRMINGHAM

Webley Pre-RIC
SN 25188 .380CF, 4 1/2" octagonal barrel, nickel, 6 shot, smooth cylinder with rear ratchet stops, smooth bone grips, spring clip on left to set hammer at half-cock, the cylinder axis pin is held by a left sided thumbscrew, ejector rod in stock is coupled to the lanyard ring, winged bullet logo on both sides of the frame.
Retailer: P.WEBLEY& SON LONDON & BIRMINGHAM

Webley Pre-RIC
SN 32523 .44RF, 4 1/4" ovate barrel, nickel, 6 shot, smooth cylinder with raised rear ratchet stops, cylinder axis pin is held by a left sided thumbscrew, lanyard ring, in blue baize lined case
Retailer: not marked

At first glance this revolver with its rounded frame appears to be a Pre-1 1/2. The lack of an S shape left sided hammer hold back spring (lack of a hammer block) and the presence of a swivel in place of a screw-in ejector rod in the butt plate precludes this designation.

Joseph L. Davis collection

18

The following illustrates the beginning of Webley's search for an appropriate frame for their solid frame RIC revolvers chambered in .380 and .320.

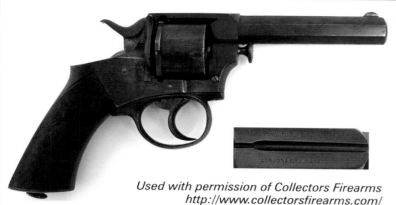

Used with permission of Collectors Firearms
http://www.collectorsfirearms.com/

Webley Pre-RIC
SN 30953   .380CF, 4" octagonal barrel, nickel, 6 shot, checkered wood grip with diamond shaped escutcheons, smooth cylinder with rear ratchet stops, ejector rod in stock, spring clip on left to set hammer at half-cock, the cylinder axis pin is held by thumbscrew, winged bullet logo both sides of frame
RETAILER: P. WEBLEY & SON LONDON & BIRMINGHAM

Roger G. Michaud collection

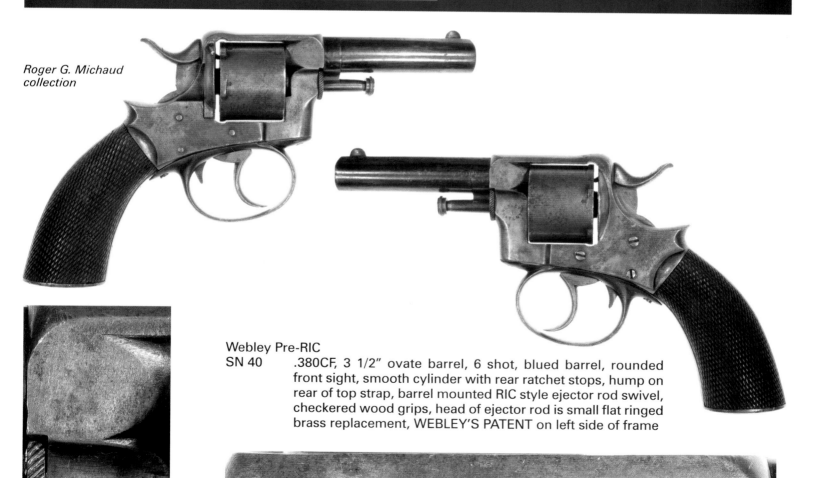

Webley Pre-RIC
SN 40   .380CF, 3 1/2" ovate barrel, 6 shot, blued barrel, rounded front sight, smooth cylinder with rear ratchet stops, hump on rear of top strap, barrel mounted RIC style ejector rod swivel, checkered wood grips, head of ejector rod is small flat ringed brass replacement, WEBLEY'S PATENT on left side of frame

Roger G. Michaud collection

19

Frank & Jean Pycha collection

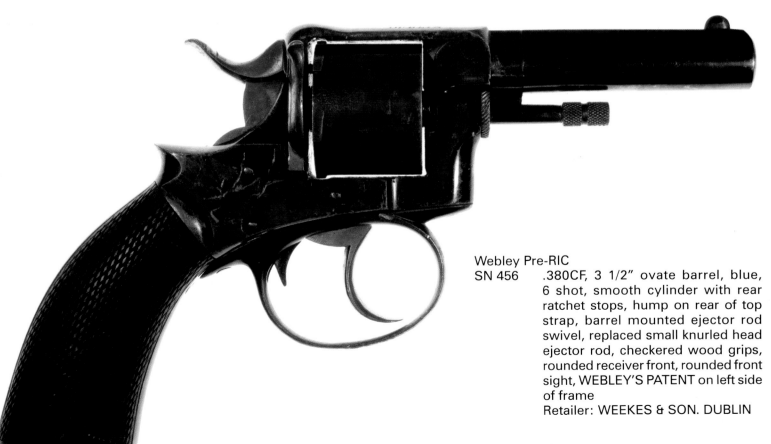

Webley Pre-RIC
SN 456 .380CF, 3 1/2" ovate barrel, blue, 6 shot, smooth cylinder with rear ratchet stops, hump on rear of top strap, barrel mounted ejector rod swivel, replaced small knurled head ejector rod, checkered wood grips, rounded receiver front, rounded front sight, WEBLEY'S PATENT on left side of frame
Retailer: WEEKES & SON. DUBLIN

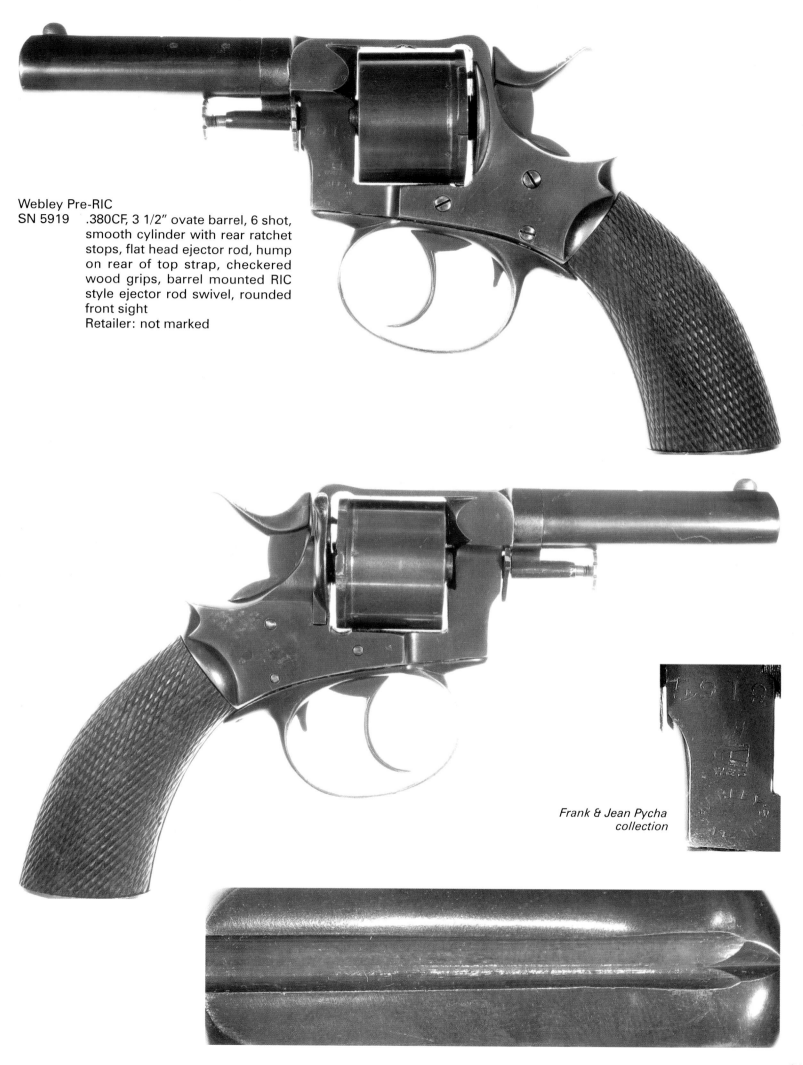

Webley Pre-RIC

SN 5919   .380CF, 3 1/2" ovate barrel, 6 shot, smooth cylinder with rear ratchet stops, flat head ejector rod, hump on rear of top strap, checkered wood grips, barrel mounted RIC style ejector rod swivel, rounded front sight
Retailer: not marked

Frank & Jean Pycha collection

21

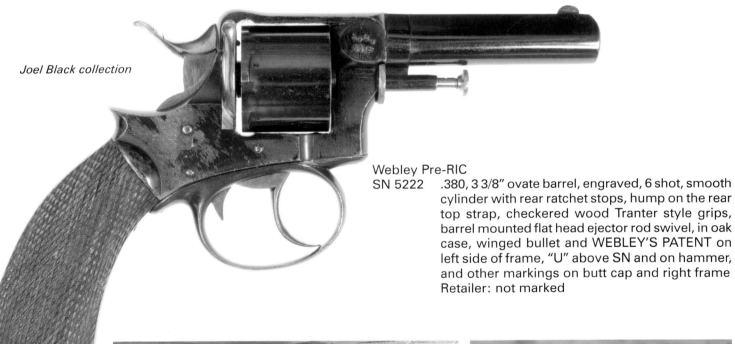

Joel Black collection

Webley Pre-RIC
SN 5222   .380, 3 3/8" ovate barrel, engraved, 6 shot, smooth cylinder with rear ratchet stops, hump on the rear top strap, checkered wood Tranter style grips, barrel mounted flat head ejector rod swivel, in oak case, winged bullet and WEBLEY'S PATENT on left side of frame, "U" above SN and on hammer, and other markings on butt cap and right frame
Retailer: not marked

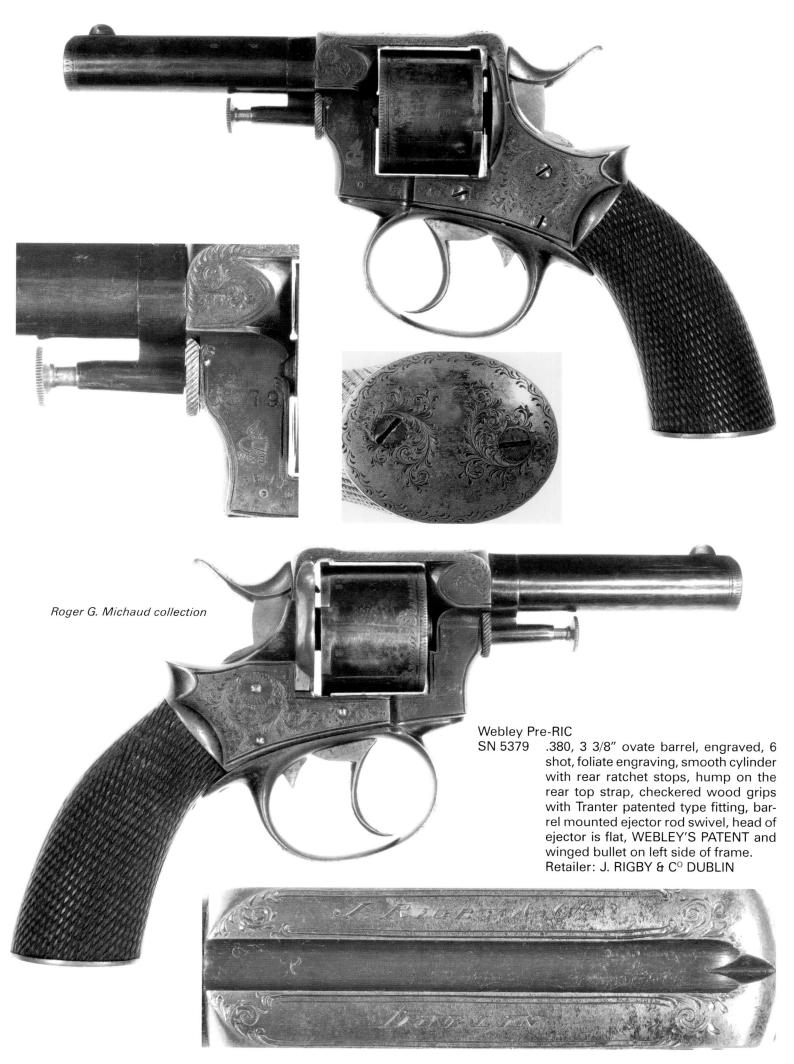

Roger G. Michaud collection

Webley Pre-RIC
SN 5379   .380, 3 3/8" ovate barrel, engraved, 6 shot, foliate engraving, smooth cylinder with rear ratchet stops, hump on the rear top strap, checkered wood grips with Tranter patented type fitting, barrel mounted ejector rod swivel, head of ejector is flat, WEBLEY'S PATENT and winged bullet on left side of frame.
Retailer: J. RIGBY & Cº DUBLIN

RIC NO. 1

As previously mentioned, until the order was received from the Royal Irish Constabulary, Webley was one of many small gun shops within the "Birmingham Trade." The revolver lock style ordered was based on William Tranter's patented lock, whereby a pointed sear entered the top rear of the trigger guard area. Tranter, also in the Birmingham gun trade, apparently licensed this patent to Webley. Tranter then simply moved the sear to the back of the trigger creating a trigger "horn," and used this new patent on his own Model 1868 revolvers. This pointed sear is what collectors use in identifying Webley made revolvers.

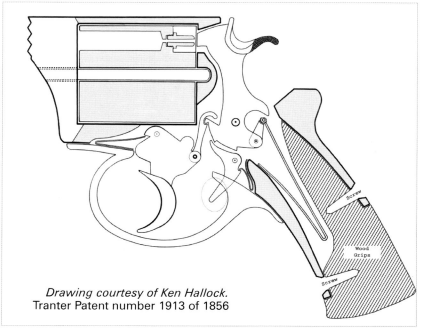

Drawing courtesy of Ken Hallock.
Tranter Patent number 1913 of 1856

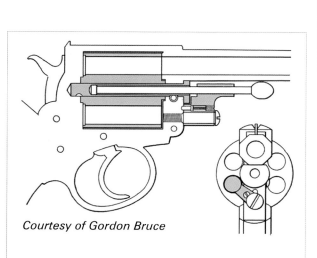

Courtesy of Gordon Bruce

Another prominent feature of the early RICs was an ejector stored in the cylinder axis pin, and rotated from a collar around the barrel. It is not known who patented this design (most likely in Belgium), but it was employed by Webley into the early 1880s. Webley also used Adams' patented ejector (shown below) beginning in 1872.

The Adams patent was in effect an amalgamation of Tranter's ejector swinging from the front of the receiver and the Belgian idea of storing a captive swinging ejector rod.

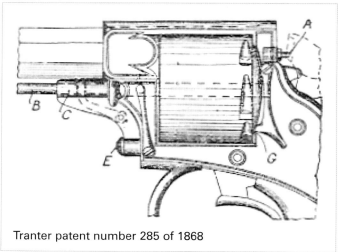

Tranter patent number 285 of 1868

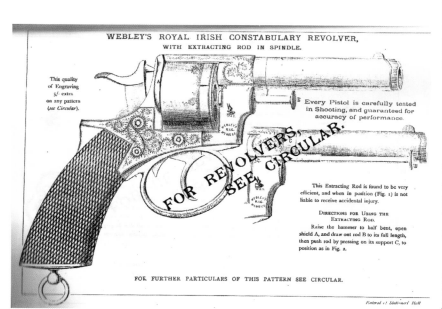

WEBLEY'S ROYAL IRISH CONSTABULARY REVOLVER,
WITH EXTRACTING ROD IN SPINDLE.

This quality of Engraving 5/- extra on any pattern (see Circular).

Every Pistol is carefully tested in Shooting, and guaranteed for accuracy of performance.

This Extracting Rod is found to be very efficient, and when in position (Fig. 1) is not liable to receive accidental injury.

DIRECTIONS FOR USING THE EXTRACTING ROD.

Raise the hammer to half bent, open shield A, and draw out rod B to its full length, then push rod by pressing on its support C, to position as in Fig. 2.

FOR FURTHER PARTICULARS OF THIS PATTERN SEE CIRCULAR.

From all the forgoing information, we conclude that Webley's early success was likely due to using other inventors' good ideas and aggressive marketing rather than their own innovation and design. There was no specific Webley patent used during this time.

Cornell Publishing reprint of an 1877 Webley catalogue. *Used with permission of Abby Mouat http://cornellpubs.com/index.htm*

Nick Preston collection

The lack of a proof mark on either side of the frame dates this and the next revolver as made prior to mid-July 1868.

Webley Pre-RIC No. 1, 1st Pattern
NVSN   .442CF, 5" ovate barrel, 6 shot, checkered 1 piece wood grip, smooth cylinder with rear projecting ratchet stops, has the RIC No. 1 style ejector that swivels from barrel, the frame is quite thin at the back of the top strap (addressed years later when the RIC No. 2 was introduced)
Retailer: not marked

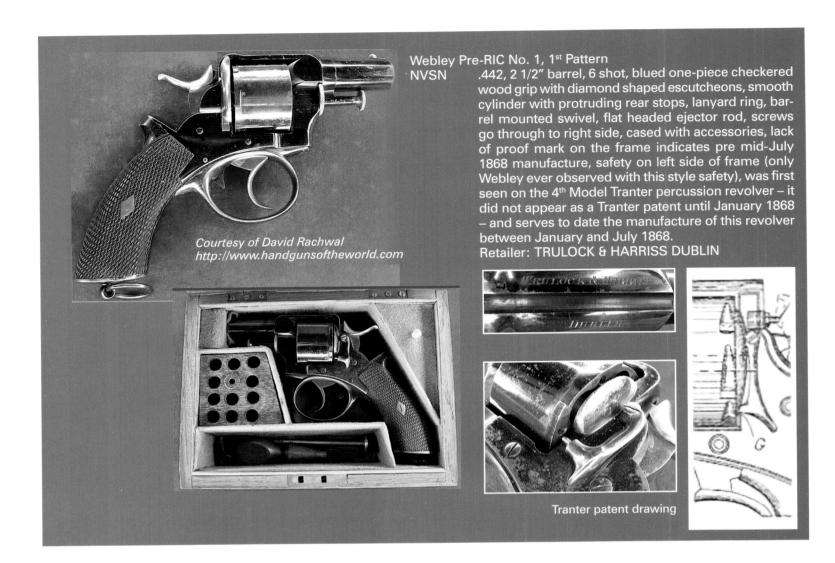

Webley Pre-RIC No. 1, 1st Pattern
NVSN   .442, 2 1/2" barrel, 6 shot, blued one-piece checkered wood grip with diamond shaped escutcheons, smooth cylinder with protruding rear stops, lanyard ring, barrel mounted swivel, flat headed ejector rod, screws go through to right side, cased with accessories, lack of proof mark on the frame indicates pre mid-July 1868 manufacture, safety on left side of frame (only Webley ever observed with this style safety), was first seen on the 4th Model Tranter percussion revolver – it did not appear as a Tranter patent until January 1868 – and serves to date the manufacture of this revolver between January and July 1868.
Retailer: TRULOCK & HARRISS DUBLIN

Courtesy of David Rachwal
http://www.handgunsoftheworld.com

Tranter patent drawing

Webley Pre-RIC No. 1, 1st Pattern
NVSN   .442, 6" barrel, 6 shot, nickel plated, two-piece checkered wood grips with diamond shaped escutcheons, smooth cylinder with protruding rear stops, barrel mounted swivel, flat headed ejector rod, lanyard ring, screws go through to right side, lack of a proof mark on the right side of the frame indicates prior to mid-July 1868 manufacture, 3 screw WEBLEY'S PATENT stamped in oval on left side. [Only 6" barrel observed in this model.]
Retailer: not marked

Courtesy of Cowans http://www.cowanauctions.com/index.asp

Webley Pre-RIC No. 1, 1st Pattern
NVSN   .442, 4 1/2" barrel, blue, 6 shot, two-piece checkered wood grips with diamond shaped escutcheons, smooth cylinder with protruding rear stops, barrel mounted swivel, flat headed ejector rod held in place by lever, swivel eye (type lanyard ring), lack of a proof mark on the frame indicates made prior to mid-July 1868.
Retailer: JNº PHILLIPS & Cº GLASGOW

Courtesy of Hermann Historica.
http://www.hermann-historica-ohg.de/gb/index.htm

Frank & Jean Pycha collection

Webley Pre-RIC No. 1, 1st Pattern
SN 21   .442, 4 1/2" barrel, blue, 6 shot, two-piece checkered wood grips with diamond escutcheons, smooth cylinder with protruding rear stops, barrel mounted swivel, flat headed ejector rod held in place by lever, lack of a proof mark on the frame indicates made prior to mid-July 1868, WEBLEY'S PATENT oval stamp on left side.

Retailer: not marked

Frank & Jean Pycha collection

Webley Pre-RIC No. 1, 1st Pattern

SN 84   .442, 4 1/2" barrel, blue, 6 shot, two-piece checkered wood grips with diamond shaped escutcheons, smooth cylinder with protruding rear stops, swivel eye, barrel mounted swivel, flat headed ejector rod held in place by lever, lack of a proof mark on the frame indicates prior to mid-July 1868 manufacture, Webleys Patent stamped in oval on left side.

Retailer: J. LANG & SONS LONDON

Joseph L. Davis collection

Webley Pre-RIC No. 1, 1ˢᵗ Pattern
SN 89   .442, 4 1/2" barrel, blue, 6 shot, 89 stamped on rear cylinder face, two-piece checkered wood grips with diamond shaped escutcheons, smooth cylinder with protruding rear stops, barrel mounted swivel, flat headed ejector rod held in place by an RIC No. 3 style lever, swivel eye, lack of a proof mark on the frame indicates pre-July 1868 manufacture, faint WEBLEY'S PATENT oval stamp on left side.
Retailer: not marked

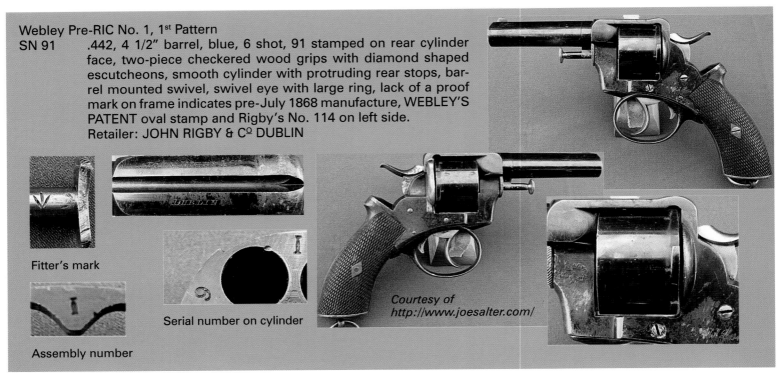

Webley Pre-RIC No. 1, 1st Pattern

SN 91   .442, 4 1/2" barrel, blue, 6 shot, 91 stamped on rear cylinder face, two-piece checkered wood grips with diamond shaped escutcheons, smooth cylinder with protruding rear stops, barrel mounted swivel, swivel eye with large ring, lack of a proof mark on frame indicates pre-July 1868 manufacture, WEBLEY'S PATENT oval stamp and Rigby's No. 114 on left side.
Retailer: JOHN RIGBY & C° DUBLIN

Fitter's mark

Assembly number

Serial number on cylinder

Courtesy of
http://www.joesalter.com/

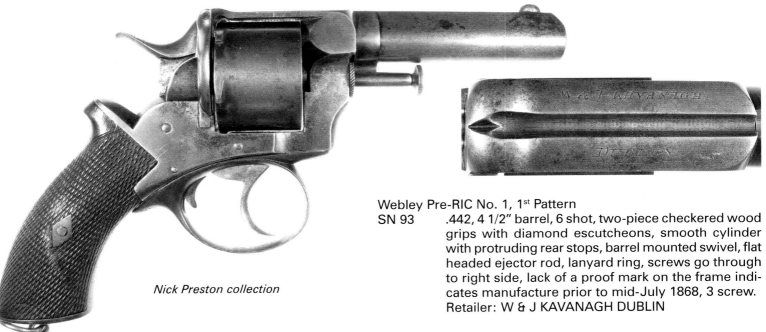

Nick Preston collection

Webley Pre-RIC No. 1, 1st Pattern

SN 93   .442, 4 1/2" barrel, 6 shot, two-piece checkered wood grips with diamond escutcheons, smooth cylinder with protruding rear stops, barrel mounted swivel, flat headed ejector rod, lanyard ring, screws go through to right side, lack of a proof mark on the frame indicates manufacture prior to mid-July 1868, 3 screw.
Retailer: W & J KAVANAGH DUBLIN

Note the flat firing pin. Filing away the bottom would make a rimfire type hammer nose.

What appears to be a broad arrow mark on the cylinder axis pin is believed to be a workman's assembly mark. On other early specimens, we have observed similar marks (such as III or VII) on various small parts or on the back side of the grips.

It is not surprising this early solid frame Webley and serial number 91 were retailed in Ireland. Richard Milner has discovered in a contemporary "Field" magazine that revolvers in the first RIC purchase were obtained from Trulock & Harriss. (Henry Webley had married Julia Harriss, the sister of John Harriss. John was a partner in the firm of Trulock & Harriss. Mr. Harriss was Trulock's son-in-law).

Webley RIC No. 1, 1st Pattern 3 Screw
SN 22 .442CF, 4 1/2" barrel, 6 shot, two-piece checkered wood grips with diamond shaped escutcheons, smooth cylinder with protruding rear stops, barrel mounted swivel, flat headed ejector rod, lanyard ring, raised top strap, WEBLEY'S RIC No. 1 .442 in an oval and winged bullet on left frame, in oak case with accessories (oil bottle, turn screw, cleaning rod).
Retailer: not marked

In our study of RICs, we believe the following photo is definitive proof that this style is the No. 1, 1st pattern. It is marked "WEBLEYS RIC No. 1." The lack of a proof mark on the right frame attests to it being made prior to mid-July 1868. It is a 3 screw model. Furthermore, all known examples of the 4 screw Webley marked "RIC No. 1" have a post mid-July proof on the right frame. Still, it is likely that the No. 1, 1st pattern 4 screw model was the frame style sold to both the RIC and Jersey Police Force (JPF) in 1868.

Joel Black collection

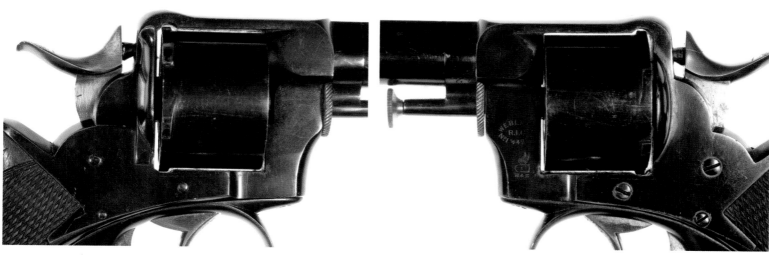

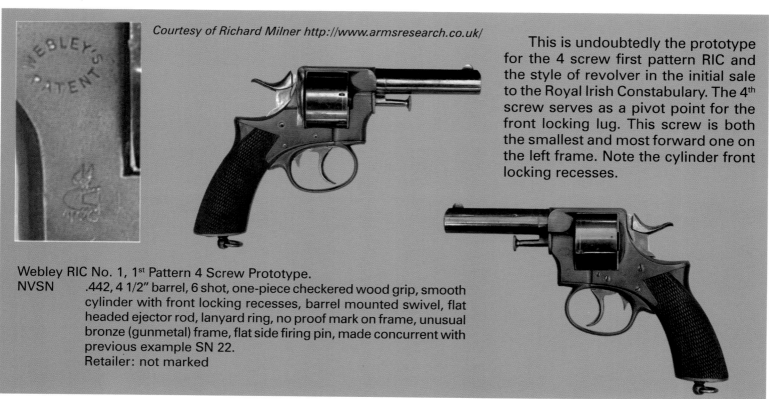

Courtesy of Richard Milner http://www.armsresearch.co.uk/

This is undoubtedly the prototype for the 4 screw first pattern RIC and the style of revolver in the initial sale to the Royal Irish Constabulary. The 4th screw serves as a pivot point for the front locking lug. This screw is both the smallest and most forward one on the left frame. Note the cylinder front locking recesses.

Webley RIC No. 1, 1st Pattern 4 Screw Prototype.
NVSN .442, 4 1/2" barrel, 6 shot, one-piece checkered wood grip, smooth cylinder with front locking recesses, barrel mounted swivel, flat headed ejector rod, lanyard ring, no proof mark on frame, unusual bronze (gunmetal) frame, flat side firing pin, made concurrent with previous example SN 22.
Retailer: not marked

Webley RIC Pre-No. 1, 4 screw Pattern

SN 4   .500CF, 5" round barrel, 6 shot, checkered two piece wood grips with diamond shaped escutcheons, smooth cylinder with forward locking recesses, ejector swivels from barrel, winged bullet and WEBLEY'S PATENT on left side of frame, proof toward rear of right frame.

Retailer: H. ALLPORT & SONS. PATRICK S^T CORK.

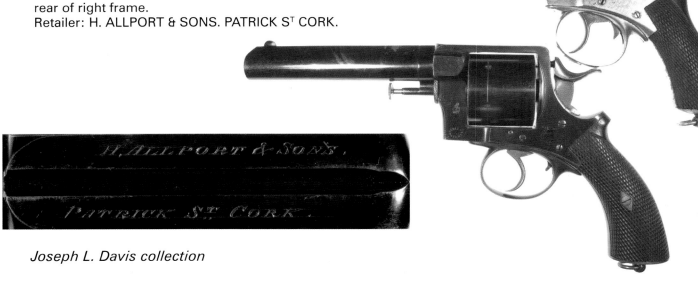

Joseph L. Davis collection

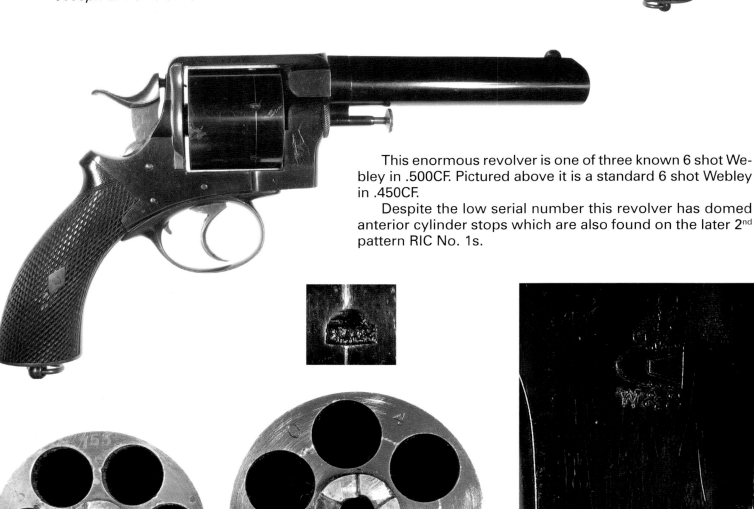

This enormous revolver is one of three known 6 shot Webley in .500CF. Pictured above it is a standard 6 shot Webley in .450CF.

Despite the low serial number this revolver has domed anterior cylinder stops which are also found on the later 2nd pattern RIC No. 1s.

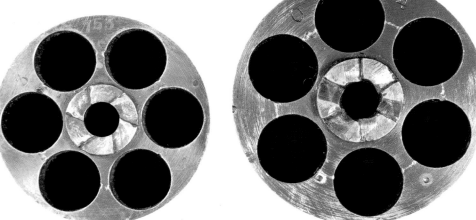

The .500 cylinder is shown to the right of a standard 6 shot .450 Webley cylinder.

Webley RIC Pre-No. 1, 1st Pattern 4 Screw
SN 15 .442CF, 4 1/2" barrel, 6 shot, one-piece checkered wood grip, smooth cylinder with front locking recesses, barrel mounted swivel, flat headed ejector rod, lanyard ring, proof mark on frame, pointed firing pin.
Retailer: FINISHED & ADJUSTED BY
JOSEPH BRADDELL & SON BELFAST

Frank & Jean Pycha collection

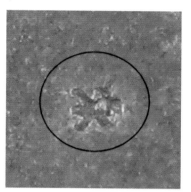

Braddell's serial number is engraved on the bottom of the trigger guard. Webley's number "15" is found on the rear cylinder face. Many early RICs were sold in Ireland due to marketing by Henry Webley's brother-in-law, John Harriss. This is undoubtedly a late 1868 revolver left over from the RIC and "JPF" contracts.

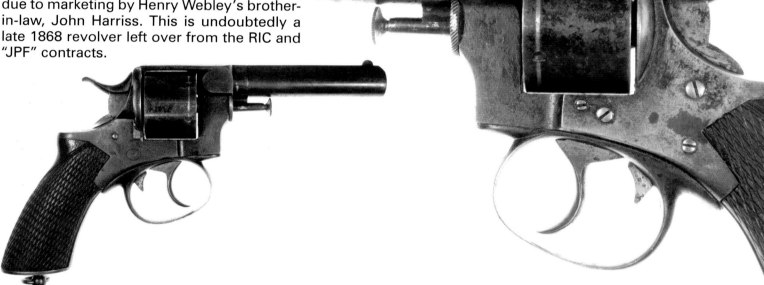

Webley RIC Pre-No. 1, 1st Pattern 4 Screw
SN 1830 .442, 2 1/2" barrel, 6 shot, one-piece checkered wood grip, smooth cylinder with front locking recesses, barrel mounted swivel, flat headed ejector rod, lanyard ring, proof mark on side of frame, no Webley markings.
Retailer: WEEKES & SON.,27, ESSEX QUAY, DUBLIN

Courtesy of Patrick Sutton

This Pre-RIC No. 1, 1st pattern 4 screw has rectangular cylinder stops only found on a few early examples. The D shaped stops are found on the later ones. The frame's proof mark dates this as a post mid-July 1868 made revolver.

Webley RIC Pre-No. 1, 1st Pattern 4 Screw

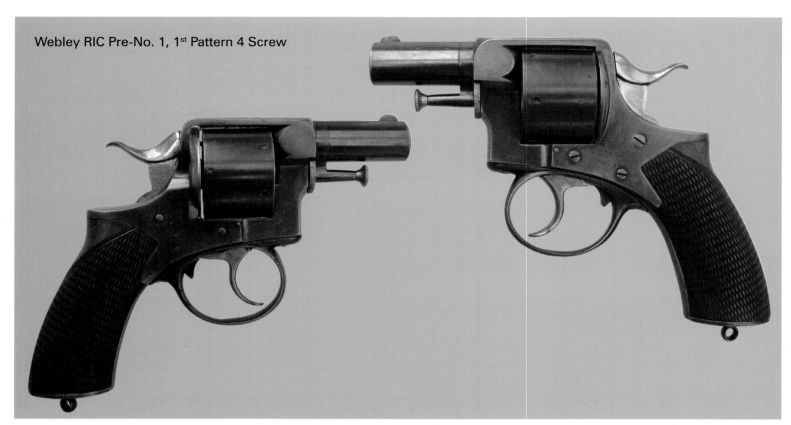

Courtesy of John Gailey

Webley RIC Pre-No. 1, 1st Pattern 4 Screw
SN 5751 .450CF, 4 1/2" barrel, nickel, 6 shot, single smooth ivory grip, smooth cylinder with front locking recesses, barrel mounted swivel, flat headed ejector rod, lanyard ring, foliate engraving, cased.
Retailer: P. WEBLEY & SON. ST JAMES'S. LONDON.

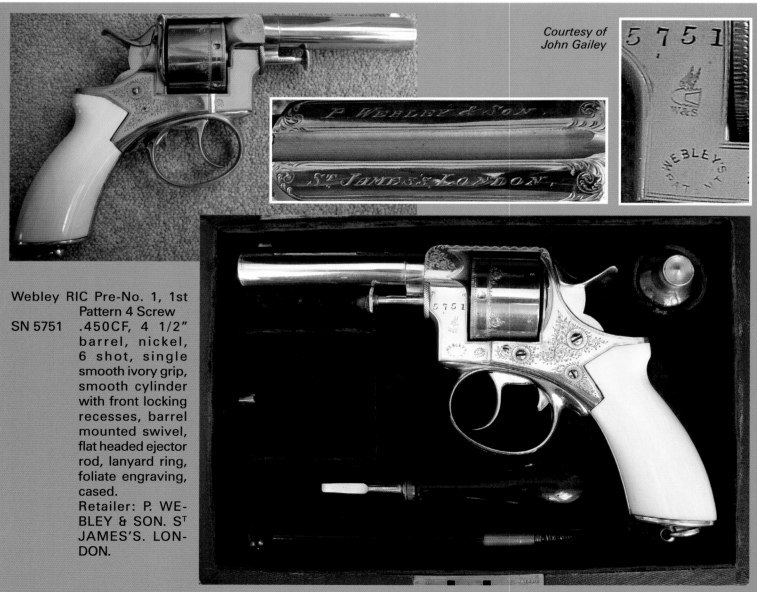

This is a very beautiful RIC cased with accessories.

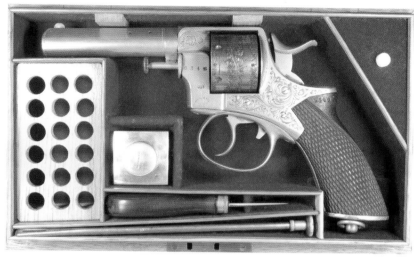

Webley RIC Pre-No. 1, 1st Pattern 4 Screw
SN 6345   .450CF, 4 1/2" barrel, nickel, 6 shot, one-piece checkered wood grip, smooth cylinder with front locking
recesses, barrel mounted swivel, flat headed ejector
rod, lanyard ring, foliate engraving, in oak case.
Retailer: T. MURCOTT 68 HAYMARKET. LONDON.

Joel Black collection

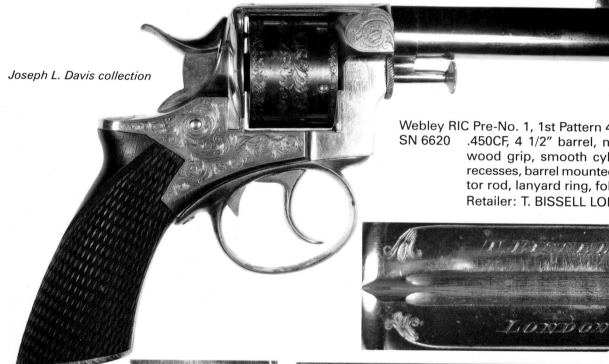

Joseph L. Davis collection

Webley RIC Pre-No. 1, 1st Pattern 4 Screw
SN 6620   .450CF, 4 1/2" barrel, nickel, 6 shot, checkered
wood grip, smooth cylinder with front locking
recesses, barrel mounted swivel, flat headed ejector rod, lanyard ring, foliate engraving, cased.
Retailer: T. BISSELL LONDON

35

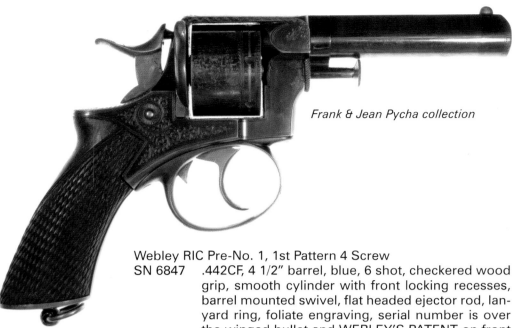

Frank & Jean Pycha collection

Webley RIC Pre-No. 1, 1st Pattern 4 Screw
SN 6847   .442CF, 4 1/2" barrel, blue, 6 shot, checkered wood grip, smooth cylinder with front locking recesses, barrel mounted swivel, flat headed ejector rod, lanyard ring, foliate engraving, serial number is over the winged bullet and WEBLEY'S PATENT on front of left frame, cased with accessories, SN 6847 is also stamped on the case's edge.
Retailer: TRULOCK BRO^S. 11 ESSEX BRIDGE DUBLIN

Webley RIC Pre-No. 1, 1st Pattern 4 Screw
SN 6864   .442CF, 4 1/2" barrel, nickel, 6 shot, smooth ivory grips, smooth cylinder with front locking recesses, barrel mounted swivel, flat headed ejector rod, lanyard ring, beautiful foliate engraving
Retailer: TRULOCK BRO^S 13 PARLIAMENT S^T. DUBLIN

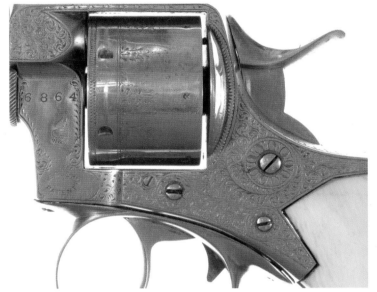

Frank & Jean Pycha collection

Webley RIC Pre-No. 1, 1st Pattern 4 Screw
SN 7042   .442CF, 2 3/8" ovate barrel, 6 shot, engraved, one-piece checkered wood grip, lanyard ring, smooth cylinder with front locking recesses, barrel mounted ejector rod swivel, flat head ejector rod, winged bullet logo on left side of frame.
Retailer: E. M. REILLY & C^O. 315 OXFORD ST. LONDON

Roger G. Michaud collection

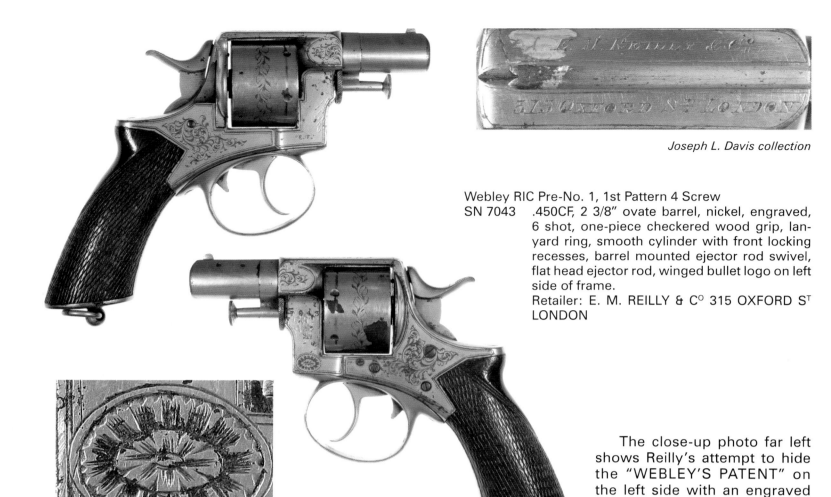

Joseph L. Davis collection

Webley RIC Pre-No. 1, 1st Pattern 4 Screw
SN 7043 .450CF, 2 3/8" ovate barrel, nickel, engraved, 6 shot, one-piece checkered wood grip, lanyard ring, smooth cylinder with front locking recesses, barrel mounted ejector rod swivel, flat head ejector rod, winged bullet logo on left side of frame.
Retailer: E. M. REILLY & C° 315 OXFORD S^T LONDON

The close-up photo far left shows Reilly's attempt to hide the "WEBLEY'S PATENT" on the left side with an engraved oval design. Reilly purposely obliterated this marking.

Joseph L. Davis collection

Webley RIC Pre-No. 1, 1st Pattern 4 Screw
SN 7544 .450, 4 1/2" barrels, 6 shot, blued, one-piece checkered wood grip, SN 7460 smooth cylinder with front locking recesses, barrel mounted swivel, flat headed ejector rod, lanyard ring, an engraved cased pair.
Retailer: J. VENABLES & SON. S^T ALDATES. OXFORD.

Webley RIC Pre-No. 1, 1st Pattern 4 Screw
SN 7965   .450, 4 1/2" barrel, 6 shot, one-piece checkered wood grip, smooth cylinder with front locking recesses, barrel mounted swivel, flat headed ejector rod, lanyard ring, WEBLEY'S PATENT in an oval and winged bullet left side of frame, cased.
Retailer: not marked

Joseph L. Davis collection

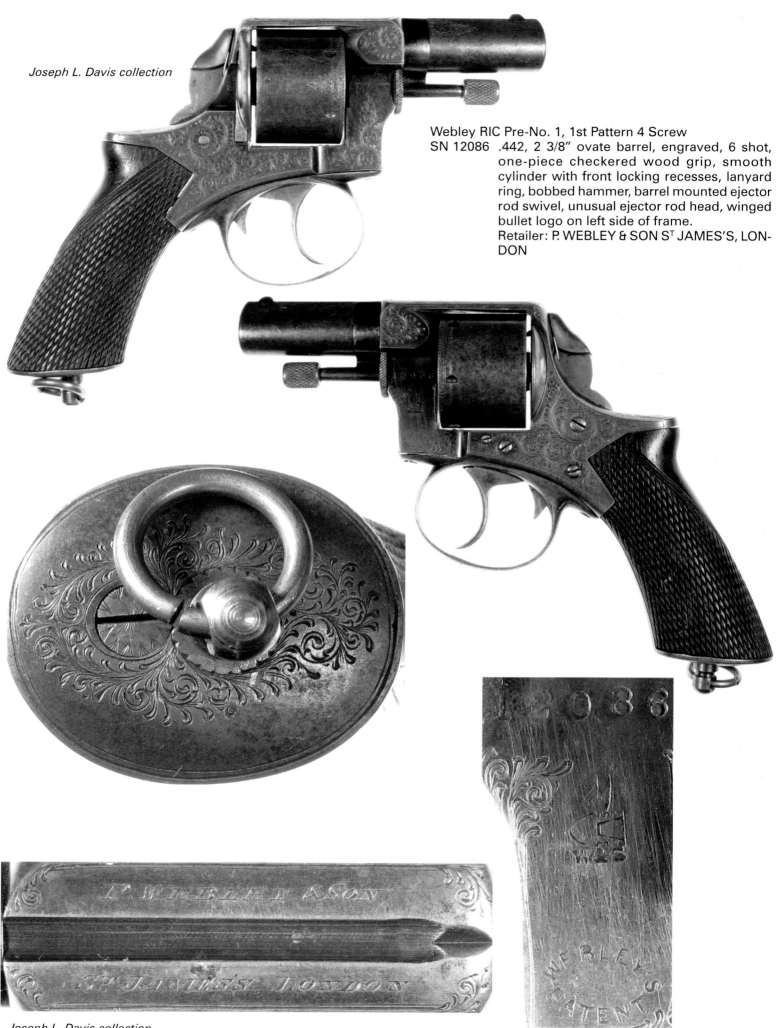

Joseph L. Davis collection

Webley RIC Pre-No. 1, 1st Pattern 4 Screw
SN 12086 .442, 2 3/8" ovate barrel, engraved, 6 shot, one-piece checkered wood grip, smooth cylinder with front locking recesses, lanyard ring, bobbed hammer, barrel mounted ejector rod swivel, unusual ejector rod head, winged bullet logo on left side of frame.
Retailer: P. WEBLEY & SON S^T JAMES'S, LONDON

Joseph L. Davis collection

Webley RIC Pre-No. 1, 1st Pattern 4 Screw
SN 12092 .442, 4 1/2" barrel, 6 shot, blued, one-piece checkered wood grip, smooth cylinder with front locking recesses, barrel mounted swivel, flat headed ejector rod, lanyard ring, WEBLEY'S PATENT in an oval and winged bullet left side of frame.
Retailer: not marked

Ejector rod is in working position.

Nick Preston collection

Webley RIC Pre-No. 1, Transitional
SN 12309   .500CF, 4 3/8" barrel, blue, 5 shot, one-piece checkered wood grip, smooth cylinder with front locking recesses, very early Adams' style receiver mounted ejector swivel, flat headed ejector rod, lanyard ring.
Retailer: P. WEBLEY & SON ST. JAMES'S LONDON

Joel Black collection

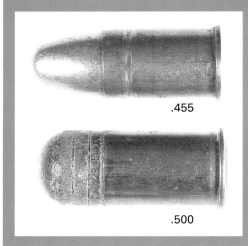

.455

.500

It is assumed that Webley decided to license and employ the Adams' style ejector on those few .500 RICs that were made after serial #4 as opposed to fabricating a more expensive larger than normal swivel ring for the thicker .500 barrel.

Webley RIC Pre-No. 1, 1st Pattern 4 Screw
SN 12930 .450, 4 1/2" barrel, 6 shot, blued, one-piece checkered wood grip, smooth cylinder with front locking recesses, barrel mounted swivel, flat headed ejector rod, lanyard ring, WEBLEY'S PATENT in an oval and winged bullet left side of frame.
Retailer: E. WOODS 106 STRAND, LONDON.

Mr. Woods was mistakenly credited as the inventor of the very first break top revolver made by Webley and retailed by Holland & Holland.

Roger G. Michaud collection

Webley RIC Pre-No. 1, 1st Pattern 4 Screw
SN 13231 .450CF, 2 1/2" barrel, 6 shot, one-piece
checkered wood grip, smooth cylin-
der with front locking recesses, barrel
mounted swivel, flat headed ejector
rod, lanyard ring, WEBLEY'S PATENT
in an oval winged bullet on left frame.
Retailer: ARMY & NAVY CO-OPERATIVE
SOCIETY LONDON

This very early
unabbreviated
marking soon
changed to Army
& Navy C.S.L.

Webley RIC Pre-No. 1, 1st Pattern 4 Screw
SN 13289 .450CF, 4 1/2" barrel, nickel, 6
shot, single smooth ivory grip,
smooth cylinder with front locking
recesses, barrel mounted swivel,
flat headed ejector rod, lanyard
ring, beautiful foliate engraving.
Retailer: LIDDLE & KAEDING SAN
FRANCISCO

Frank & Jean Pycha collection

43

Webley RIC Pre-No. 1, 1st Pattern 4 Screw
SN 14130 .442CF, 4 1/2" barrel, 6 shot, one-piece
checkered wood grip, smooth cylinder
with front locking recesses, barrel mounted
swivel, flat headed ejector rod, lanyard ring,
winged bullet over oval WEBLEY'S PATENT
on left front frame.
Retailer: ARMY & NAVY CO-OPERATIVE
SOCIETY LONDON

Courtesy of Hermann Historica.
http://www.hermann-historica-ohg.de/gb/index.htm

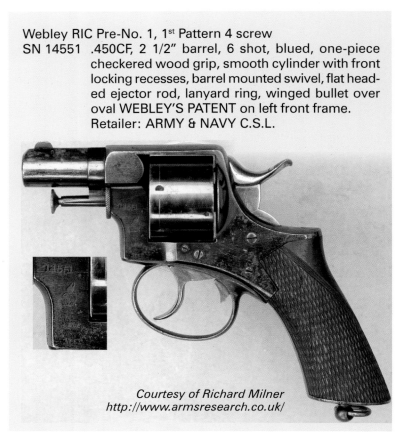

Webley RIC Pre-No. 1, 1st Pattern 4 screw
SN 14551 .450CF, 2 1/2" barrel, 6 shot, blued, one-piece
checkered wood grip, smooth cylinder with front
locking recesses, barrel mounted swivel, flat headed ejector rod, lanyard ring, winged bullet over
oval WEBLEY'S PATENT on left front frame.
Retailer: ARMY & NAVY C.S.L.

Courtesy of Richard Milner
http://www.armsresearch.co.uk/

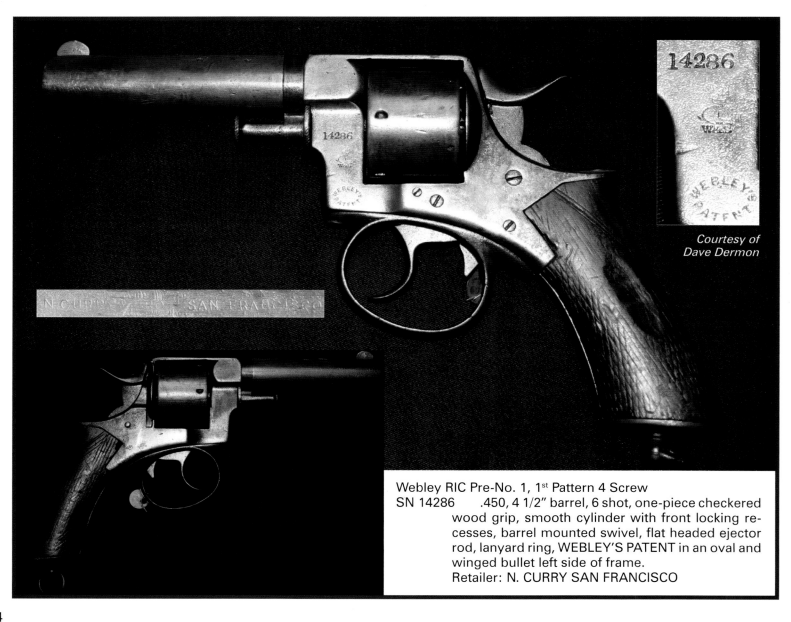

*Courtesy of
Dave Dermon*

Webley RIC Pre-No. 1, 1st Pattern 4 Screw
SN 14286 .450, 4 1/2" barrel, 6 shot, one-piece checkered
wood grip, smooth cylinder with front locking recesses, barrel mounted swivel, flat headed ejector
rod, lanyard ring, WEBLEY'S PATENT in an oval and
winged bullet left side of frame.
Retailer: N. CURRY SAN FRANCISCO

Webley RIC No. 1 [3], Transitional 4 screw
SN 15109 .500CF, 4 1/2" ovate barrel, blue, 5 shot, one-piece checkered wood grip, smooth cylinder with front locking recesses, marked as RIC No. 3 but actually not, features are more RIC No. 1 with a flat headed Adams type ejector rod (rather than barrel mounted swivel type)
Retailer: LIDDLE & KAEDING SAN FRANCISCO

Roger G. Michaud collection

Webley RIC No. 1, Transitional 4 screw
SN 15279.500CF, 4 1/2" barrel, fading nickel, 5 shot, one-piece checkered wood grip, smooth cylinder with front locking recesses, Adams type flat headed ejector rod, lanyard ring, winged bullet logo on left frame.
Retailer: LIDDLE & KAEDING SAN FRANCISCO

This is the lowest serial number 4 screw RIC observed with the standard markings.

Courtesy of Dave Dermon

Courtesy of Rock Island Auction http://www.rockislandauction.com/

Webley RIC No. 1, 1st Pattern 4 Screw
SN 15678 .450CF, 4 1/2" barrel, nickel, 6 shot, single smooth ivory grip, smooth cylinder with front locking recesses, barrel mounted swivel, flat headed ejector rod, lanyard ring, brass collection ID tag, profuse foliate engraving, "R. Garvey" engraved on front grip strap
Retailer: LIDDLE & KAEDING SAN FRANCISCO

Roger G. Michaud collection

Webley RIC No. 1, 1st Pattern 4 screw
SN 15435 .450CF, 4 1/2" barrel, fading gold wash over bluing, 6 shot, smooth cylinder with front locking recesses, checkered wood grip, barrel mounted swivel, flat headed ejector rod, lanyard ring, winged bullet logo on left frame, in oak case with blue baize lining.
Retailer: LIDDLE & KAEDING SAN FRANCISCO

Webley RIC No. 1, 1st Pattern 4 screw
SN 16136 .450CF, 4 1/2" barrel, blue, 6 shot,
checkered wood grip, smooth cylinder with front locking recesses,
lanyard ring, barrel mounted
swivel, flat headed ejector rod,
winged bullet logo on left frame.
Retailer: ARMY & NAVY C.S.L.

*Joseph L. Davis
collection*

Webley RIC No. 1, Transitional
SN 16691 .500CF, 4 1/2" barrel, nickel, 5 shot, one-piece
checkered wood grip, smooth cylinder with front
locking recesses, frame mounted swivel (Adam's
type) flat headed ejector rod, winged bullet logo
("flying bullet") on left side of left frame.
Retailer: G. FAURE LE PAGE A PARIS

Joseph L. Davis collection

Webley RIC No. 1, 1st Pattern 4 screw
SN 16870 .450CF, 3 1/2" barrel, blue, 6 shot, one-piece
checkered wood grip, smooth cylinder with front
locking recesses, barrel mounted swivel, flat headed
ejector rod, lanyard ring, SWS TRADE MARK on right
side of gun and back of period leather holster.
Retailer: S.W.SILVER & Co. 66 CORNHILL LONDON

Roger G. Michaud collection

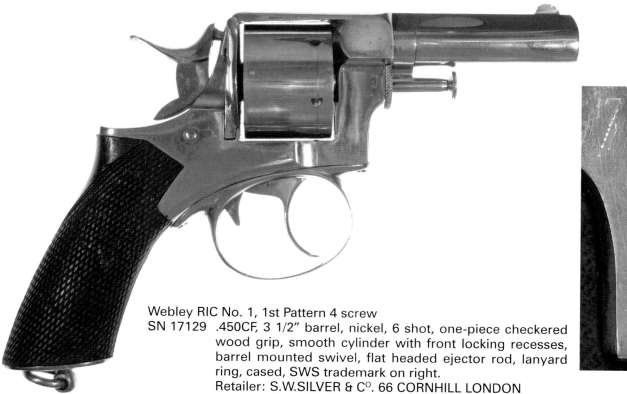

Webley RIC No. 1, 1st Pattern 4 screw
SN 17129 .450CF, 3 1/2" barrel, nickel, 6 shot, one-piece checkered wood grip, smooth cylinder with front locking recesses, barrel mounted swivel, flat headed ejector rod, lanyard ring, cased, SWS trademark on right.
Retailer: S.W.SILVER & Cº. 66 CORNHILL LONDON

This revolver was in the Webley factory collection until 1997.
Frank & Jean Pycha collection

Webley RIC No. 1, 1st Pattern 4 screw
SN 17935 .450CF, 3 1/2" barrel, blue, 6 shot, one-piece
checkered wood grip, smooth cylinder with
front locking recesses, barrel mounted swiv-
el, flat headed ejector rod, lanyard ring, SWS
TRADE MARK on right front, 6 / D ^ D (WWII
Australian government ownership mark) on
lower rear of right side.
Retailer: S.W.SILVER & C° 66 CORNHILL
LONDON

*Joseph L. Davis
collection*

During WWII,
Australia pressed
many obsolete arms
like this into service.

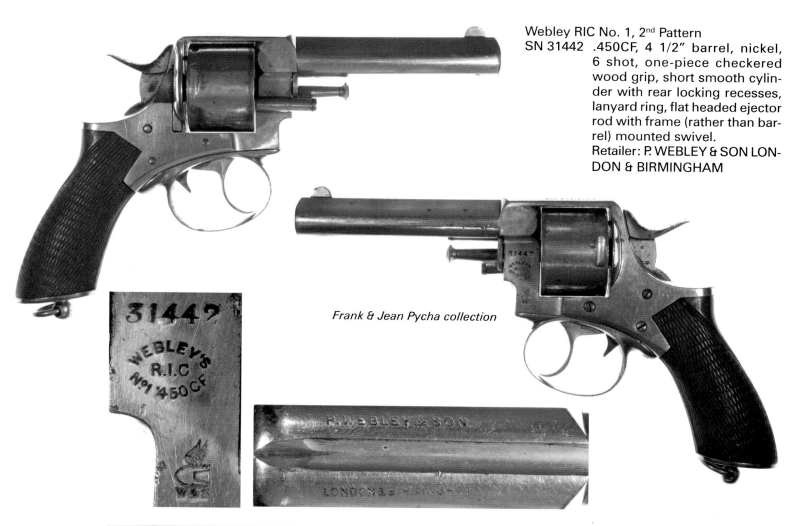

Webley RIC No. 1, 2nd Pattern
SN 31442 .450CF, 4 1/2" barrel, nickel,
6 shot, one-piece checkered
wood grip, short smooth cylinder with rear locking recesses,
lanyard ring, flat headed ejector
rod with frame (rather than barrel) mounted swivel.
Retailer: P. WEBLEY & SON LON-
DON & BIRMINGHAM

Frank & Jean Pycha collection

This cut, from a January 1884
Army & Navy C.S.L. price list, still pic-
tures an RIC No. 1 1st pattern 4 screw,
rather than the expected 2nd pattern
or RIC No. 1 New Model. To add to
confusion, the Queensland contract
was filled with RIC No. 3.

Courtesy of Gordon Bruce

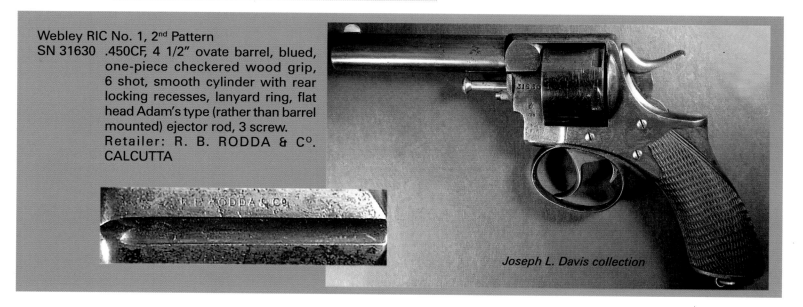

Webley RIC No. 1, 2nd Pattern
SN 31630 .450CF, 4 1/2" ovate barrel, blued,
one-piece checkered wood grip,
6 shot, smooth cylinder with rear
locking recesses, lanyard ring, flat
head Adam's type (rather than barrel
mounted) ejector rod, 3 screw.
Retailer: R. B. RODDA & Cº.
CALCUTTA

Joseph L. Davis collection

Webley RIC No. 1, 2nd Pattern
SN 70659 .450CF, 4 1/2" ovate barrel, blued, 6 shot, one-piece checkered wood grip, rear locking recesses, lanyard ring, flat head ejector rod, in oak case lined with blue baize plus accessories.
Retailer: J. PATSTONE SOUTHAMPTON

SILVER MEDAL PARIS 1878
inscription engraved on barrel.

Frank & Jean Pycha collection

Webley RIC No. 1, 2ⁿᵈ Pattern
SN 70850 .450CF, 4 1/2" ovate barrel, nickel, 6 shot, one-piece checkered wood grip, mushroom head ejector rod, smooth cylinder with rear locking recess, lanyard ring.
Retailer: ARMY & NAVY C.S.L.

Joel Black collection

Joel Black collection

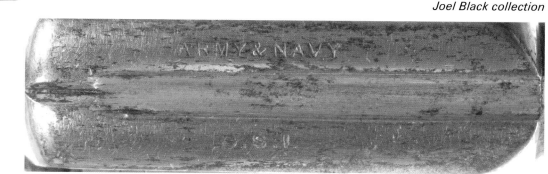

Webley RIC No. 1, 2ⁿᵈ Pattern
SN 518 .450CF, 5" ovate barrel, 6 shot, one-piece checkered wood grip, short smooth cylinder with rear recessed stops, mushroom head ejector pivoting from front of frame, Bentley's "TRADE MARK LONDON TOWER" and "FOR 450 CENTRAL FIRE CARTRIDGES" designation on left side.
Retailer: BLAND & SONS 106 STRAND LONDON

Bentley's London Tower trademark and "FOR 450 CENTRALFIRE CARTRIDGES"

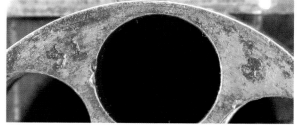

Frank & Jean Pycha collection

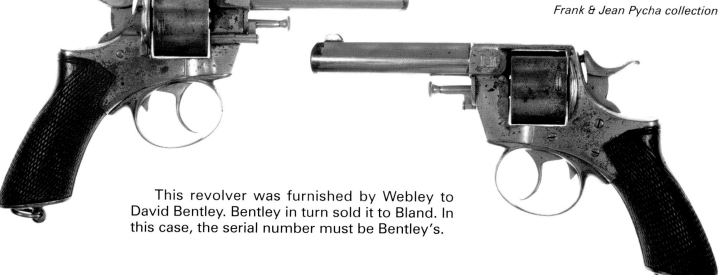

This revolver was furnished by Webley to David Bentley. Bentley in turn sold it to Bland. In this case, the serial number must be Bentley's.

RIC NO. 1 New Model

The RIC No. 1 New Model was introduced in 1882. An Adam's type ejector rod replaced the barrel mounted swivel ejector mechanism. The ejector head was altered to the form of an acorn. The cylinder for this model was fluted and lengthened to accept up to six .455, .476 or .44 Russian cartridges. One-piece checkered wood grip, lanyard ring, and screw in ovate barrel were standard features.

This February 1883 A&N C.S.L. record is the earliest date of delivery of the Webley RIC New Model observed. Above there was a delivery of New Models from Pryse.

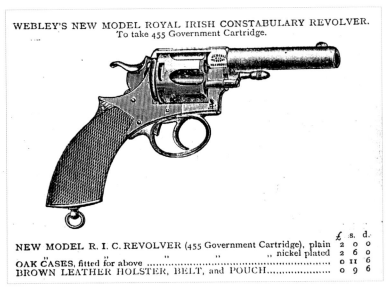

Courtesy of Gordon Bruce

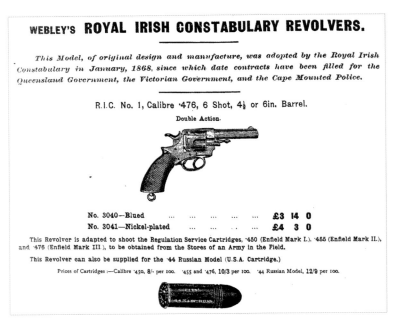

Original Webley 1898 catalog. *Joel Black collection*

This cut from a July 1882 Army & Navy (A&N) catalogue depicts a "New Model" RIC. Webley did not consistently use this title in marking the gun.

Used with permission of Glasgow University.
http://www.gla.ac.uk/archives/

This drawing by Ken Hallock is representative of the lock and firing mechanism of the RIC No. 1, 2nd pattern (transitional) and the New Model.

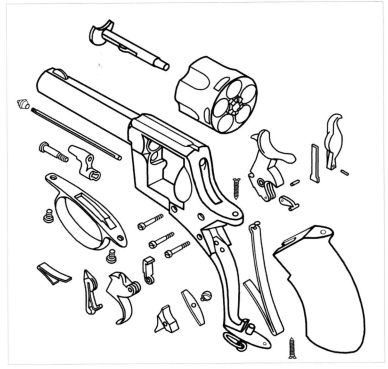

On this 1898 catalogue page, Webley did not even use the "New Model" name. In all likelihood, they ceased using this model name when they stopped making the 1st pattern ("old pattern") RIC around 1885. With the enormous success of break top revolvers such as the WG and Mk I, by 1893 Webley ceased ordering new solid frames from their supplier, the Soho Drop Forge Company of Smithwick. Webley continued to supply solid frame weapons through the 1930s, but these were from frames left in inventory up to 40 years earlier. So few solid frame revolvers were assembled after the 1897 merger with Scott that Webley did not bother to have a Webley & Scott stamp made for their solid frame handguns until the final two hundred RIC/83s were assembled. By that time the P. WEBLEY & SON stamp no longer existed.

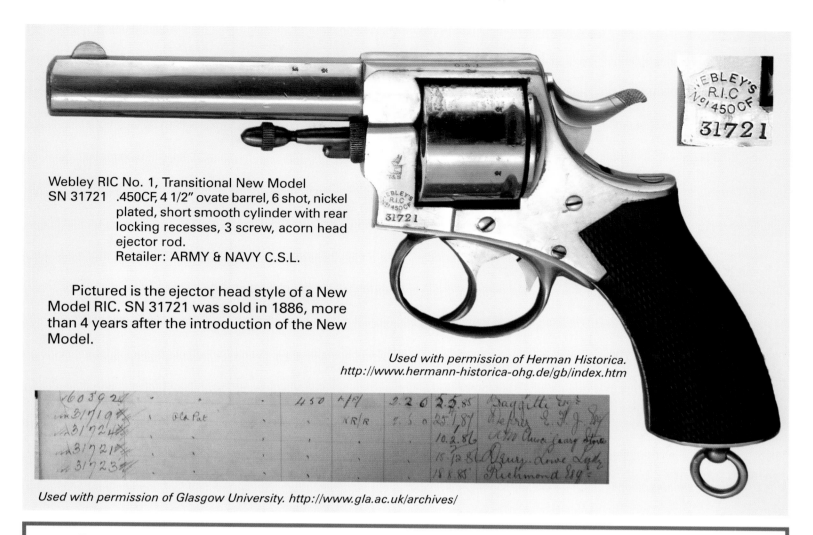

Webley RIC No. 1, Transitional New Model
SN 31721 .450CF, 4 1/2" ovate barrel, 6 shot, nickel plated, short smooth cylinder with rear locking recesses, 3 screw, acorn head ejector rod.
Retailer: ARMY & NAVY C.S.L.

Pictured is the ejector head style of a New Model RIC. SN 31721 was sold in 1886, more than 4 years after the introduction of the New Model.

Used with permission of Herman Historica.
http://www.hermann-historica-ohg.de/gb/index.htm

Used with permission of Glasgow University. http://www.gla.ac.uk/archives/

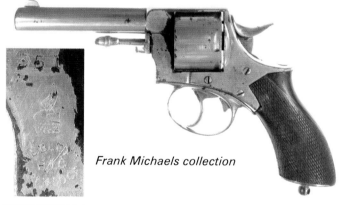

Frank Michaels collection

Used with permission of Glasgow University.
http://www.gla.ac.uk/archives/

Webley RIC No. 1, Transitional New Model
SN 351 .450CF, 5" ovate barrel, 6 shot, nickel plated, short smooth cylinder with rear recessed stops (no front locking type), late ejector with elongated acorn finial pivoting from front of frame, winged bullet logo over WEBLEY'S RIC No. 1 .450 on left side.
Retailer: LIDDLE & KAEDING SAN FRANCISCO

Around the time Webley introduced the "RIC No. 1 New Model", they started a second serial number group beginning at number 100. For several years, A&N C.S.L. records showed Webley continuing to use the older serial number sequence on some New Models along with the new sequence. We speculate this situation originated from Webley having to outsource some of their solid frame production in order to meet numerous military and civilian orders of their hinge-frame Government Service Mark I and the WG Models.

55

Webley RIC No. 1, Transitional New Model
SN 753   .450CF, 5" ovate barrel, 6 shot, blue ("plain"), long smooth cylinder with rear recessed stops, late ejector with acorn finial pivoting from front of frame, winged bullet logo and WEBLEY'S PATENT RIC No. 1 .450 marking on left side, Arabic script on right side.
Retailer: WILLIAMS & POWELL LIVERPOOL

Joseph L. Davis collection

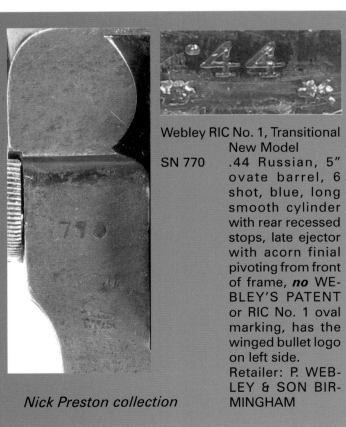

Nick Preston collection

Webley RIC No. 1, Transitional New Model
SN 770   .44 Russian, 5" ovate barrel, 6 shot, blue, long smooth cylinder with rear recessed stops, late ejector with acorn finial pivoting from front of frame, **no** WEBLEY'S PATENT or RIC No. 1 oval marking, has the winged bullet logo on left side.
Retailer: P. WEBLEY & SON BIRMINGHAM

This revolver has the longer albeit unfluted cylinder and the acorn finial, but it is not marked "New Model". In fact, the "NEW MODEL" marking was only used sporadically. The .44 Russian is one of the least encountered chambering.

Webley RIC No. 1, New Model
SN 1137 .455CF, 4 1/2" barrel, blue,
6 shot, conventional fluting,
lanyard ring, elongated acorn
finial to ejector rod, one-piece
checkered wood grip.
Retailer: ARMY & NAVY
C.S.L.

This was sold to Sir A. Sullivan in April 1884.

Courtesy of Glasgow University

Joseph L. Davis collection

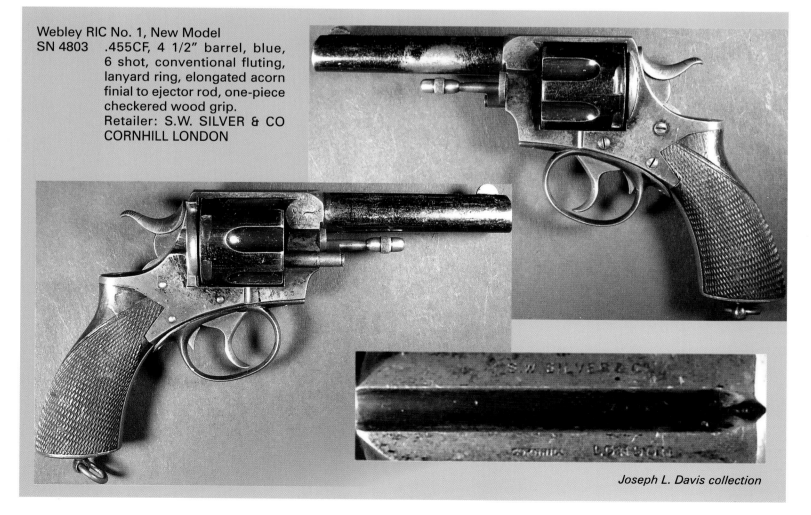

Webley RIC No. 1, New Model
SN 4803 .455CF, 4 1/2" barrel, blue,
6 shot, conventional fluting,
lanyard ring, elongated acorn
finial to ejector rod, one-piece
checkered wood grip.
Retailer: S.W. SILVER & CO
CORNHILL LONDON

Joseph L. Davis collection

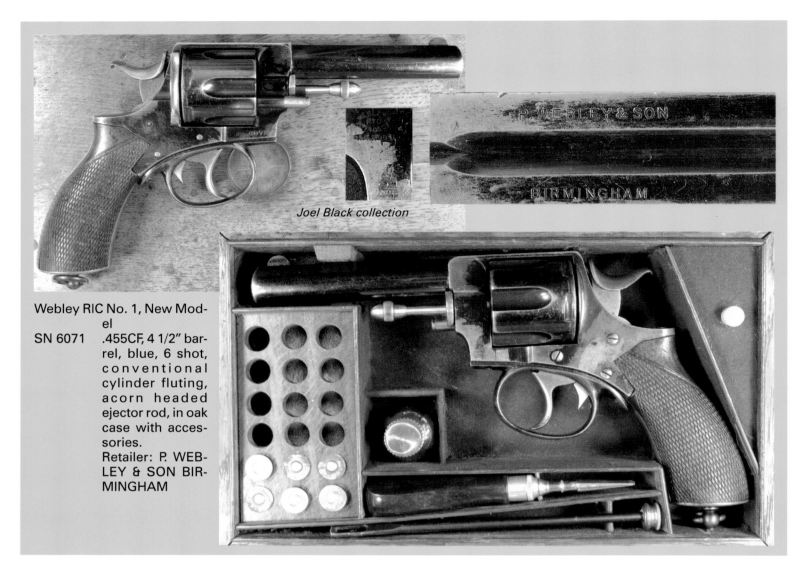

Joel Black collection

Webley RIC No. 1, New Model
SN 6071 .455CF, 4 1/2" barrel, blue, 6 shot, conventional cylinder fluting, acorn headed ejector rod, in oak case with accessories.
Retailer: P. WEBLEY & SON BIRMINGHAM

Webley RIC No. 1, New Model
SN 6280 .455CF, 4 1/2" barrel, 6 shot, nickel plated acorn headed ejector rod, in oak case with blue baize lining.
Retailer: ARMY & NAVY C.S.L.

Courtesy of Glasgow University

Joseph L. Davis collection

Sold to Bidwell, Esq. September 1882, and is recorded as a "New Pattern" in the records.

Webley RIC No. 1, New Model
SN 6903   .455CF, 4 1/2" barrel, plated bright nickel, 6 shot, lanyard ring, elongated acorn finial to ejector rod, one-piece checkered wood grip of a lighter color and with a diamond shaped escutcheon on right side.
Retailer: FRED BARNES & Co LONDON.

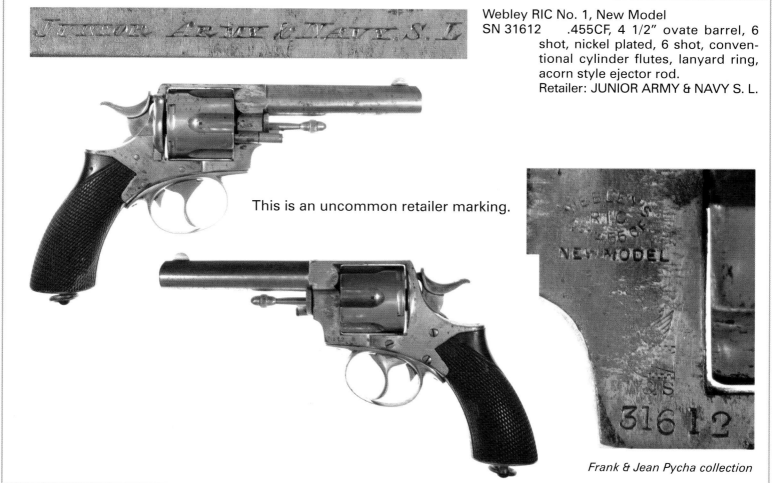

Webley RIC No. 1, New Model
SN 31612   .455CF, 4 1/2" ovate barrel, 6 shot, nickel plated, 6 shot, conventional cylinder flutes, lanyard ring, acorn style ejector rod.
Retailer: JUNIOR ARMY & NAVY S. L.

This is an uncommon retailer marking.

Webley RIC No. 1, New Model
SN 32180 .476CF, 4 1/2″ ovate barrel, 6 shot, plated
bright nickel, conventional cylinder flutes,
lanyard ring, Adams patent acorn style
ejector rod, sold to Col. Agnew in 1886.
Retailer: ARMY & NAVY C.S.L.

*Roger G. Michaud
collection*

Used with permission of Glasgow University http://www.gla.ac.uk/archives/

Webley RIC No. 1, New Model
SN 32577 .476CF, 4 1/2″ ovate barrel, 6 shot, blue, acorn headed ejector
rod, conventional cylinder flutes, lanyard ring.
Retailer: YORK HOUSE REGENT ST LONDON

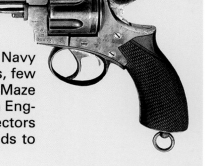

York House is a somewhat mysterious entity. It was also named Junior Army & Navy
C.S.L. While the Army & Navy C.S.L. organization sold a huge number of firearms, few
examples of York House marked firearms are extant. Noted historian Dr. Robert J. Maze
was unsuccessful in his efforts to research this English company. Richard Milner in England relates that York House was a breakaway company formed by a group of directors
who left A&N C.S.L. to compete in the business of specialized supplies and goods to
younger, more junior officers.

Courtesy of Hermann Historica. http://www.hermann-historica-ohg.de/gb/index.htm

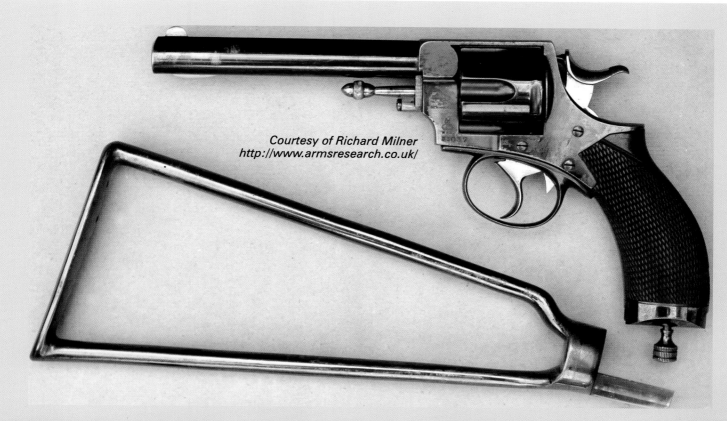

Courtesy of Richard Milner
http://www.armsresearch.co.uk/

Webley RIC No. 1, New Model
SN 33037 .476CF, 6" ovate barrel, 6 shot, blue ("plain"), acorn style ejector rod, retains one-
        piece checkered wood grip, metal cap and screw to butt, very rare metal shoulder
        stock version.
        Retailer: not marked

Webley RIC No. 1, New Model
SN 33039   .476CF, 4 1/2″ ovate barrel, 6 shot, blue,
          conventional cylinder flutes, lanyard ring,
          acorn style ejector rod.
          Retailer: MANTON & CO LONDON &
          CALCUTTA

Joseph L. Davis collection

Webley RIC No. 1, New Model
SN 34024 .450CF, 4 1/2" ovate barrel, 6 shot, nickel plated, conventional cylinder flutes, lanyard ring, acorn style ejector rod, has Cogwell & Harrison's trademark: TRADE MARK / facing lion / VENIVIDIVICI
Retalier: COGSWELL & HARRISON
226 STRAND & 142 NEW BOND ST LONDON

Cogswell & Harrison was among very few retailers to whom Webley would sell revolvers devoid of all marking except serial numbers.

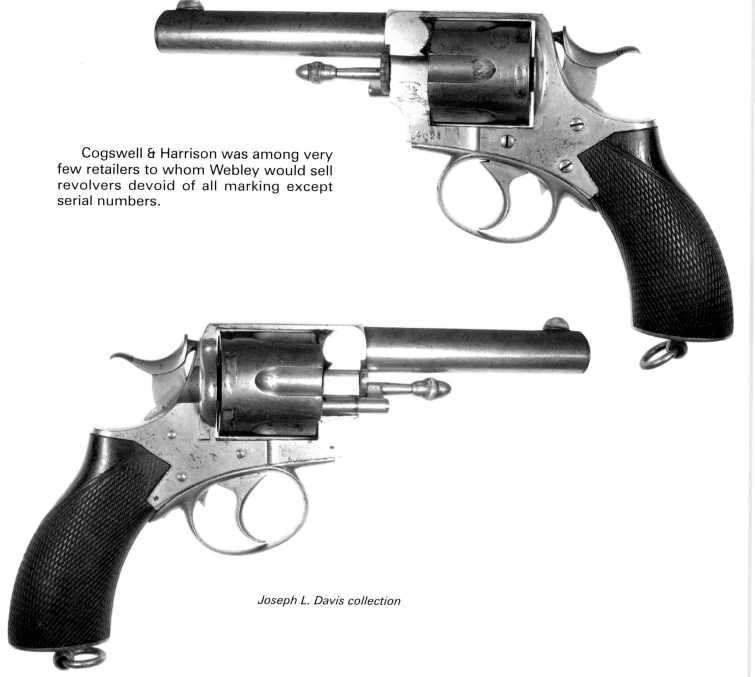

Joseph L. Davis collection

Webley RIC No. 1, New Model
SN 34462 .450CF, 4 1/2" barrel, nickel plated, 6 shot, conventional cylinder flutes, thick acorn style ejector rod, S&F #203, round blade front sight, lanyard ring, fitted with ejector and hammer safety, rare PATENT gun (less than 500 made with patent) SILVER&FLETCHER'S PATENT "THE EXPERT." stamped on top of barrel, P. WEBLEY & SON stamped in the groove of the top strap.
Retailer: S.W. SILVER & Co. CORNHILL LONDON

Joseph L. Davis collection

The hook-like mechanism that pivots near the top rear of the receiver rides in the rebated edge of the cylinder. When the hammer hits it (as in this case) and the primer, the gun is fired and at the same time the previously fired cased is ejected by the hook. Of course, this requires the loading gate to be left ajar, which explains why these were not popular. When the pennant-like object on the hammer is rotated to the left, it withdraws the firing pin to a position where it cannot reach the primer. The authors believe if this safety was offered as a separate accessory it would have been successful.

Webley RIC No. 1, New Model
SN 35160 .450CF, 4 1/2" barrel, blue, 6 shot, conventional cylinder flutes, thick acorn style ejector rod, S&F #265, bead on rear of blade front sight, lanyard ring, fitted with ejector and hammer safety, rare patent gun (less than 500 made with PATENT), SILVER&FLETCHER'S PATENT "THE EXPERT." stamped on top of barrel.
Retailer: S.W. SILVER & Co. CORNHILL LONDON

Greg Reddick collection

SAFETY OFF

SAFETY ON

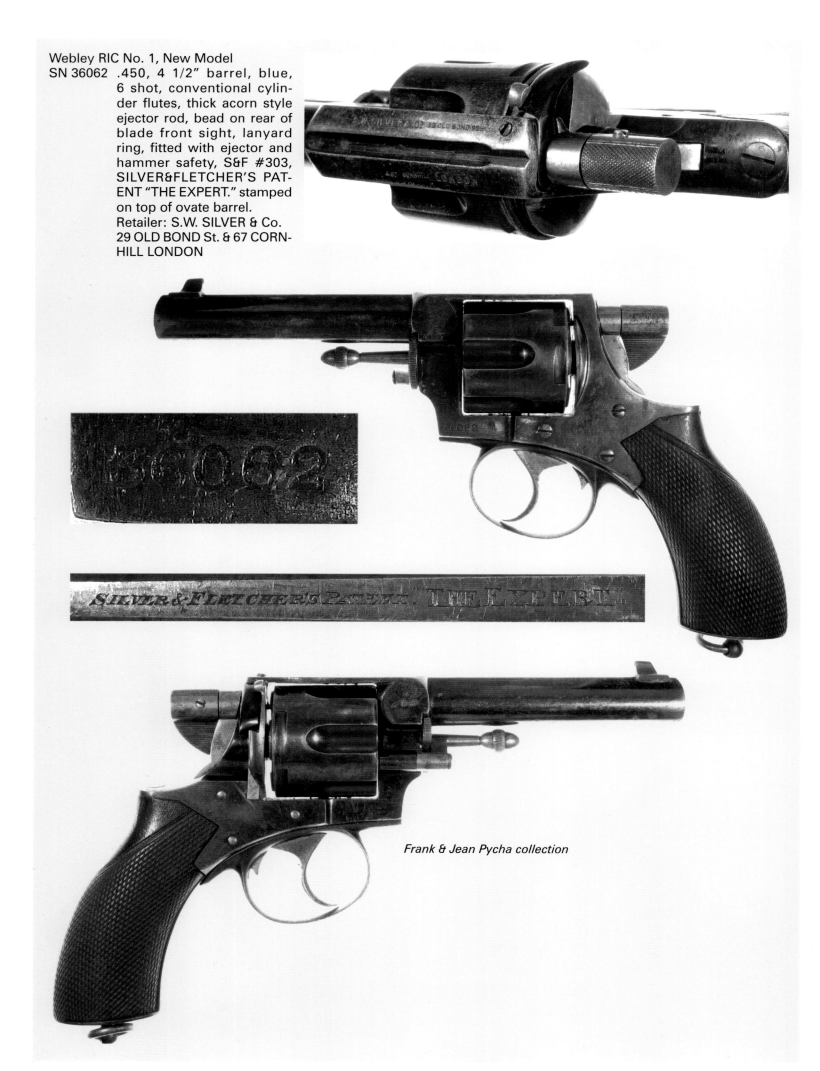

Webley RIC No. 1, New Model
SN 36062 .450, 4 1/2" barrel, blue, 6 shot, conventional cylinder flutes, thick acorn style ejector rod, bead on rear of blade front sight, lanyard ring, fitted with ejector and hammer safety, S&F #303, SILVER&FLETCHER'S PATENT "THE EXPERT." stamped on top of ovate barrel.
Retailer: S.W. SILVER & Co. 29 OLD BOND St. & 67 CORNHILL LONDON

Frank & Jean Pycha collection

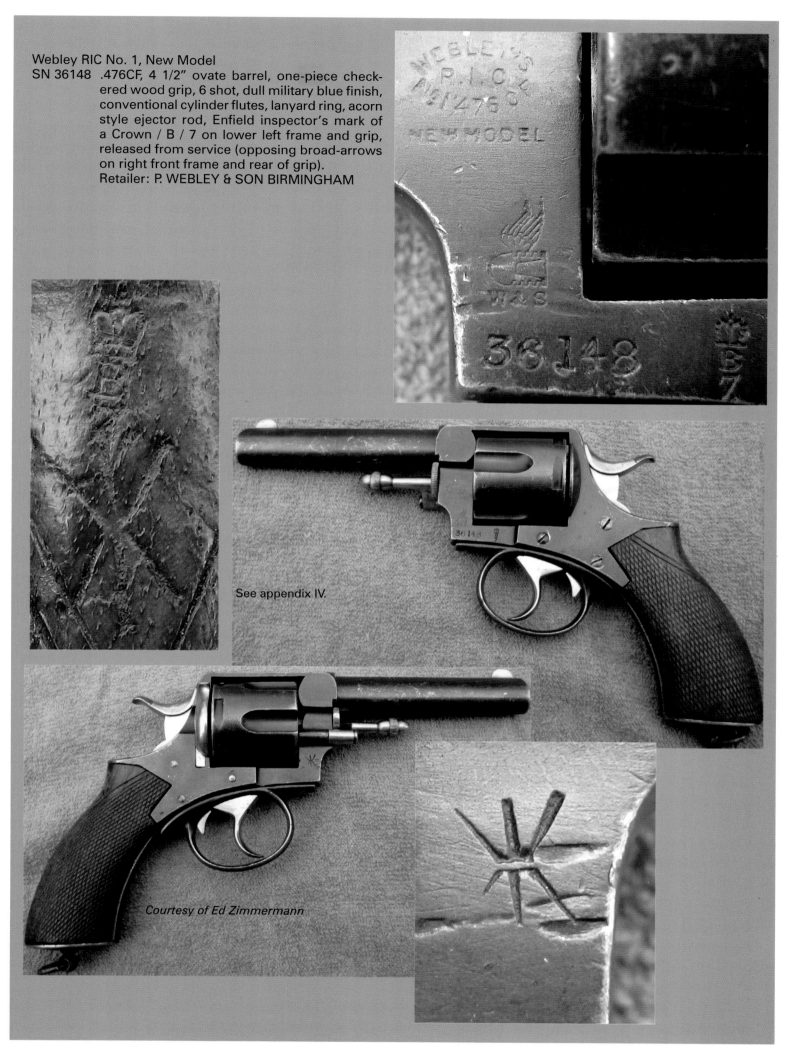

Webley RIC No. 1, New Model
SN 36148 .476CF, 4 1/2" ovate barrel, one-piece check-ered wood grip, 6 shot, dull military blue finish, conventional cylinder flutes, lanyard ring, acorn style ejector rod, Enfield inspector's mark of a Crown / B / 7 on lower left frame and grip, released from service (opposing broad-arrows on right front frame and rear of grip).
Retailer: P. WEBLEY & SON BIRMINGHAM

See appendix IV.

Courtesy of Ed Zimmermann

67

Roger G. Michaud collection

Webley RIC No. 1, New Model
SN 36387 .476, 4 1/2" barrel, blue, 6 shot, conventional cylinder flutes, thick acorn style ejector rod, S&F #336, bead on rear of blade front sight, lanyard ring, fitted with ejector and hammer safety, SILVER&FLETCHER'S PATENT "THE EXPERT." stamped on top of ovate barrel.
Retailer: S.W. SILVER & Co.
29 OLD BOND ST. & 67 CORNHILL LONDON

Webley RIC No. 1, New Model
SN 36394 .450CF, 4 1/2" ovate barrel, nickel, 6 shot, conventional cylinder flutes, thick acorn style ejector rod, S&F #203, round blade front sight, lanyard ring, fitted with ejector and hammer safety, rare patent gun (less than 500 made with PATENT), SILVER&FLETCHER'S PATENT "THE EXPERT.", the wooden stock is integral with the grip.
Retailer: S.W. SILVER & Co.
29 OLD BOND ST CORNHILL LONDON

> ILLUSTRATED   FAA Category:S1
>
> 785 A UNIQUE .450 SILVER AND FLETCHERS PATENT SIX SHOT "THE EXPERT" solid frame double action ejecting nickel plated revolver, Serial No.36394. With it's original non detachable carbine type walnut butt stock, chequered at the grip. The barrel flat marked "SILVER AND FLETCHERS PATENT THE EXPERT" the top strap with address S.W. SLIVER Co., 29 OLD BOND STREET, CORNHILL, LONDON. Patent retractable firing pin, lanyard ring and blued foresight. Grade One plus with 98% nickel leather plating in it's original Leg O mutton style case. Grade 3. An excellent lot for the collector of unusual revolvers. Grade 3 plus. Brl.4.5".
> ILLUSTRATED   FAA Category:S1

This one of a kind New Model was featured in a Weller & Dufty auction.

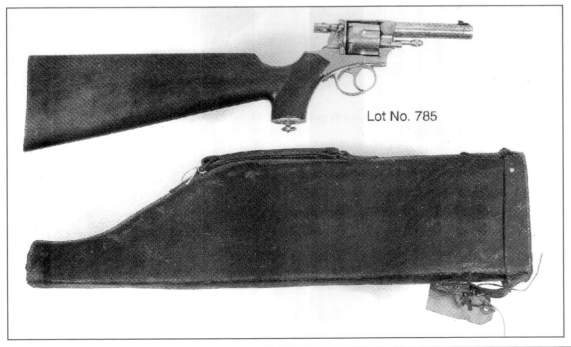

Lot No. 785

Courtesy of Richard Milner
http://www.armsresearch.co.uk/

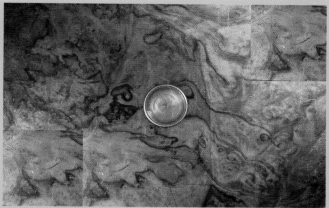

Webley RIC No. 1, New Model
SN 36675 .476CF, 4 1/2″ ovate barrel, 6 shot, nickel plated, conventional cylinder flutes, lanyard ring, acorn style ejector rod, in beautiful burl walnut case.
Retailer: WESTLEY RICHARDS& C° LONDON

Joseph L. Davis collection

Webley RIC No. 1, New Model
SN 69737 .450CF, 4 1/2″ ovate barrel, 6 shot, blue, conventional cylinder flutes, lanyard ring, acorn style ejector rod, short cylinder.
Retailer: P. WEBLEY & SON LONDON & BIRMINGHAM

Marked MP over L on butt plate.

Frank & Jean Pycha collection

Webley RIC No. 1, New Model
SN 70017 .476CF, 4 1/2" ovate barrel, 6 shot, blue, conventional cylinder flutes, lanyard ring, acorn style ejector rod, sold in 1898 to James Bradick.
Retailer: ARMY & NAVY C.S.L.

Used with permission of Glasgow University http://www.gla.ac.uk/archives/

Joseph L. Davis collection

This revolver is a New Model having all the characteristics of that model, yet it was not so marked. The Date of Invoice is March 12, 1898. The A&N C.S.L. description is "RIC plain" (blued). Note the spread of serial numbers on the invoice sheet.

Webley RIC No. 1, New Model
SN 73178   .450CF, 4 1/2" ovate barrel, 6 shot, blue, conventional cylinder flutes, short cylinder, lanyard ring, acorn style ejector rod, not marked NEW MODEL.
Retailer: P. WEBLEY & SON LONDON & BIRMINGHAM

Frank & Jean Pycha collection

Butt plate marked MP over 39 by Melbourne Police.

Webley RIC No. 1, New Model
SN 73754 .450CF, 4 1/2" ovate barrel, 6 shot, blue, lanyard ring, thin acorn ejector rod, has a short smooth cylinder with rear locking recesses.
Retailer: P. WEBLEY & SON BIRMINGHAM

This revolver is an example of Webley trying to use up old parts on hand. Both the frame and cylinder were for an old model while the ejector was for a new model.

Courtesy of Kerry Guerin. http://www.firearmsmuseum.org.au/index.htm

71

Webley RIC No. 1, New Model
SN 79208 .476CF, 4 1/2" ovate barrel, 6
        shot, nickel plated, larger acorn
        style ejector rod, conventional
        fluting, lanyard ring.
     Retailer: W^M. MOORE & GREY
  8 CRAVEN S^T. STRAND LONDON

Joseph L. Davis collection

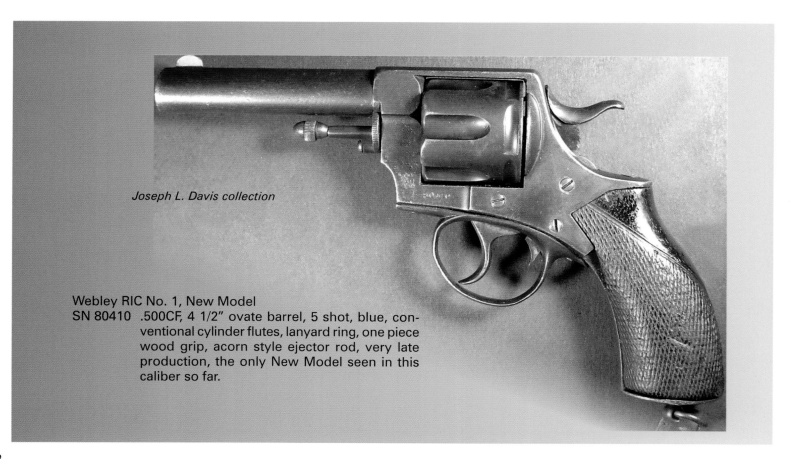

Joseph L. Davis collection

Webley RIC No. 1, New Model
SN 80410 .500CF, 4 1/2" ovate barrel, 5 shot, blue, con-
        ventional cylinder flutes, lanyard ring, one piece
        wood grip, acorn style ejector rod, very late
        production, the only New Model seen in this
        caliber so far.

New Model Finials

As with all things Webleys, nothing was ever written in stone. Even the simple acorn finials came in at least 3 varieties. It is assumed that these kinds of variations were a product of Webley's reliance on outsourcing when the demand for hinge frame revolvers far outdistanced the dwindling solid frame business.

Roger G. Michaud collection

Webley RIC No. 1, New Model
SN 80657 .450CF, 4 1/2" ovate barrel, blue, 6 shot, checkered wood grip, lanyard ring, larger acorn-style ejector rod, short cylinder with conventional fluting.
Retailer: P. WEBLEY LONDON & BIRMINGHAM

Joseph L. Davis collection

73

Webley RIC No. 1, New Model
SN 84059 .450CF, 4 1/2" ovate barrel, 6 shot, blue, short
smooth cylinder with rear locking recesses, larger
acorn-style ejector rod, lanyard ring, checkered
wood grip, Webley is using up parts left on hand.
Retailer: P. WEBLEY & SON BIRMINGHAM

Joseph L. Davis collection

Roger G. Michaud collection

Webley RIC No. 1, New Model
SN 84551 .476CF, 4 1/2" ovate barrel, 6 shot,
bright nickel plating larger acorn-style
ejector rod, conventional fluting, one
piece light brown checkered wood
grip, lanyard ring, L1588 (South African
registration #) on the right frame.
Retailer: HOLLAND & HOLLAND
98 NEW BOND S^T LONDON.

Webley RIC No. 1, New Model
SN 84814 .450, 4 1/2" barrel, blue, 6 shot, conventional cylinder flutes, thick style ejector rod, S&F #390, bead on rear of blade front sight, lanyard ring, fitted with ejector and hammer safety, SILVER & FLETCHER'S PATENT "THE EXPERT." Stamped on top of ovate barrel.
Retailer: S.W. SILVER & C°. CORNHILL LONDON

Joseph L. Davis collection

Webley RIC No. 1, New Model
SN 85556 .476CF, 4 1/2" ovate barrel, 6 shot, blue, larger acorn-style ejector rod, 3 screw frame, conventional fluting, one-piece checkered wood grip, lanyard ring, has winged bullet logo, left frame stamped: WEBLEY'S RIC N° 1 476CF NEW MODEL.
Retailer: COGSWELL & HARRISON
226 STRAND & 142 NEW BOND ST LONDON

Frank & Jean Pycha collection

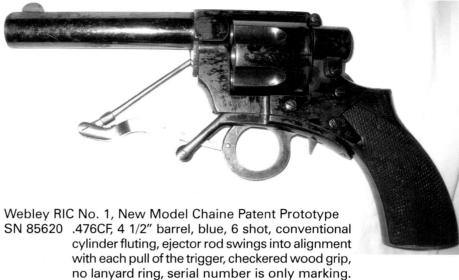

Webley RIC No. 1, New Model Chaine Patent Prototype
SN 85620 .476CF, 4 1/2" barrel, blue, 6 shot, conventional cylinder fluting, ejector rod swings into alignment with each pull of the trigger, checkered wood grip, no lanyard ring, serial number is only marking.
Retailer: not marked

This was an unsuccessful attempt to make an auto ejecting, auto-loading revolver.

Webley RIC No. 1, New Model
SN 85886 .450CF, 4 1/2" ovate barrel, blue, short stubby acorn finial, short cylinder with conventional fluting, lanyard ring, butt cap stamped M. P. 242 (Melbourne police).
Retailer: P. WEBLEY & SON LONDON & BIRMINGHAM

Roger G. Michaud collection

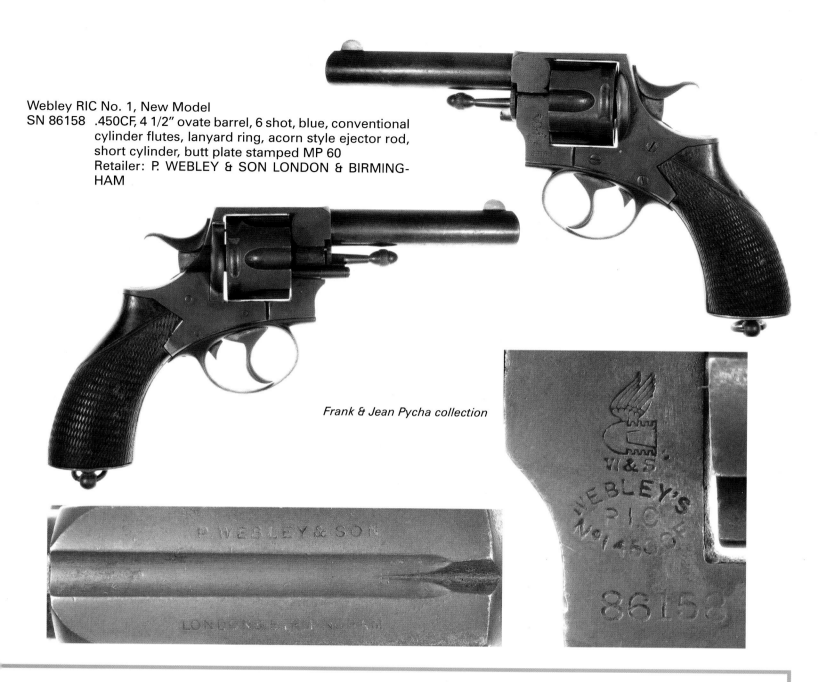

Webley RIC No. 1, New Model
SN 86158 .450CF, 4 1/2" ovate barrel, 6 shot, blue, conventional
cylinder flutes, lanyard ring, acorn style ejector rod,
short cylinder, butt plate stamped MP 60
Retailer: P. WEBLEY & SON LONDON & BIRMING-
HAM

Frank & Jean Pycha collection

P. WEBLEY & SON

LONDON & BIRMINGHAM

W & S.
WEBLEY'S
P.I.C.
No. 1 450 CF

86158

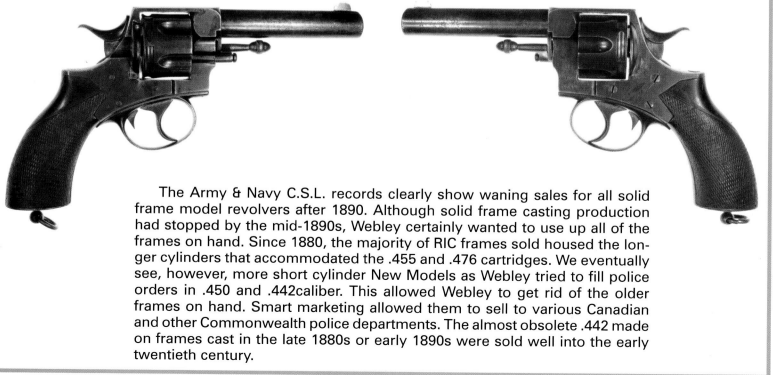

The Army & Navy C.S.L. records clearly show waning sales for all solid frame model revolvers after 1890. Although solid frame casting production had stopped by the mid-1890s, Webley certainly wanted to use up all of the frames on hand. Since 1880, the majority of RIC frames sold housed the longer cylinders that accommodated the .455 and .476 cartridges. We eventually see, however, more short cylinder New Models as Webley tried to fill police orders in .450 and .442 caliber. This allowed Webley to get rid of the older frames on hand. Smart marketing allowed them to sell to various Canadian and other Commonwealth police departments. The almost obsolete .442 made on frames cast in the late 1880s or early 1890s were sold well into the early twentieth century.

Webley RIC No. 1, New Model
SN 88653 .455CF, 4 1/2" ovate barrel, blue, 6 shot, conventional fluting, acorn ejector rod, lanyard ring, Farsi type markings on lower right frame, stamped 7 E.P. (Egyptian Police) on left front frame, commercial Birmingham proofs (no military British proof mark).
Retailer: P. WEBLEY & SON LONDON & BIRMINGHAM

Roger G. Michaud collection

Webley RIC No. 1, New Model
SN 90906 .476CF, 4 1/2" ovate barrel, 6 shot, blue, long cylinder, conventional cylinder fluting, acorn ejector rod, very rough surface.
Retailer: ARMY & NAVY C.S.L.

Used with permission of Glasgow University

This was sold to Mr. Reeves, Esq. in 1898.

Frank & Jean Pycha collection

Webley RIC No. 1, New Model
SN 91993 .455CF, 4 1/2" ovate barrel, blue,
        6 shot, not marked NEW MODEL,
        long cylinder with conventional
        fluting, acorn ejector rod.
Retailer: P. WEBLEY & SON LON-
        DON & BIRMINGHAM

Joseph L. Davis collection

Webley RIC No.1, New Model
SN 94492 .455CF, 4 1/2" ovate barrel, blue, 6 shot, not marked
        NEW MODEL, long cylinder with conventional fluting,
        acorn ejector rod.
Retailer: ARMY & NAVY C.S.L. LONDON

Joseph L. Davis collection

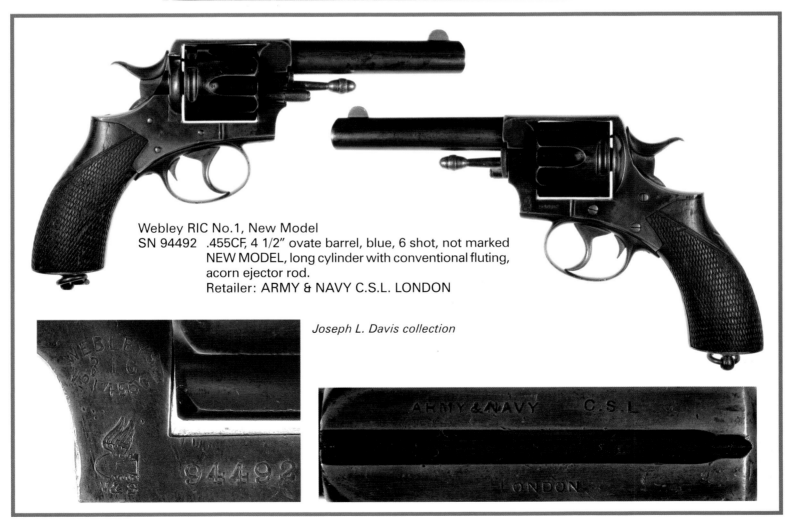

Webley RIC No. 1, New Model

SN 94862 .450CF, 4 1/2" barrel, blue, 6 shot, short cylinder with conventional fluting, acorn ejector rod.

Retailer: ARMY & NAVY C.S.L. LONDON

This A&N C.S.L. page dating from the early 1890s demonstrates just how many old frames the Webley factory had lying around. In this case, these RICs had longer frames capable of chambering the .476 and .455. Eventually, there was a concerted effort to get rid of the short frames on hand. Also, by offering longer frame RICs in 38/40, 44/40, and .45 Colt, Webley hoped to rid themselves of frames still in stock. Shooters still preferred the simultaneous ejection offered by hinge frame Webleys, Smith & Wessons, and even the Colt Model 1889, and later side swinging cylinder revolvers.

Used with permission of Glasgow University.
http://www.gla.ac.uk/archives/

No.	Description	Size of Bore	Cost	Selling	When Sold
37124	R.I.C.Plain	.476	M.N.A.R	5.00	
37129	"	"	"	"	
37130	"	"	"	"	
37135	"	"	"	"	
37121	"	"	"	R 37.8	
37122	"	"	"	"	
37123	"	"	"	"	
37127	"	"	"	"	
37128	"	"	"	"	
6104	"	"	"	"	
6226	"	"	"	"	
6228	"	"	"	"	
6239	"	"	"	"	
87002	"	"	"	"	
36998	"	"	"	"	
36994	"	"	"	"	
87050	"	"	"	"	
87051	"	"	"	5.00	
87053	"	"	"	"	

Joseph L. Davis collection

The Bentley and
Commonwealth Police Department RIC

During the percussion era, the Webley brothers and Joseph Bentley's firm were closely linked. Philip's elder brother James was probably apprenticed to Joseph Bentley. Philip, upon finishing his apprenticeship under Benjamin Watson (the younger), went into partnership with James. When Philip married in 1838, the partnership split up. In 1851, James is recorded as working at No.14 St. Mary's Row, an address shared by Joseph Bentley. At this time he employed 24 men making pepperbox pistols, and eventually, percussion revolvers. James is best remembered for the "Longspur" revolver which he patented in 1853, and which Philip exploited after James sudden death in 1856. When he married, Philip was lodged in Tower Road, where the Bentley family house was also situated. Bentley's London Tower trademark was named after the Tower Gun manufactory run by Joseph's son David, who appears to have been particularly active in obtaining orders from both domestic and foreign constabularies. He naturally went to P. Webley & Son to supply these orders. By the last decade of the nineteenth century, Webley was selling direct to many of England's colonial police and law enforcement agencies throughout the world. In May 1912, Webley & Scott sold 47 T.P.F marked revolvers directly to Rice, Lewis and Son at Toronto. In April 1914, they sold to Rice, Lewis & Son another 44 T.P.F marked .442CF revolvers.

Joel Black collection

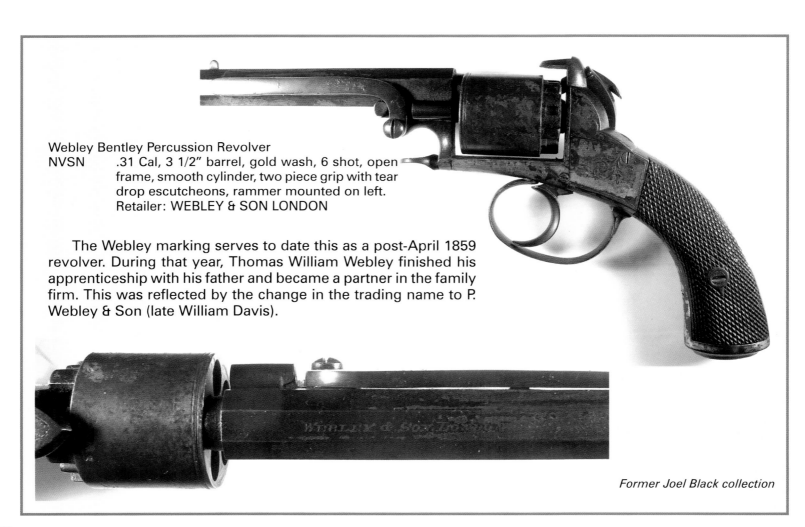

Webley Bentley Percussion Revolver
NVSN   .31 Cal, 3 1/2" barrel, gold wash, 6 shot, open frame, smooth cylinder, two piece grip with tear drop escutcheons, rammer mounted on left.
Retailer: WEBLEY & SON LONDON

The Webley marking serves to date this as a post-April 1859 revolver. During that year, Thomas William Webley finished his apprenticeship with his father and became a partner in the family firm. This was reflected by the change in the trading name to P. Webley & Son (late William Davis).

Former Joel Black collection

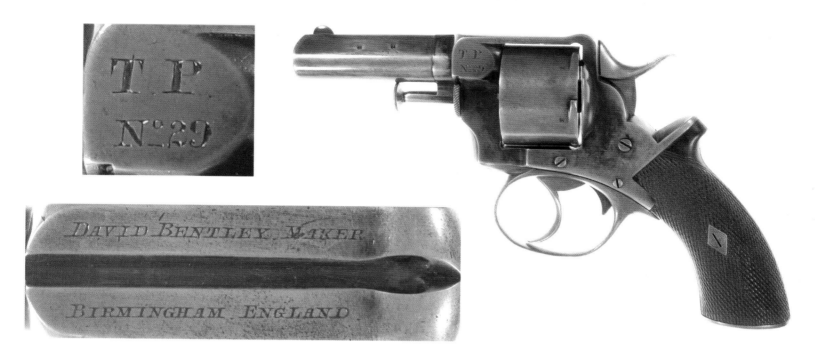

Webley Pre-RIC No. 1, 1st Pattern
SN 40 .442, 4" barrel, blue, 6 shot, two-piece checkered wood grips with diamond escutcheons, smooth cylinder with protruding rear stops, barrel mounted swivel, TP No 29 flat headed, lack of a proof mark on frame means it was made prior to July 1868, while the frame style indicates a likely 1867 date.
Retailer: DAVID BENTLEY MAKER BIRMINGHAM ENGLAND

This revolver and number 99 are perhaps most important finds in retelling the history of Webley solid frame revolvers. They appear to represent the first sale by Webley (via David Bentley) to a police department. The frame style, serial number, and lack of July 1868 proof mark, indicate they were sold in 1867. This was a year after the Fenian raids into Canada, a year before the JPF and RIC sales. The latter is considered the seminal event, which propelled Webley into the realm of manufacturers. This sale to the Toronto police likely was used as a selling point when they were making the next year's sales.

Marking on butt cap.

Joel Black collection

Note the flat sided hammer that could be filed to suit either rimfire or centerfire cartridges.

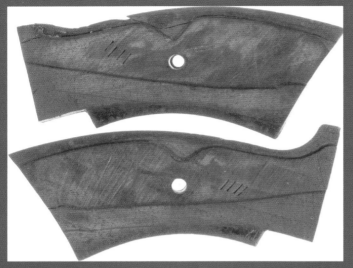

The assembly number 70 can be seen faintly penciled in, while the //// is the worker's mark.

Inside of loading gate.

Cylinder axis pin.

When Serial number 96 was first studied, it was thought that the apprentice who was assigned to applying the serial numbers to the back of the cylinder had mistakenly held his stamp upside down and transformed a 99 into a 96. When serial number 40 and 22 were disassembled it became obvious that Webley used the number on the frame and grips as assembly numbers to ensure that those hand fitted pieces stayed together. S&W used the same method marking the crane, with its mating point on the frame and on the underside of the barrel. The Roman numerals on the grips, cylinder axis pin, and loading gate identified the workers who fitted them and were paid on a piecework basis.

Inside of rear gripstrap.

Webley Pre-RIC No. 1, 1st Pattern
SN 96 .442, 4" barrel, blue, 6 shot, two-piece checkered wood grips with diamond escutcheons, smooth cylinder with protruding rear stops, barrel mounted swivel, TP № 1, flat headed, no proof mark on frame (required after July 1868).
Retailer: DAVID BENTLEY MAKER BIRMINGHAM ENGLAND

Norman Lanthier collection, Yves Lanthier photos

This revolver and serial number 40 were undoubtedly among a group of approximately 30 bought by the Toronto Police in 1867. This was in reaction to the Fenian raids of 1866.

In this very early photo *(right)* of decidedly relaxed Toronto police officers, side arms in holsters are visible.

In this later photo *(left)*, Canadian police officers are seen in a military stance proudly displaying their newly furnished Ross rifles. *Courtesy of Peter Vronsky http://www.russianbooks.org/crime/cph3.htm*

The history of the purchase and use of side arms by the Toronto Police serves as a microcosm of the rise and fall of Webley as a firearms manufacturer. The following photo from the 1960s is emblematic of the end of Webley as a serious player in the firearms world. Here a Toronto police officer is shown shooting his Colt Police Positive revolver rather than one of the previously issued Webley MK IV hinge frame revolvers.

Courtesy of Peter Vronsky http://www.russianbooks.org/crime/cph3.htm

$10.00

A Genuine

WEBLEY Revolver

Royal Irish Constabulary Model. Complete with Holster.

These revolvers cost over $40.00 to import, and were used by the Police Dept. of one of our biggest Cities, from whom we bought them. Every one is in perfect order, and except for the bluing on the barrel being slightly worn, are as good as when they left the factory. They take .44 cal. WEBLEY cartridges. Will stop anything in the woods and a real protection for the home or store.

State whether you want 2¾ or 3½ inch barrel. We will sell to

Canadian or American Citizens Only Please Furnish Reference

Send Money Order or we will ship C.O.D.

Money returned if not satisfied. The Publishers of *Rod and Gun* will guarantee our good faith.

A. K. COULTER, 70 Lombard St., Toronto

The following advertisement from the early 1950s indicates the Toronto Police kept these obsolete Webleys in service until they purchased MK IV .38s.

Courtesy of http://www.joesalter.com/

Webley RIC Pre-No. 1, 1st Pattern 4 Screw
SN 141   .442CF, 3" barrel, blue, 6 shot, smooth
cylinder with front locking recesses,
flat headed ejector swivels from barrel,
J.P.F. 49 on the left frame, no lanyard
ring, proof on frame.
Retailer: DAVID BENTLEY MAKER.
BIRMINGHAM, ENGLAND

Norman Lanthier collection, Yves Lanthier photos

Norman Lanthier collection, Yves Lanthier photos

Norman Lanthier collection,
Yves Lanthier photos

Note the post July 1868 proof mark.
Norman Lanthier collection, Yves Lanthier photos

Norman Lanthier collection, Yves Lanthier photos

Norman Lanthier collection, Yves Lanthier photos

Frank & Jean Pycha collection

Webley RIC Pre-No. 1, 1st Pattern 4 Screw SN 151 .442CF, 3" barrel, blue, 6 shot, smooth cylinder with front locking recesses, flat headed ejector swivels from barrel, J.P.F. 57 on the left frame, no lanyard ring, note proof on right frame.
Retailer: DAVID BENTLEY MAKER. BIRMINGHAM, ENGLAND

Webley RIC Pre-No. 1, 1st Pattern 4 Screw
SN 987   .442CF, 3" barrel, blue, 6 shot, smooth cylinder with front locking
recesses, unusual oval headed ejector swivels from barrel, J.P.F. 70
on the left frame, no lanyard ring, no proof on frame.
Retailer: DAVID BENTLEY MAKER. BIRMINGHAM, ENGLAND

Nick Preston collection

Webley RIC Pre-No. 1, 1st Pattern 4 Screw
SN 980   .442CF, 3 3/4" barrel, blue, 6 shot, one-piece checkered wood grip, smooth cylinder with front locking
recesses, barrel mounted swivel, flat headed ejector rod, lanyard ring is removed, J.P.F 76 on left, no
proof mark on frame.
Retailer: DAVID BENTLEY, MAKER BIRMINGHAM
ENGLAND

Although we are not sure, we believe these "JPF"
RICs were supplied to the Jersey Police Force (Channel
Island). J.P.F. numbers 70, 76, and 78, along with T.P.F.
No. 103, were all made and proofed prior to mid-July
1868. J.P.F. number 57 was proofed after mid-July 1868.
This convinces us that the 4 screw RIC style was made
concurrently with the RIC version with rear projecting
cylinder stops. Because these 4 screw 1st Pattern RICs
were sold throughout 1868, the year of the Royal Irish
Constabulary's first contract, it was likely this pattern was
also delivered to both Jersey and Toronto police forces
(although in this case after the first 30, which were 1st
pattern 3 screw Pre-RICs).

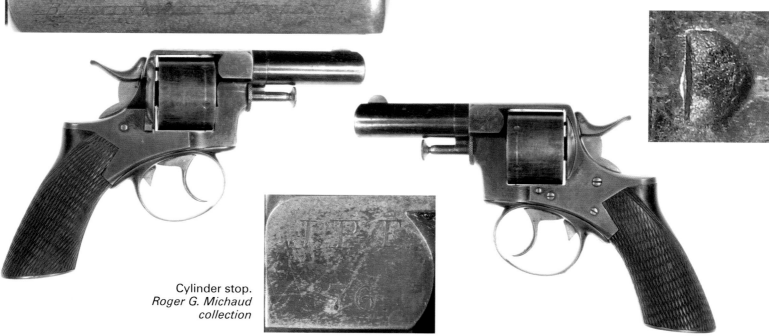

Cylinder stop.
*Roger G. Michaud
collection*

Webley RIC Pre-No. 1, 1st Pattern 4 Screw
SN 989   .442CF, 3 3/8" barrel, blue, 6 shot, one-piece checkered wood grip, smooth cylinder with front locking recesses, barrel mounted swivel, flat headed ejector rod, lanyard ring is removed, J.P.F 75 on left, proof mark on right frame.
Retailer: DAVID BENTLEY, MAKER BIRMINGHAM ENGLAND

Webley RIC Pre-No. 1, 1st Pattern 4 Screw
SN 11   .442CF, 3" barrel, blue, 6 shot, smooth cylinder with front locking recesses, ejector swivels from barrel, lanyard ring, J.P.F. 78 on the left frame, no proof mark on frame.
Retailer: DAVID BENTLEY, MAKER BIRMINGHAM, ENGLAND

This is the lowest known serial number of a 4 screw RIC Pre-No. 1.

Once Webley was in a position of power, they moved to stop Bentley from marking "MAKER" on subsequent lots.

Joel Black collection

Webley Pre-RIC No. 1
NVSN .442CF, 2 1/2" barrel, blue, 6 shot, cylinder with conventional fluting, DMP on right frame, TRADE MARK LONDON TOWER on left frame, Crown BR 18 government inspector's mark on butt plate, lanyard ring is missing, one-piece checkered wood grip.
Retailer: DAVID BENTLEY BIRMINGHAM

Nick Preston collection

In place of "Maker", David Bentley started to stamp RICs retailed by him with the "London Tower" trademark. It is thought that this revolver was sold to the Dublin police.

Webley RIC Model/82
SN 34150 .442CF, 2 1/2" barrel, blue, 6 shot, smooth cylinder with rear locking recesses, ejector swivels from frame, no lanyard ring, T.P.F. 7 (Toronto Police Force) on the left frame.
Retailer: DAVID BENTLEY BIRMINGHAM

Joel Black collection

This is an early RIC/82, and proves that "THE TOWER BULL DOG" trademark was owned by Bentley at this time. This is the only known RIC/82 with this marking. Mr. Black believes Webley acquired both the Tower Bull Dog and London Tower trademarks from Bentley around 1884.

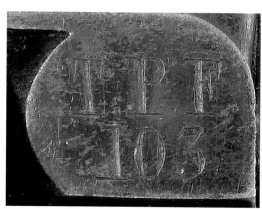

Webley RIC Pre-No. 1, 1st Pattern 4 Screw
SN 236 .442CF, 3 1/2" barrel, blue, 6 shot,
smooth cylinder with front locking
recesses, flat headed swivel type ejector rod, lanyard ring hole plugged,
T.P.F 103 (Toronto Police Force) is
engraved, no frame proof mark.
Retailer: DAVID BENTLEY
BIRMINGHAM, ENGLAND

Frank Pycha collection

Webley RIC No. 1, Transitional New Model
SN 35001 .442CF, 3 1/2" barrel, blue, 6 shot, one-piece checkered
wood grip, smooth cylinder with elongated rear locking recesses, acorn headed ejector rod, no lanyard
ring, T. P. F. 196, has winged bullet logo above SN on
lower left frame.
Retailer: DAVID BENTLEY BIRMINGHAM.

Joseph L. Davis collection

Webley RIC No. 1, Transitional New Model
SN 36263 .442CF, 3 1/2" barrel, blue, 6 shot, smooth
cylinder with elongated rear locking recesses, acorn ejector rod, no lanyard ring,
T.P.F. 227 on upper front portion of the left
frame.
Retailer: DAVID BENTLEY BIRMINGHAM

Note that this revolver has a flat butt plate
and no provision for a lanyard ring.

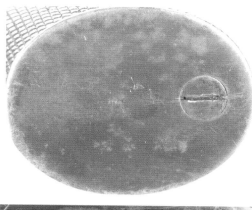

Joseph L. Davis collection

David Bentley was a gun and pistol maker at
Birmingham, England, between 1845 and 1883.
Between 1871 and 1883, his business address was
listed at Tower Works, 45 Tower Road, Aston. His use
of the Tower of London trademark began by 1875.

Webley RIC No. 1, Transitional New Model
SN 82159 .442CF, 3 1/2" barrel, blue, 6 shot, smooth cylinder with elongated rear locking recesses, acorn ejector rod, no lanyard ring, T.P.F. 230 TPF and inventory number are on opposite sides of frame, one-piece checkered wood grip, flat bottom to grip.
Retailer: P. WEBLEY & SON BIRMINGHAM

Roger G. Michaud collection

The serial number, paired with an acorn ejector rod finial, places this revolver in the New Model period. As previously mentioned, Webley assembled older RIC frames with short length smooth cylinders to unsuspecting Canadian municipal police departments. For most Canadians at the turn of the twentieth century, the .442 was uncommon relative to the more available .455 or .38 calibers.

(Webley?) RIC No. 1
NVSN   .442CF, 3 1/2" barrel, blue, 6 shot, smooth cylinder with elongated
        rear locking recesses, Tranter style ejector rod, lanyard ring, T.P.F.
        279 on left frame, angled at base of butt.
        Retailer: BENTLEY & PLAYFAIR L^{TD}
                  BIRMINGHAM ENGLAND

Courtesy of Paul Breakey

The Tranter Model 1868 style ejector is unusual. The firm of Bentley & Playfair at Summer Lane, Birmingham, manufactured arms, but for a time were tenants of Tranter.

(Webley?) RIC No. 1, New Model
SN 45   .442CF, 3 1/2" barrel, blue, 6 shot, fluted cylinder with elongated rear locking recesses, Tranter style ejector rod, missing lanyard ring, T.P.F. 292 on left frame, angled butt.
Retailer: BENTLEY & PLAYFAIR LTD BIRMINGHAM ENGLAND

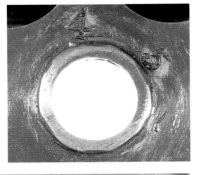

Frank & Jean Pycha collection

Webley RIC No. 1, New Model
SN 94055 .442CF, 3 1/2" barrel, in the white, 6 shot, conventional fluting, acorn ejector rod, T.P.F. 356 on the left frame, lanyard ring.

Ian McPherson collection

Retailer: P. WEBLEY & SON LONDON & BIRMINGHAM

Webley RIC No. 1, New Model
SN 95520 .22LR, 6" barrel, blue, short cylinder with conventional fluting, no lanyard ring, thin acorn ejector rod, stamped T.P.F 598, permanently converted to .22 with target sights installed for practice.

Retailer: P. WEBLEY & SON LONDON & BIRMINGHAM

Joseph L. Davis collection

Webley RIC No. 1, New Model
SN 95551 .442CF, 3 1/2" barrel, blue, 6 shot, conventional fluting, acorn ejector rod,
T.P.F. 425 on the left frame, lanyard ring.
Retailer: P. WEBLEY & SON LONDON & BIRMINGHAM

Joseph L. Davis collection

Webley RIC No. 1, New Model
SN 95641 .442CF, 3 1/2" barrel, blue, 6 shot, conventional fluting, acorn ejector rod, grip has the rare head crusher buttcap, T.P.F. 436 on the left frame.
Retailer: P. WEBLEY & SON LONDON & BIRMINGHAM

Courtesy of Greg Crockett

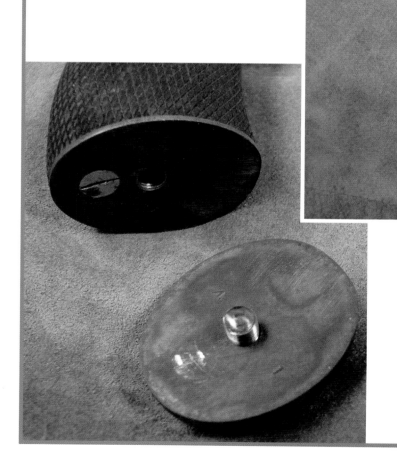

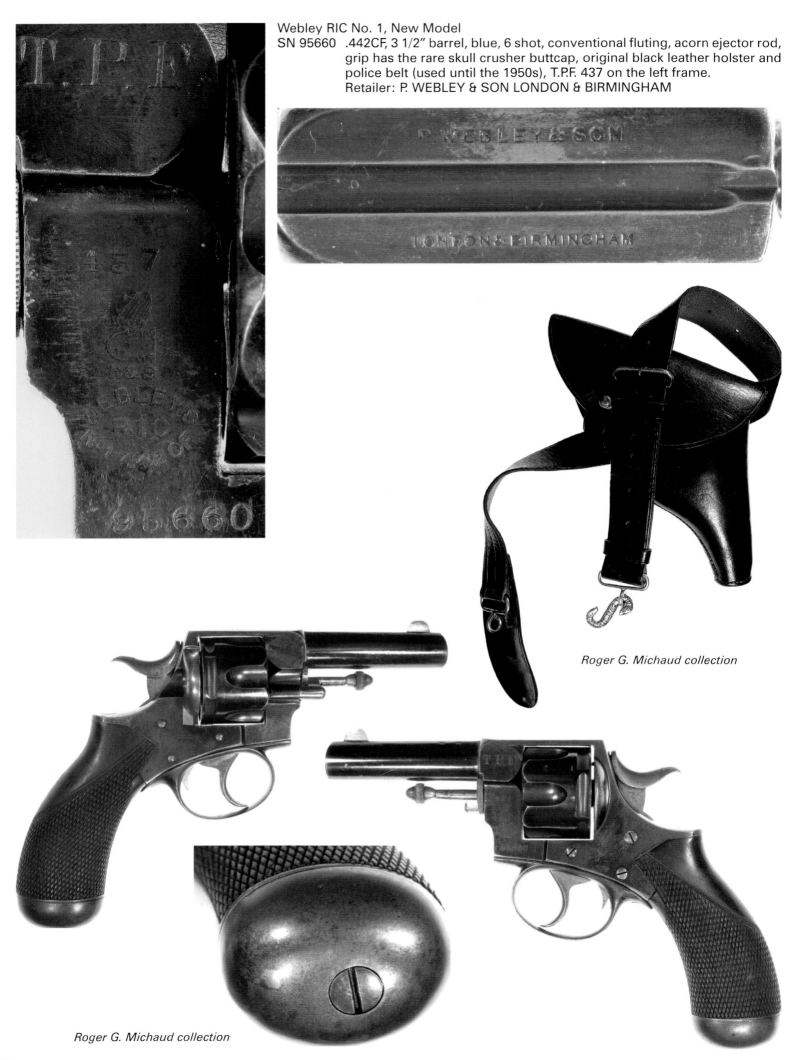

Webley RIC No. 1, New Model
SN 95660 .442CF, 3 1/2" barrel, blue, 6 shot, conventional fluting, acorn ejector rod, grip has the rare skull crusher buttcap, original black leather holster and police belt (used until the 1950s), T.P.F. 437 on the left frame.
Retailer: P. WEBLEY & SON LONDON & BIRMINGHAM

Roger G. Michaud collection

Roger G. Michaud collection

Webley RIC No. 1, New Model
SN 99289 .442CF, 3 1/2" barrel, blue, 6 shot, conventional fluting, acorn ejector
rod, grip has the rare skull crusher buttcap, T.P.F. 449 on the left front
frame.
Retailer: P. WEBLEY & SON LONDON & BIRMINGHAM

Joseph L. Davis collection

*Joseph L. Davis
collection*

Webley RIC No. 1, New Model
SN 99317 .442CF, 3 5/8" barrel, blue, 6 shot, conventional fluting, acorn ejector rod, designed without a lanyard ring, T.P.F. 480 on left frame.
Retailer: P. WEBLEY & SON LONDON & BIRMINGHAM

Frank & Jean Pycha collection

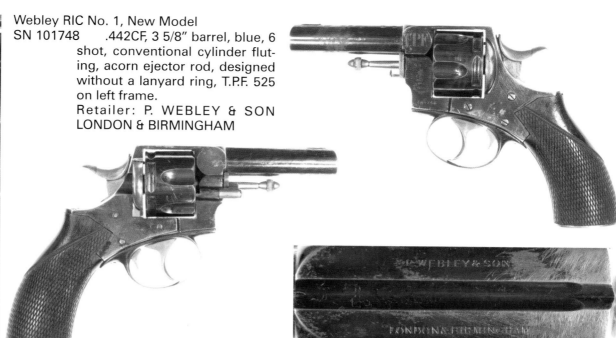

Webley RIC No. 1, New Model
SN 101748   .442CF, 3 5/8" barrel, blue, 6 shot, conventional cylinder fluting, acorn ejector rod, designed without a lanyard ring, T.P.F. 525 on left frame.
Retailer: P. WEBLEY & SON LONDON & BIRMINGHAM

Roger G. Michaud collection

Roger G. Michaud collection

Webley Metropolitan Police (Late pattern)
SN 101758   .442, 2 1/2" barrel, blue, conventional cylinder flutes, acorn style ejector rod, broader grip base design, serial number on the left side of frame, stamped TPF 81 above Webley's M.P. logo on left frame, trigger guard cut away at a later date
Retailer: P. WEBLEY & SON LONDON & BIRMINGHAM

This is the only marked MP observed in a caliber other than .450. As previous noted the short barrel Webleys were in a numbering sequence separate from the others.

Courtesy of Normand Lanthier

RIC Model/82, W.J. Hill and Metropolitan Police

As with the standard RIC, this model existed before being named due to a major sale to an important police agency. At first it carried no model designation. In 1882, it was called the RIC Model/82. A year later, it was adopted by the London Metropolitan Police and renamed the MP. All initial purchase and future MPs were chambered for .450CF, and marked with a Crown over MP Any Webley with the same webbed swivel as an early MP but not in .450 is an RIC Model/82. Unless otherwise noted, all MP **** revolvers have a lanyard ring, one-piece checkered wood grip, commercial British proofs, a rounded front sight, and V notch rear sight. Metropolitan Police revolvers are all 6 shot. They have the logo of two manacled hands beneath which are the initials MP – Webley's trademark created for police models. In 1905, in order to address safety issues, 370 of 931 Metropolitan Police revolvers had a second set of cylinder stops added, and a rebounding, blocked hammer installed. The total number of revolvers bought by the force is unknown. Some MPs were bought by the public. It also appears that the New South Wales Police purchased several hundred MPs.

No. 8, GUN Department—Second Floor.

WEBLEY'S REVOLVER, AS ADOPTED BY THE METROPOLITAN POLICE, November, 1883.

R. I. C. Model /82.   ·450, 6 Shot.   2½ in. Barrel.

Scale, ⅓ size.

Courtesy of Gordon Bruce

This cut from an original January 1884 Army & Navy C.S.L. catalog nicely serves to both confirm the date of introduction and configuration of this model. Note that this was printed just before the name change.

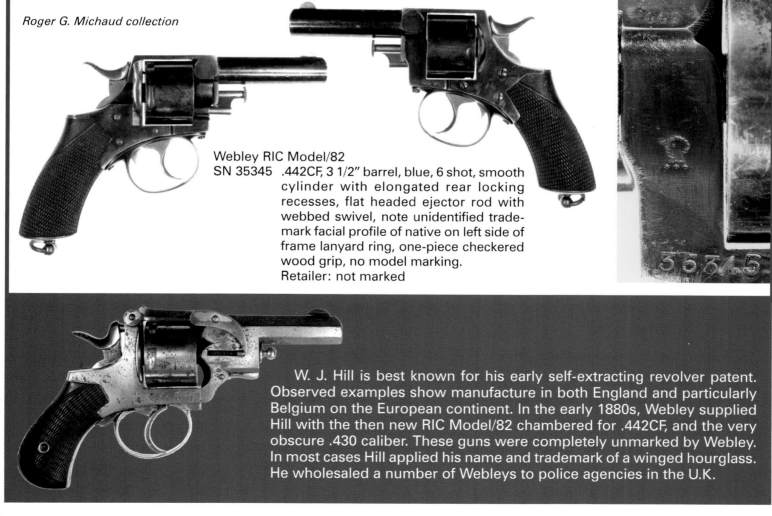

Roger G. Michaud collection

Webley RIC Model/82
SN 35345 .442CF, 3 1/2" barrel, blue, 6 shot, smooth cylinder with elongated rear locking recesses, flat headed ejector rod with webbed swivel, note unidentified trademark facial profile of native on left side of frame lanyard ring, one-piece checkered wood grip, no model marking.
Retailer: not marked

W. J. Hill is best known for his early self-extracting revolver patent. Observed examples show manufacture in both England and particularly Belgium on the European continent. In the early 1880s, Webley supplied Hill with the then new RIC Model/82 chambered for .442CF, and the very obscure .430 caliber. These guns were completely unmarked by Webley. In most cases Hill applied his name and trademark of a winged hourglass. He wholesaled a number of Webleys to police agencies in the U.K.

"HILL'S PATENT BULL DOG SELF EXTRACTOR"

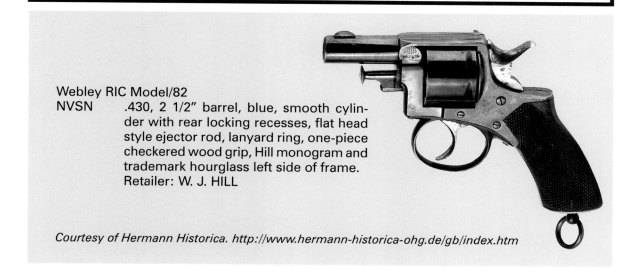

Webley RIC Model/82
NVSN   .430, 2 1/2" barrel, blue, smooth cylinder with rear locking recesses, flat head style ejector rod, lanyard ring, one-piece checkered wood grip, Hill monogram and trademark hourglass left side of frame.
Retailer: W. J. HILL

Courtesy of Hermann Historica. http://www.hermann-historica-ohg.de/gb/index.htm

Nick Preston collection

Webley RIC Model/82
NVSN   .430, 2 1/2" barrel, blue, smooth cylinder with rear locking recesses, flat head style ejector rod (note webbed swivel), faint trademark flying hourglass right side of frame, crown on left side.
Retailer: W. J. HILL

Webley RIC Model/82
SN 2135   .430, 2 1/2" barrel, blue, smooth cylinder with
rear locking recesses, flat head style ejector rod,
crown above RIC on upper frame left side, Hill
trademark hourglass on upper frame right side.
Retailer: W. J. HILL

*Nick Preston
collection*

This crown over
RIC indicates this
revolver was sold by
Hill to the Royal Irish
Constabulary.

Joseph L. Davis collection

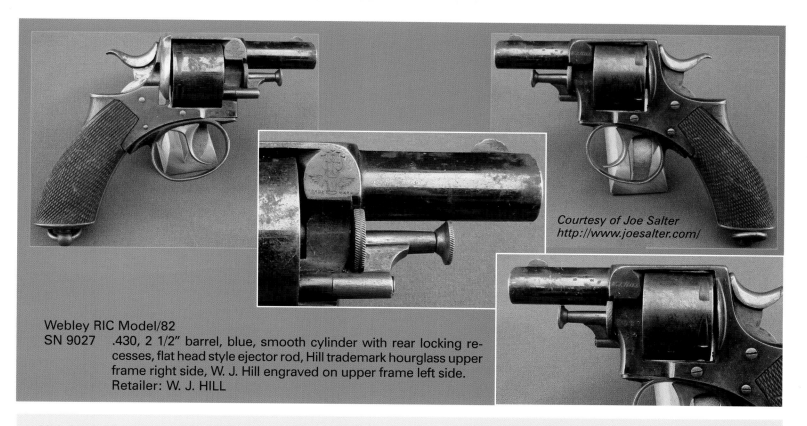

Webley RIC Model/82
SN 9027   .430, 2 1/2" barrel, blue, smooth cylinder with rear locking recesses, flat head style ejector rod, Hill trademark hourglass upper
frame right side, W. J. Hill engraved on upper frame left side.
Retailer: W. J. HILL

Courtesy of Joe Salter
http://www.joesalter.com/

Webley RIC Model/82
NVSN   .442, 2 1/2" barrel, original dull nickel finish,
smooth cylinder with rear locking recesses,
lanyard ring, Adams' style flat headed ejector rod (webbed swivel), tapered stock,
marked Wolverhampton Police No. 11.
Retailer: W. J. HILL

Courtesy of Richard Milner http://www.armsresearch.co.uk/

Webley RIC Model/82
NVSN   .442, 2 1/2" barrel, blued, smooth
cylinder with rear locking recesses,
Adams' style ejector rod, lanyard ring,
tapered stock, lanyard ring, marked
Wolverhampton Police No. 12.
Retailer: W. J. HILL

Courtesy of Richard Milner http://www.armsresearch.co.uk/

Webley RIC Model/82
NVSN .442, 2 1/2" barrel, original dull nickel with engraving on
top strap, Adams' style ejector rod with webbed swivel,
tapered stock, lanyard ring, smooth cylinder with rear
locking recesses, gripstrap is marked: WOLVERHAMPTON
POLICE Nº 27.
Retailer: not marked

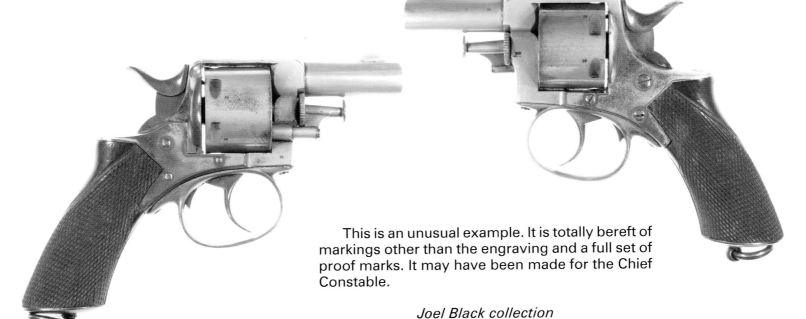

This is an unusual example. It is totally bereft of markings other than the engraving and a full set of proof marks. It may have been made for the Chief Constable.

Joel Black collection

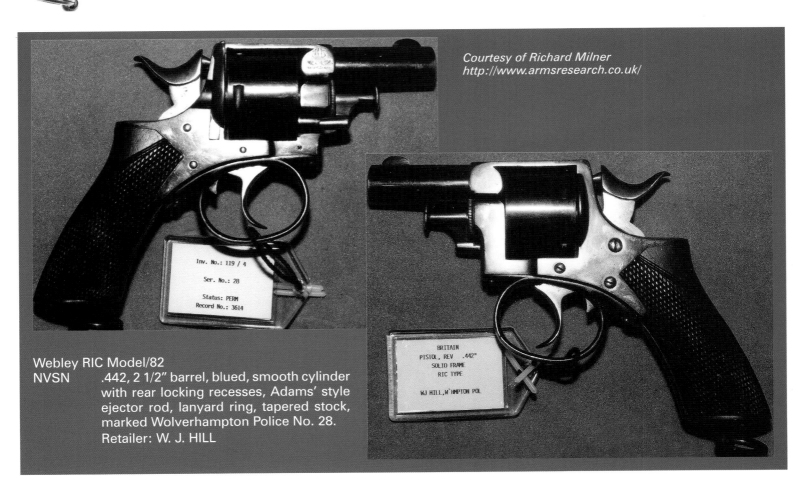

Courtesy of Richard Milner
http://www.armsresearch.co.uk/

Webley RIC Model/82
NVSN .442, 2 1/2" barrel, blued, smooth cylinder
with rear locking recesses, Adams' style
ejector rod, lanyard ring, tapered stock,
marked Wolverhampton Police No. 28.
Retailer: W. J. HILL

Webley RIC Model/82

SN 481   .442, 2 1/2" barrel, blue, Adam's style ejector rod, smooth cylinder with rear locking recesses, lanyard ring, tapered stock, N° 2734 (rack number) and Crown RIC on front of left frame indicates Royal Irish Constabulary ownership.
Retailer: TRULOCK & HARRISS DUBLIN

Frank & Jean Pycha collection

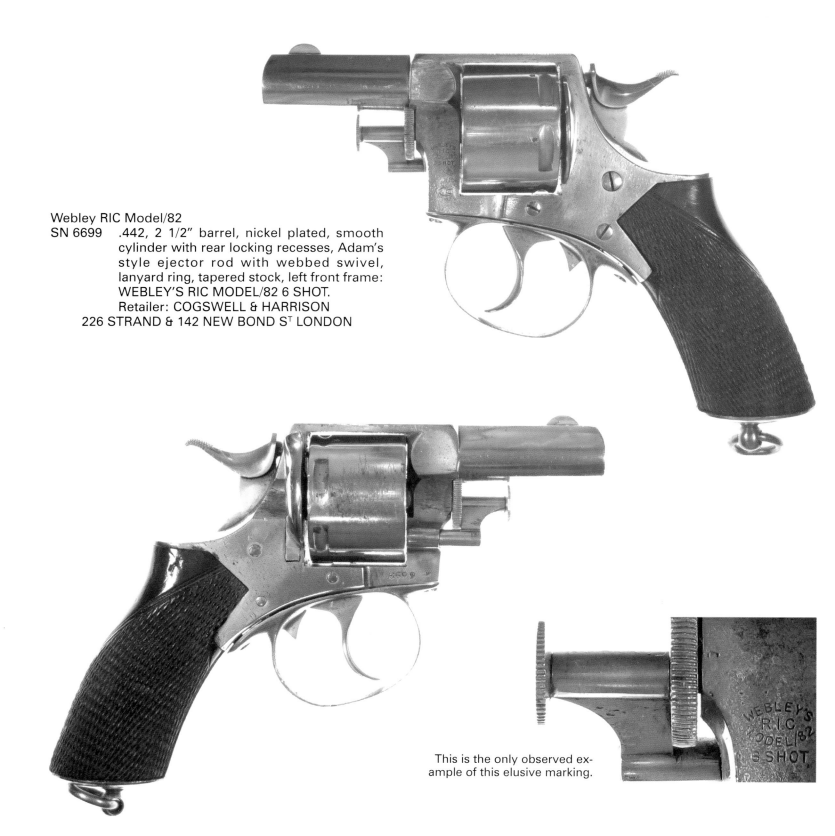

Webley RIC Model/82
SN 6699 .442, 2 1/2" barrel, nickel plated, smooth
cylinder with rear locking recesses, Adam's
style ejector rod with webbed swivel,
lanyard ring, tapered stock, left front frame:
WEBLEY'S RIC MODEL/82 6 SHOT.
Retailer: COGSWELL & HARRISON
226 STRAND & 142 NEW BOND S^T LONDON

This is the only observed example of this elusive marking.

*Frank & Jean Pycha
collection*

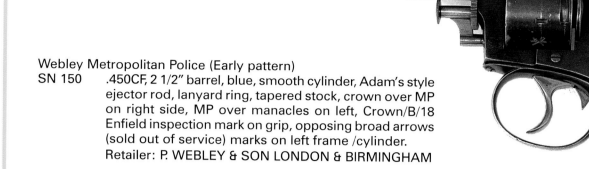

Webley Metropolitan Police (Early pattern)
SN 150   .450CF, 2 1/2" barrel, blue, smooth cylinder, Adam's style ejector rod, lanyard ring, tapered stock, crown over MP on right side, MP over manacles on left, Crown/B/18 Enfield inspection mark on grip, opposing broad arrows (sold out of service) marks on left frame /cylinder.
Retailer: P. WEBLEY & SON LONDON & BIRMINGHAM

This is an extremely rare 1st pattern MP which in 1905, along with 369 others, were fitted with an extra set of cylinder stops to accommodate a rebounding, blocked hammer. This was meant to address safety issues expressed by the Met.

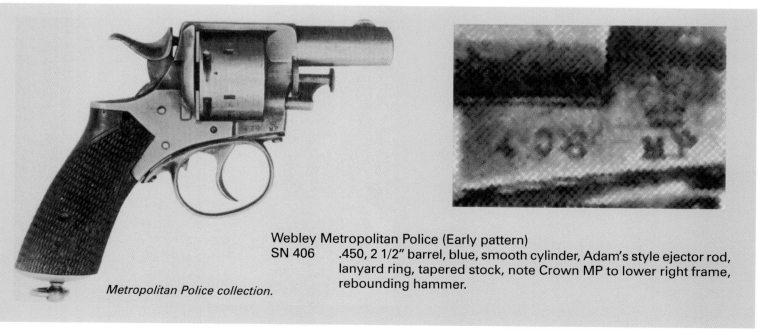

Webley Metropolitan Police (Early pattern)
SN 406   .450, 2 1/2" barrel, blue, smooth cylinder, Adam's style ejector rod, lanyard ring, tapered stock, note Crown MP to lower right frame, rebounding hammer.

Metropolitan Police collection.

Webley Metropolitan Police (Early pattern)
SN 135   .450, 2 1/2" barrel, nickel, smooth cylinder, Adam's style ejector rod, lanyard
ring, tapered stock, lanyard ring.
Retailer: COGSWELL & HARRISON
226 STRAND & 142 NEW BOND S^T LONDON

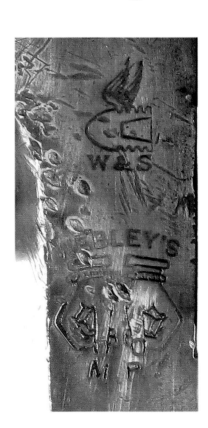

112

Webley Metropolitan Police (Early pattern)
SN 31788 .450, 2 1/2" barrel, blue, smooth
cylinder, Adam's style ejector rod,
lanyard ring, tapered stock.
Retailer: COGSWELL & HARRISON
226 STRAND LONDON

Joseph L. Davis collection

Roger G. Michaud collection

Webley Metropolitan Police (Early pattern)
SN 34566 .450 (stamped over .442), 2 1/2" barrel, blue, smooth cylinder, Adam's style ejector rod, lanyard ring, tapered stock, no police number.
Retailer: P. WEBLEY & SON BIRMINGHAM

The .442 marking can be seen below the .450.

Webley Metropolitan Police (Early pattern) SN 34837 .450, 2 1/2" barrel, blue, smooth cylinder, flat headed ejector rod with webbed swivel, lanyard ring, tapered stock, no police number, in oak case with accessories and P. C. Harris' Victoria Jubilee Police medal.
Retailer: P. WEBLEY & SON BIRMINGHAM & LONDON

Joel Black collection

This is one of the very few known cased MPs. It was presented by Lord Burton to Police Constable R. Harris of K division (Bow St) in 1888. P. C. Harris' Victoria Jubilee medal is still with the revolver. At the time of this presentation, Lord Burton was reputed to be the richest industrialist in England. He is still known for Bass Beer and was the first "Beer Baron". The most likely explanation for this presentation to a mere P.C. from so lofty a personage is that Harris was assigned to protect him after the "Bloody Sunday" labor riots.

Webley RIC No 1 [Metropolitan Police (Early pattern)]
SN 35840 .450, 2 1/2" barrel, blue, smooth cylinder, flat headed ejector rod
with webbed swivel, lanyard ring, tapered stock, government
inspection marks on stock and frame
Retailer: TRULOCK & HARRISS DUBLIN

Courtesy of Pat Donnelly
http://www.patdonnellyantiquearms.com/index.htm

This is one of the most interesting Webleys to come to light. It certainly is an early pattern MP in the expected .450 caliber. With the over stamped caliber marking on MP serial number 34566 we can see Webley was hard pressed to keep up demand for solid frame revolvers while filling large orders for their new, more modern, hinge frame revolvers. In this case they fitted a 2 1/2" barrel along with a smooth short .450 cylinder and an MP webbed ejector rod swivel to a frame in stock marked RIC No. 1. It is assumed the front of the frame rather than the left side (as seen on RIC/82 serial number 481) was used because the model number already occupied that space. It is also possible Trulock & Harriss had it marked RIC No. 1 to avoid possible confusion if it was marked MP. In any case this revolver in another of the rarely seen Webleys used by the RIC.

Bottom to top: Early pattern, Transitional pattern, Late pattern.

Badges, whistles and a truncheon all used
by London's Metropolitan Police.

Roger G. Michaud collection

Webley Metropolitan Police (Transitional pattern)
SN 69590 .450, 2 1/2" barrel, blue,
smooth cylinder, acorn
style ejector rod, thicker
grip design, stamped PO-
LICE 488 on right lower
frame.
Retailer: P. WEBLEY & SON
LONDON & BIRMING-
HAM

First observed use of the acorn finial.
Frank & Jean Pycha collection

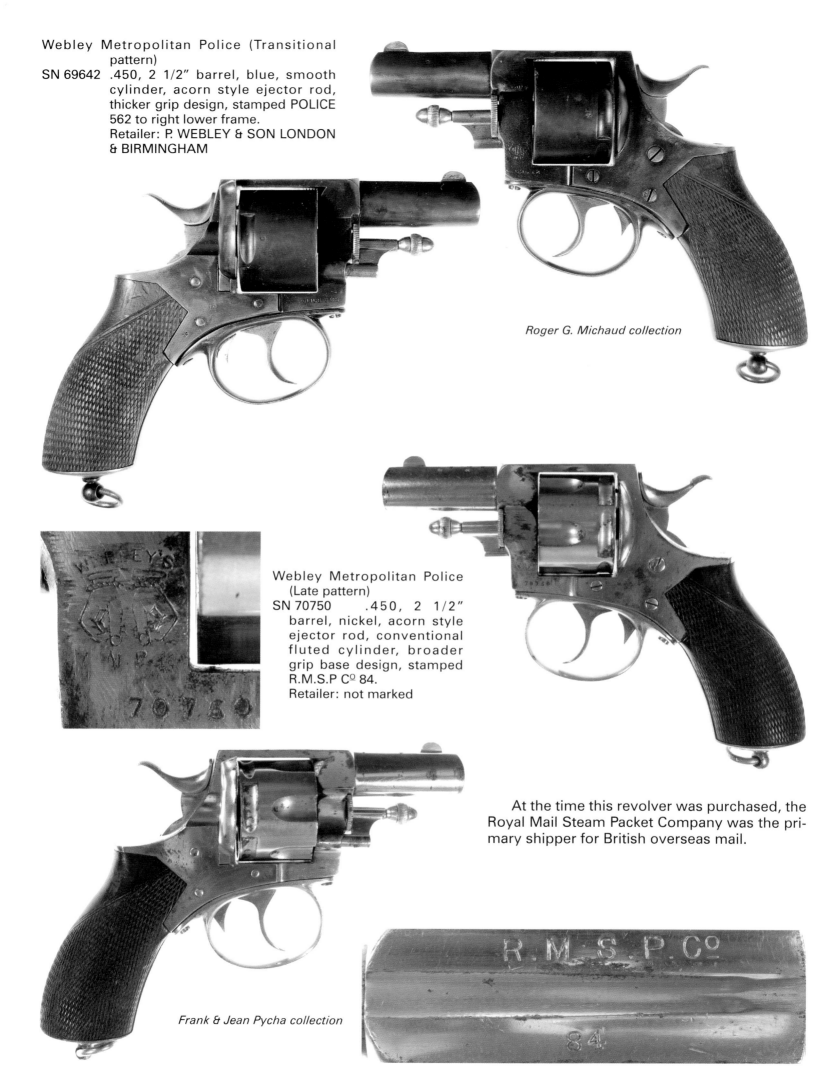

Webley Metropolitan Police (Transitional
   pattern)
SN 69642 .450, 2 1/2" barrel, blue, smooth
   cylinder, acorn style ejector rod,
   thicker grip design, stamped POLICE
   562 to right lower frame.
   Retailer: P. WEBLEY & SON LONDON
   & BIRMINGHAM

Roger G. Michaud collection

Webley Metropolitan Police
   (Late pattern)
SN 70750   .450, 2 1/2"
   barrel, nickel, acorn style
   ejector rod, conventional
   fluted cylinder, broader
   grip base design, stamped
   R.M.S.P Cᵒ 84.
   Retailer: not marked

At the time this revolver was purchased, the
Royal Mail Steam Packet Company was the pri-
mary shipper for British overseas mail.

Frank & Jean Pycha collection

Webley Metropolitan Police (Early pattern)
SN 74342 .450, 2 1/2" barrel, blue, flat head ejector rod, broader grip base design, smooth cylinder with rear locking recesses, police number 423 on front of frame.
Retailer: P. WEBLEY & SON BIRMINGHAM

Frank & Jean Pycha collection

Frank & Jean Pycha collection

Webley Metropolitan Police (Late pattern)
SN 79429 .450, 2 1/2" barrel, blue, acorn style ejector rod, conventional fluted cylinder, broader grip base design, stamped POLICE on left top strap, police No.824 under loading gate.
Retailer: P. WEBLEY & SON LONDON & BIRMINGHAM

Webley Metropolitan Police (Late pattern)
SN 79437 .450, 2 1/2" barrel, blue, acorn style ejector rod, conventional fluted cylinder, broader grip base design, stamped POLICE on left top strap.
Retailer: P. WEBLEY & SON LONDON & BIRMINGHAM

First observed use of the new style ejector swivel housing.
Joseph L. Davis collection

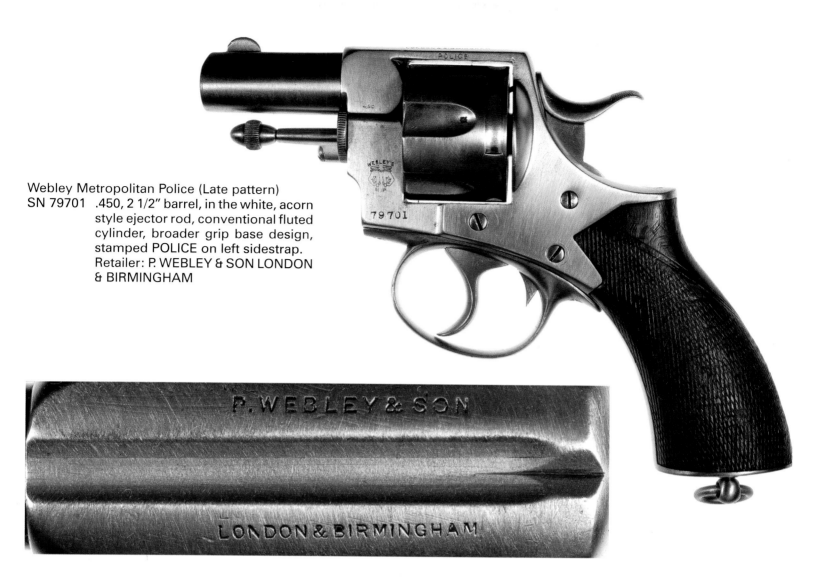

Webley Metropolitan Police (Late pattern)
SN 79701 .450, 2 1/2" barrel, in the white, acorn
style ejector rod, conventional fluted
cylinder, broader grip base design,
stamped POLICE on left sidestrap.
Retailer: P. WEBLEY & SON LONDON
& BIRMINGHAM

Webley Metropolitan Police (Late pattern)
SN 79726 .450, 2 1/2" barrel, blue, acorn style ejector rod, conventional fluted cylinder, broader grip base design, stamped POLICE on left top strap and 1102 on right frame behind the loading gate.
Retailer: P. WEBLEY & SON LONDON & BIRMINGHAM

P. WEBLEY & SON

LONDON & BIRMINGHAM

POLICE

Roger G. Michaud collection

Webley Metropolitan Police (Late pattern)
SN 80661 .450, 2 1/2" barrel, blue, acorn style ejector rod, conventional fluted cylinder, broader grip base design, stamped NSW POLICE and 1639 on left frame.
Retailer: P. WEBLEY & SON LONDON & BIRMINGHAM

Frank & Jean Pycha collection

Webley Metropolitan Police (Early pattern)
SN 82249 .450, 2 1/2" barrel, blue, smooth cylinder, flat headed ejector rod with web
swivel, thicker grip design, marked "HERTS CONSTABULARY" on barrel.
Retailer: TAYLOR & SON IRONMONGERS & C. HERTFORD

For a short time Webley started to use up old ejector swivel assemblies that must have remained in inventory. In this example we see both the old webbed swivel and flat ejector head.

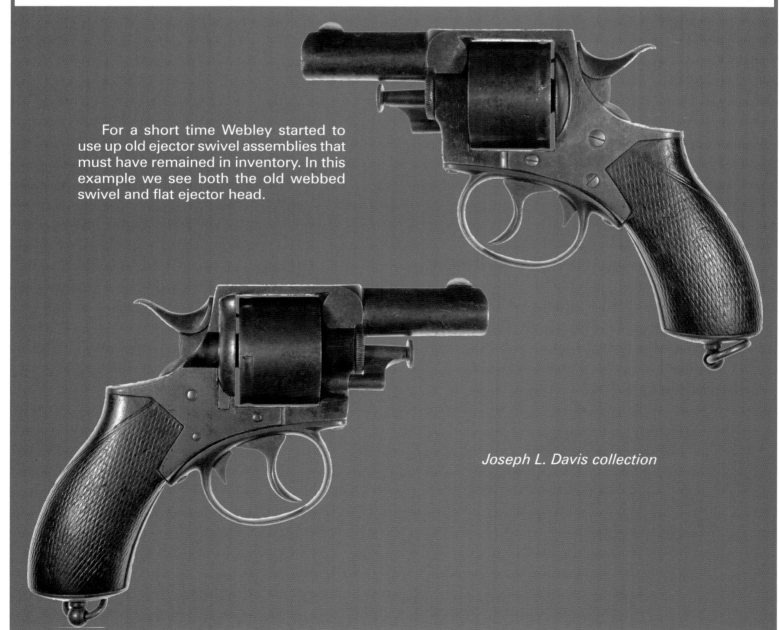

Joseph L. Davis collection

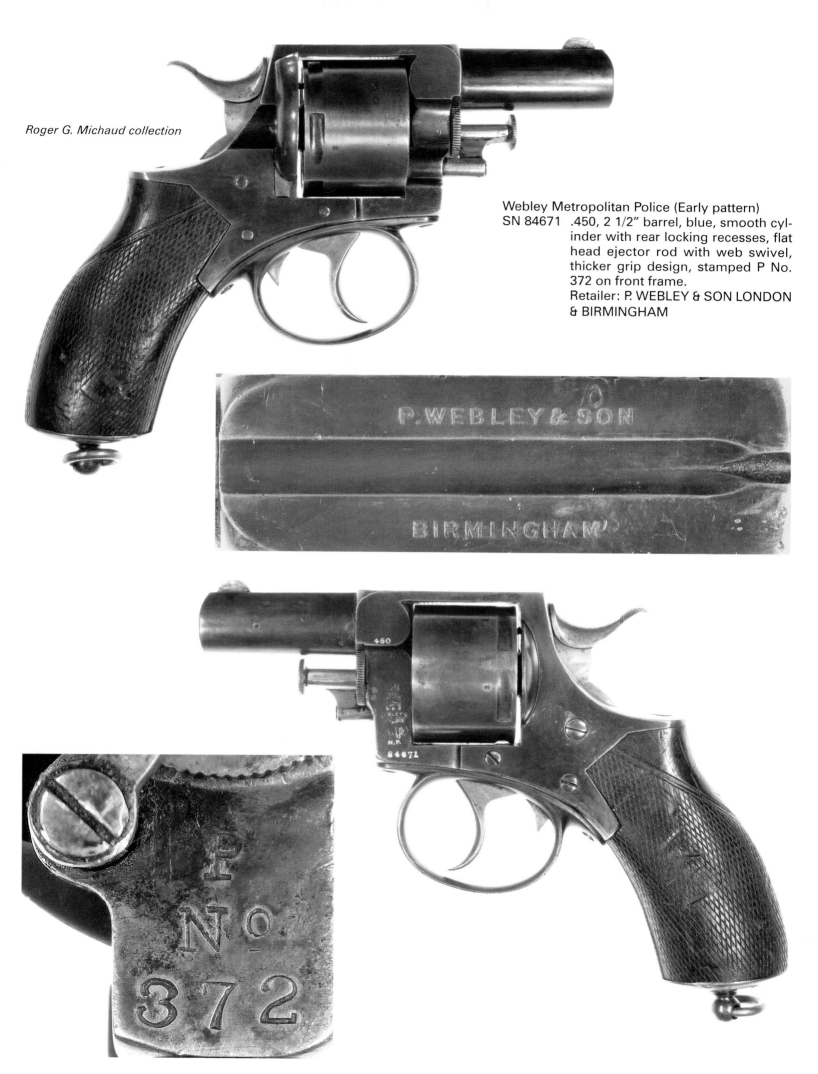

Roger G. Michaud collection

Webley Metropolitan Police (Early pattern)
SN 84671 .450, 2 1/2" barrel, blue, smooth cylinder with rear locking recesses, flat head ejector rod with web swivel, thicker grip design, stamped P No. 372 on front frame.
Retailer: P. WEBLEY & SON LONDON & BIRMINGHAM

125

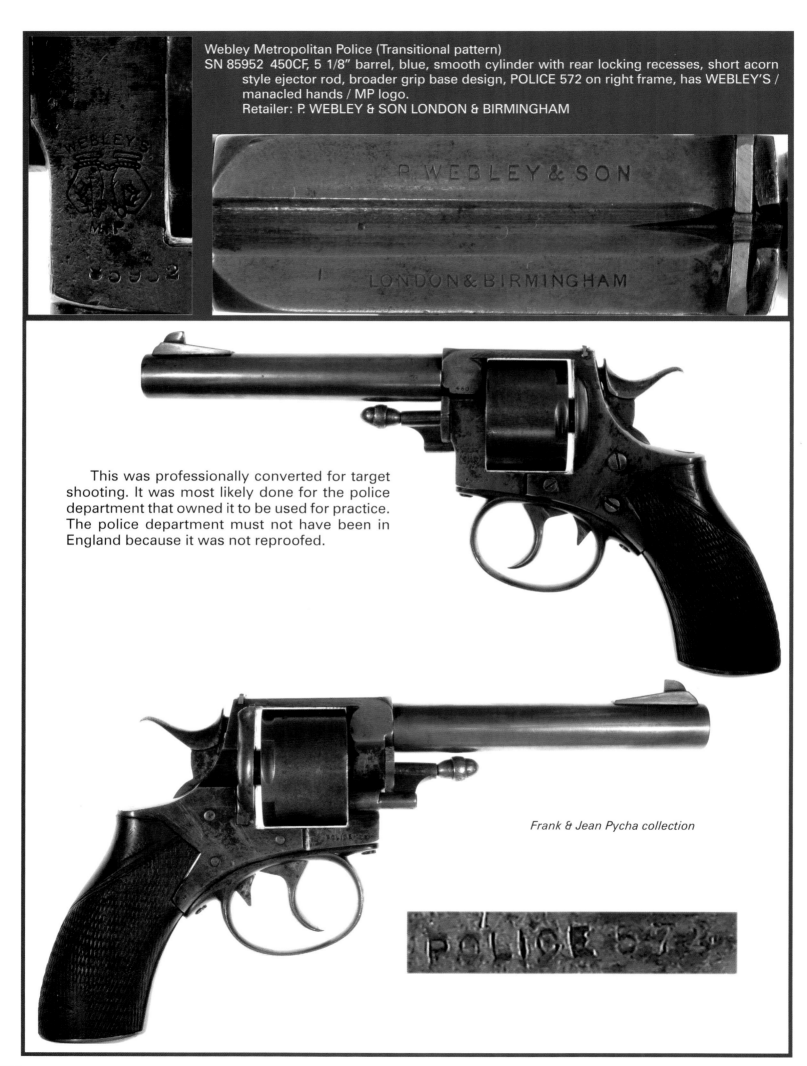

Webley Metropolitan Police (Transitional pattern)
SN 85952 450CF, 5 1/8" barrel, blue, smooth cylinder with rear locking recesses, short acorn
style ejector rod, broader grip base design, POLICE 572 on right frame, has WEBLEY'S /
manacled hands / MP logo.
Retailer: P. WEBLEY & SON LONDON & BIRMINGHAM

This was professionally converted for target shooting. It was most likely done for the police department that owned it to be used for practice. The police department must not have been in England because it was not reproofed.

Frank & Jean Pycha collection

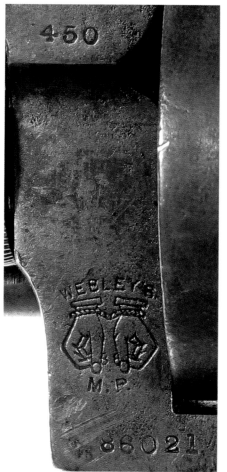

Frank & Jean Pycha collection

Webley Metropolitan Police (Later pattern)
SN 86021 .450, 7" barrel, blue, smooth cylinder, short acorn style
     ejector rod, broader grip base design, POLICE 755 on right
     frame.
     Retailer: P. WEBLEY & SON LONDON & BIRMINGHAM

Another conversion done outside of England.

Webley Metropolitan Police (Transitional pattern)
SN 86033 .450, 2 1/2" barrel, blue, smooth cylinder, acorn style ejector rod, thicker
    grip design, stamped POLICE 704 on right frame.
    Retailer: P. WEBLEY & SON LONDON & BIRMINGHAM

Roger G. Michaud collection

Webley Metropolitan Police (Transitional pattern)
SN 86046 .450, 2 1/2" barrel, blue, smooth cylinder, acorn style ejector rod, thicker grip design, stamped POLICE 708 and L.P. (possibly Leeds or Liverpool police) on right frame.
Retailer: P. WEBLEY & SON LONDON & BIRMINGHAM

Frank & Jean Pycha collection

Joseph L. Davis collection

Webley Metropolitan Police (Transitional pattern)
SN 86204   .450, 2 1/2" barrel, blue, smooth cylinder, acorn style ejector rod and webbed swivel, thicker grip design, stamped POLICE 634 on right frame, elongated cylinder recesses.
Retailer: P. WEBLEY & SON LONDON & BIRMINGHAM

Joseph L. Davis collection

Frank & Jean Pycha collection

Webley Metropolitan Police (Late pattern)
SN 88902 .450, 2 1/2" barrel, blue, conventional fluted cylinder, acorn style ejector rod, broader grip base design, serial numbering now moved to right lower frame, stamped POLICE above Webley's MP logo and 1373 below it on left frame.
Retailer: P. WEBLEY & SON LONDON & BIRMINGHAM

Frank & Jean Pycha collection

Webley Metropolitan Police (Late pattern)
SN 88944 .450, 2 1/2" barrel, blue, conventional fluted cylinder, acorn style ejector rod, broader grip base design, serial numbering now moved to right lower frame, stamped PO-LICE above Webley's MP logo and 1413 (rack or inventory number) on left frame.
Retailer: P. WEBLEY & SON LONDON & BIRMINGHAM

Frank & Jean Pycha collection

Webley Metropolitan Police (Late pattern)
SN 88992 .450, 2 1/2" barrel, blue, conventional fluted cylinder, acorn style ejector rod, broader grip base design, serial numbering now moved to right lower frame, stamped POLICE above Webley's MP logo and 1459 on left frame, front of receiver is deeper.
Retailer: P. WEBLEY & SON LONDON & BIRMINGHAM

Roger G. Michaud collection

Webley Metropolitan Police (Late pattern)
SN 92148 .450, 2 1/2" barrel, blue, conventional cylinder flutes, acorn style ejector rod, broader grip base design, serial number on the right side of frame, stamped 1665 "N.S.W. POLICE" (New South Wales) below the Webley's MP logo on the left frame.
Retailer: P. WEBLEY & SON LONDON & BIRMINGHAM

Frank & Jean Pycha collection

Roger G. Michaud collection

Webley Metropolitan Police (Late pattern)
SN 94991 .450, 2 1/2" barrel, blue, conventional cylinder flutes, acorn style ejector rod, broader grip base design, serial number on the right side of frame, on left frame stamped 1857 "N.S.W. POLICE" below Webley's MP logo.
Retailer: P. WEBLEY & SON LONDON & BIRMINGHAM

Roger G. Michaud collection

Webley Metropolitan Police (Late pattern)
SN 95004 .450, 2 1/2" barrel, blue, conventional cylinder flutes, acorn style ejector rod, broader grip base design, serial number on right side of frame, stamped 1877 "N.S.W. POLICE" below the Webley's MP logo on left frame.
Retailer: P. WEBLEY & SON LONDON & BIRMINGHAM

Joseph L. Davis collection

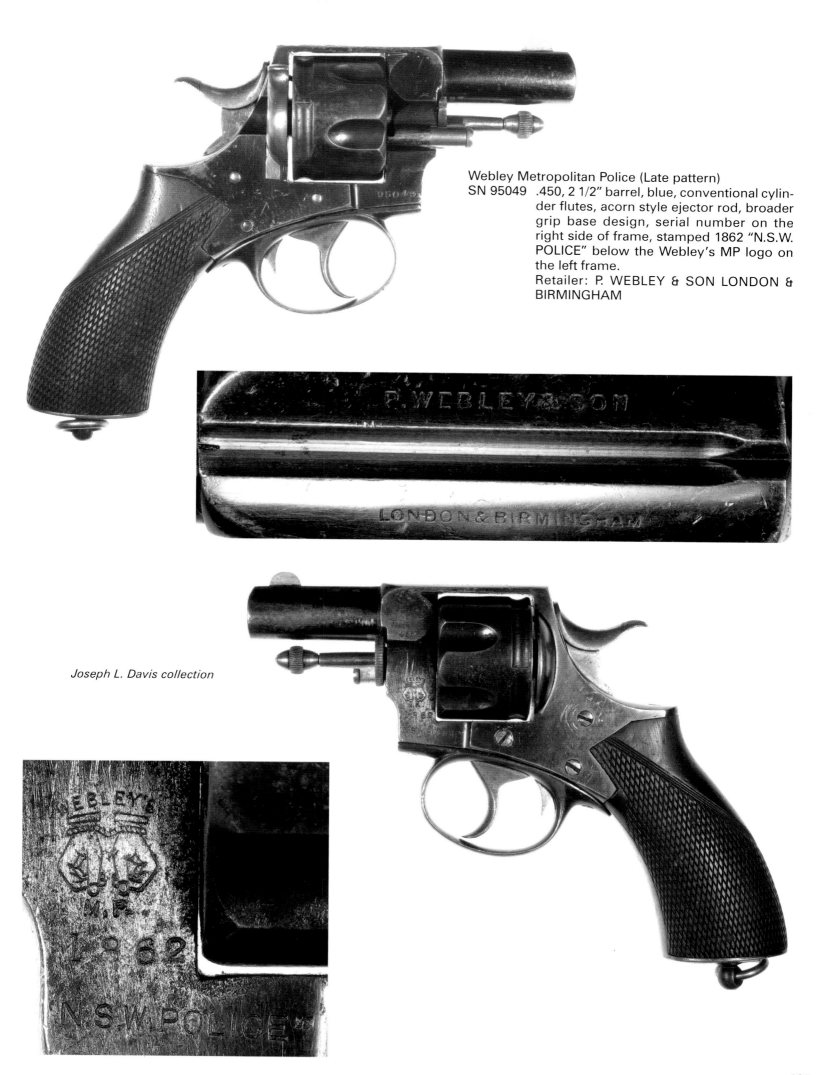

Webley Metropolitan Police (Late pattern)
SN 95049 .450, 2 1/2" barrel, blue, conventional cylinder flutes, acorn style ejector rod, broader grip base design, serial number on the right side of frame, stamped 1862 "N.S.W. POLICE" below the Webley's MP logo on the left frame.
Retailer: P. WEBLEY & SON LONDON & BIRMINGHAM

Joseph L. Davis collection

Webley Metropolitan Police (Late pattern)
SN 95808 .450, 2 1/2" barrel, blue, conventional cylinder flutes, acorn style ejector rod, broader grip base design, serial number on the right side of frame, stamped 2034 "N.S.W. POLICE" below the Webley's MP logo on the left frame.
Retailer: P. WEBLEY & SON LONDON & BIRMINGHAM

There appears to be an aboriginal symbol engraved on the left side. *Greg Reddick collection*

Webley Metropolitan Police
NVSN   .450 blank, 2 1/2" barrel, blue, conventional cylinder flutes, flat style ejector rod with early webbed swivel ejector, broader grip base design, Webley's MP logo on the left frame.
Retailer: P. WEBLEY & SON LONDON & BIRMINGHAM

Note the plugs in each chamber. Lack of serial number indicates this was made as a blank gun, most likely for "school sports days".
Joseph L. Davis collection

139

RIC No. 2

Most, but not all, RIC No. 2s in caliber .442 or larger have a ramped barrel, a top strap with raised rear sight, and a one piece grip with an angled bottom. In regard to smaller calibers, no generalizations can be made. Despite standardization of large caliber RICs, Webley spent years trying to decide on a set frame configuration for the smaller calibers. To add confusion, at different periods of time the smaller caliber revolvers were designated as the No. 2, the RIC No. 1 or the RIC No. 2.

Webley Pre-RIC No. 2
SN 2722   .380CF, 2 7/8" ovate barrel, 6 shot, nickel, checkered wood grips with diamond shaped escutcheons, smooth cylinder with rear ratchet cylinder stops, mushroom head ejector swivels from frame, winged bullet on left and WEBLEY'S PATENT on right side, Tranter Model 1868 patent style sear on back of trigger.
Retailer: RICHARDSON & SONS CORK

Joel Black collection

Webley Pre-RIC No. 2
SN 2802 .320CF, 2 7/8" ovate barrel, 6 shot, nickel, smooth ivory grips with round escutcheons, smooth cylinder with rear ratchet cylinder stops, mushroom head ejector swivels from frame, engraved, cased winged bullet on left and WEBLEY'S PATENT on right side. Retailer: P. WEBLEY & SON S^T JAMES'S LONDON

Joel Black collection

Webley Pre-RIC No. 2
SN 2844 .380CF, 2 7/8" ovate barrel, 6 shot, nickel, checkered wood grips with diamond shaped escutcheons, smooth cylinder with rear recessed cylinder stops, RIC style ejector swivels from frame, moderate foliate engraving, winged bullet on left side and WEBLEY'S PATENT on right side of frame.
Retailer: CHAS. INGRAM GLASGOW

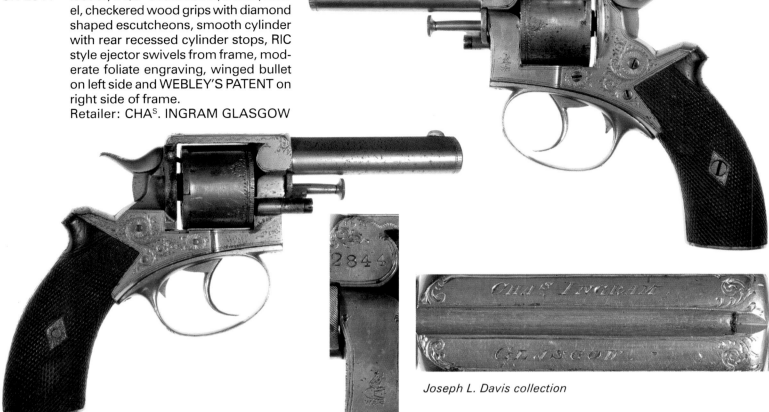

Joseph L. Davis collection

Webley Pre-RIC No. 2
SN 2990 .380CF, 2 7/8" ovate barrel, 6 shot, nickel, checkered wood grips with diamond shaped escutcheons, smooth cylinder with rear ratchet cylinder stops, mushroom head ejector swivels from frame, winged bullet on left and WEBLEY'S PATENT on right side.
Retailer: J. BRADDELL & SON CASTLE PLACE BELFAST

Greg Reddick collection

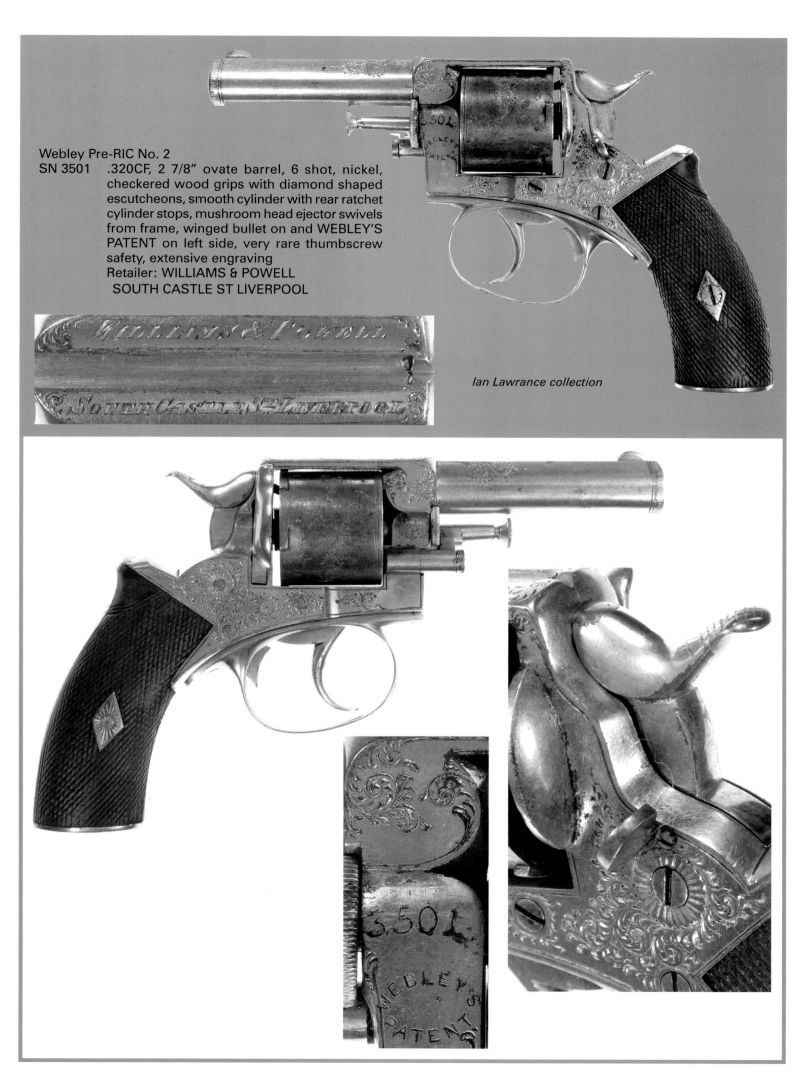

Webley Pre-RIC No. 2
SN 3501   .320CF, 2 7/8" ovate barrel, 6 shot, nickel, checkered wood grips with diamond shaped escutcheons, smooth cylinder with rear ratchet cylinder stops, mushroom head ejector swivels from frame, winged bullet on and WEBLEY'S PATENT on left side, very rare thumbscrew safety, extensive engraving
Retailer: WILLIAMS & POWELL
  SOUTH CASTLE ST LIVERPOOL

Ian Lawrance collection

143

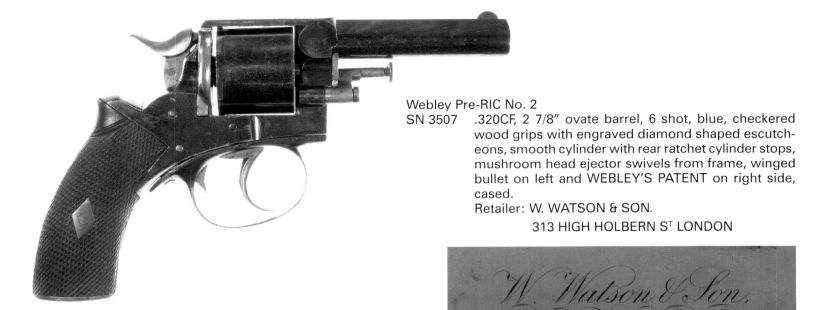

Webley Pre-RIC No. 2
SN 3507   .320CF, 2 7/8" ovate barrel, 6 shot, blue, checkered wood grips with engraved diamond shaped escutcheons, smooth cylinder with rear ratchet cylinder stops, mushroom head ejector swivels from frame, winged bullet on left and WEBLEY'S PATENT on right side, cased.
Retailer: W. WATSON & SON.

313 HIGH HOLBERN ST LONDON

Frank & Jean Pycha collection

Joel Black collection

Webley Pre-RIC No. 2
SN 3515   .380CF, 2 7/8" ovate barrel, 6 shot, blued and engraved, checkered wood grips with engraved diamond shaped escutcheons, smooth cylinder with rear ratchet cylinder stops, mushroom head ejector swivels from frame, in oak case winged bullet on left and WEBLEY'S PATENT on right side.
Retailer: J. RIGBY & Cº DUBLIN.

Webley Pre-RIC No. 2
SN 3627   .380CF, 6 shot, blue, checkered wood grips with diamond shaped escutcheons, smooth cylinder with rear ratchet cylinder stops, later smokeless powder proof marks, flat mushroom head ejector.
Retailer: ARMY & NAVY CO-OPERATIVE SOCIETY
LIMITED, LONDON

Roger G. Michaud collection

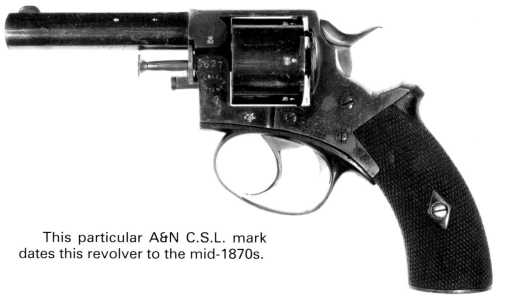

This particular A&N C.S.L. mark dates this revolver to the mid-1870s.

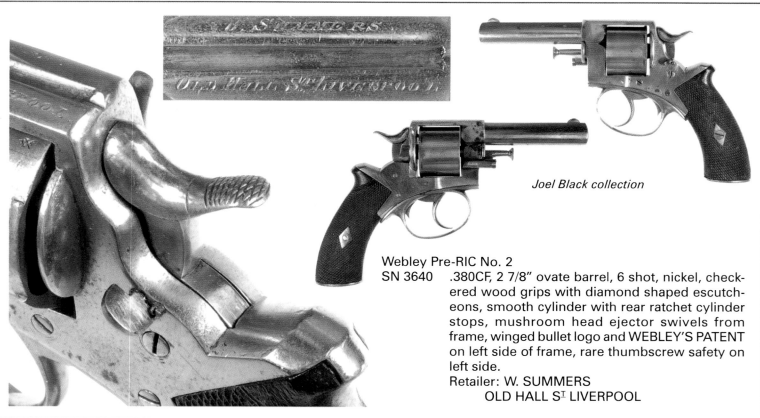

Joel Black collection

Webley Pre-RIC No. 2
SN 3640   .380CF, 2 7/8" ovate barrel, 6 shot, nickel, checkered wood grips with diamond shaped escutcheons, smooth cylinder with rear ratchet cylinder stops, mushroom head ejector swivels from frame, winged bullet logo and WEBLEY'S PATENT on left side of frame, rare thumbscrew safety on left side.
Retailer: W. SUMMERS
OLD HALL S^T LIVERPOOL

Webley Pre-RIC No. 2
SN 3568 .442, 3 3/4" screwed in barrel, not ramped, blue, 6 shot, no lanyard ring, one-piece checkered wood grip, smooth cylinder with rear stops, Adams type ejector rod with mushroom head, angled grip, serial number engraved on right side.
Retailer: W. S. RILEY 63 BISHOPSGATE S^T WITHIN LONDON

Frank & Jean Pycha collection

147

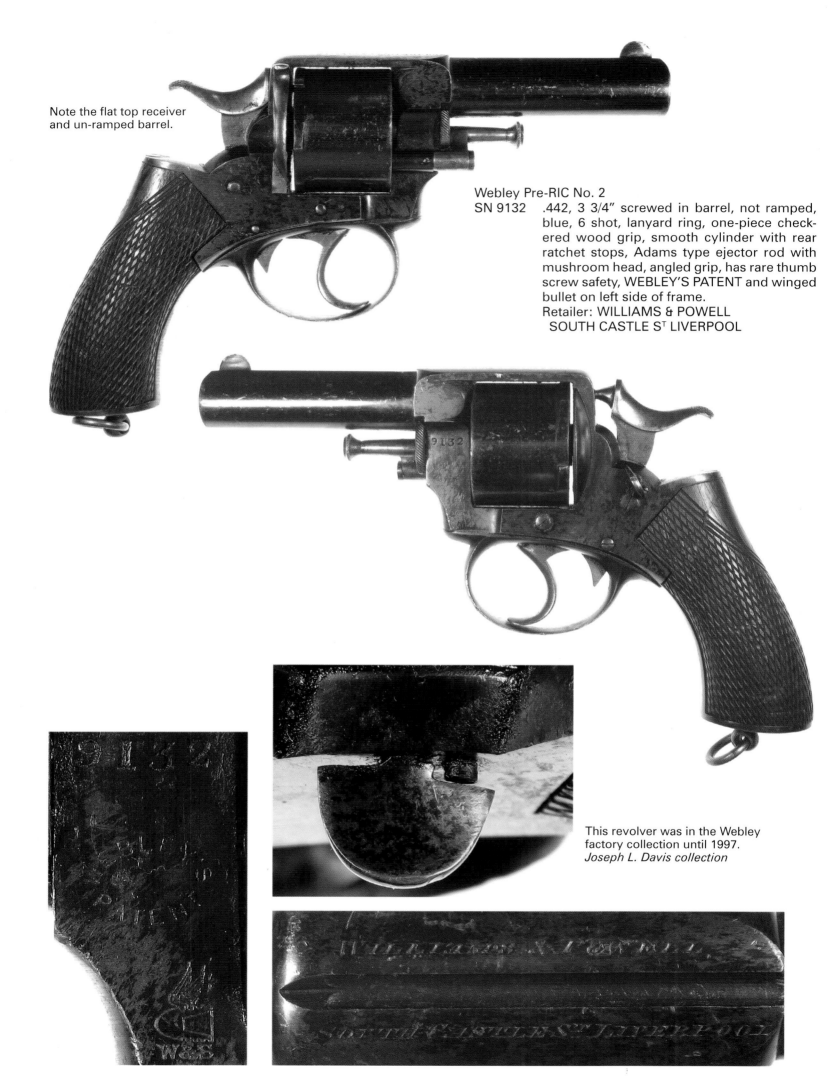

Note the flat top receiver and un-ramped barrel.

Webley Pre-RIC No. 2
SN 9132   .442, 3 3/4" screwed in barrel, not ramped, blue, 6 shot, lanyard ring, one-piece checkered wood grip, smooth cylinder with rear ratchet stops, Adams type ejector rod with mushroom head, angled grip, has rare thumb screw safety, WEBLEY'S PATENT and winged bullet on left side of frame.
Retailer: WILLIAMS & POWELL
  SOUTH CASTLE ST LIVERPOOL

This revolver was in the Webley factory collection until 1997.
Joseph L. Davis collection

148

Webley Pre-RIC No. 2
SN 9147   .442, 3 3/4" screwed in barrel, not ramped, nickel, 6 shot, lanyard ring, one-piece checkered wood grip, smooth cylinder with rear ratchet stops, Adams type ejector rod with mushroom head, angled grip, WEBLEY'S PATENT and winged bullet on left side of frame.
Retailer: E & G HIGHAM RANELAGH S^T LIVERPOOL

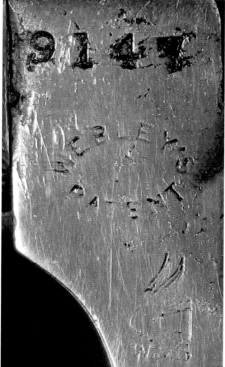

Joseph L. Davis collection

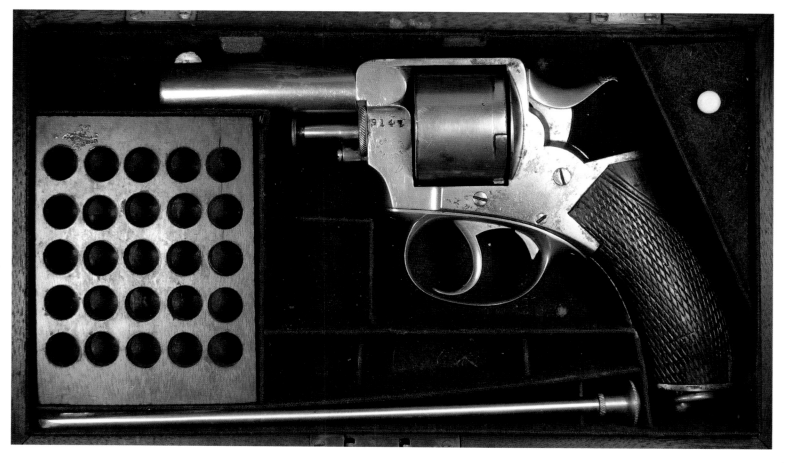

Webley Pre-RIC No. 2
SN 9409   .442CF, 3 3/4" screwed in barrel, not ramped, blue, 6 shot,
lanyard ring, one-piece checkered wood grip, smooth
cylinder with rear ratchet stops, Adams type ejector rod
with mushroom head, angled grip, WEBLEY'S PATENT
and winged bullet on left side of frame
Retailer: J. BRADDELL & SON BELFAST

Frank & Jean Pycha collection

Webley Pre-RIC No. 2
NVSN .450, 3 3/4" screwed in barrel, not ramped, blue, 6 shot, no lanyard ring, one-piece checkered wood grip, smooth cylinder with rear stops, Adams type ejector rod with mushroom head, angled grip, cased with dealer's ivory name plate added to inside of lid.
Retailer: W. S. RILEY 63 BISHOPSGATE S^T WITHIN LONDON.

At some point this revolver was resold by F. Lassetter & Co. at Sydney, Australia.
Joel Black collection

Webley (Charles Pryse) Pre-RIC No. 2
SN 3209 .442, 3 3/4" screwed in, ramped barrel, nickel, 6 shot, lanyard ring, one-piece checkered wood grip, grip is angled, the rear ratchet cylinder, cylinder axis pin and ejector rod are missing.
Retailer: not marked

Pryse's serial number is marked on the bottom of the barrel where it meets the frame.

Despite its relic condition, this is an important revolver. An article by Gordon Bruce in the August 2008 issue of *Man at Arms* mentions "Charles Pryse's Aston Factory" and the theory that Pryse made some revolvers for Webley. The author informed Mr. Black that Pryse operated his factory at 84 Aston Street, Birmingham, until 1873. At that point, Charles Jr. took over and ran it until 1888. Pryse apparently assembled and sold RICs on his own. Army & Navy C.S.L. records show purchases of RICs directly from Pryse.

Joel Black collection

Used with permission of Glasgow University. http://www.gla.ac.uk/archives/

Webley (Charles Pryse) RIC No. 1 [No. 2 style]
SN 7   .442, 3 3/4" screwed in ramped barrel, 6 shot,
          nickel plated, one-piece checkered wood grip,
          angled grip, lanyard ring conventional cylinder
          flutes.
          Retailer: not marked

Pryse's Trademark. *Frank & Jean Pycha collection*

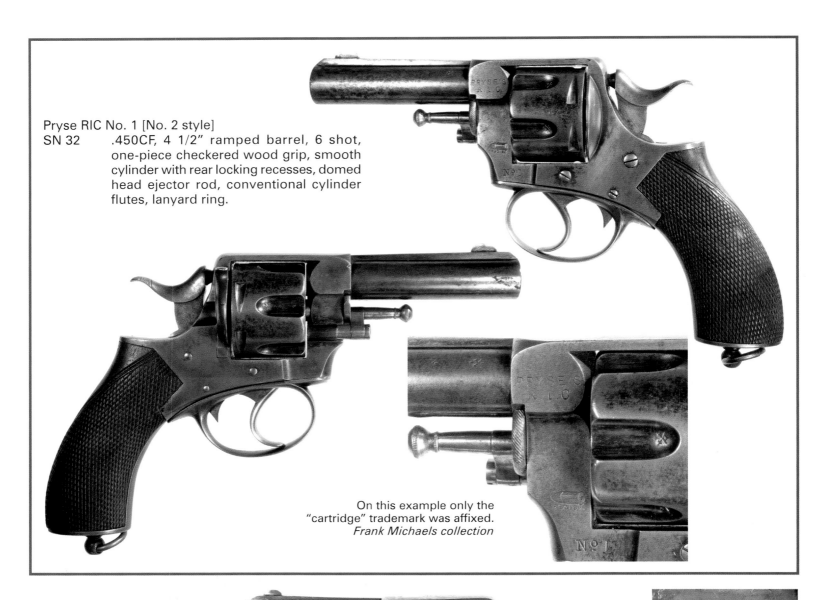

Pryse RIC No. 1 [No. 2 style]
SN 32 .450CF, 4 1/2" ramped barrel, 6 shot, one-piece checkered wood grip, smooth cylinder with rear locking recesses, domed head ejector rod, conventional cylinder flutes, lanyard ring.

On this example only the "cartridge" trademark was affixed.
Frank Michaels collection

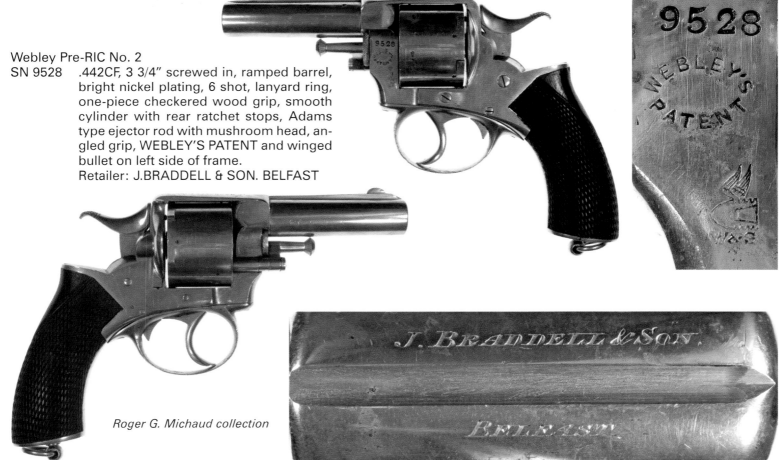

Webley Pre-RIC No. 2
SN 9528 .442CF, 3 3/4" screwed in, ramped barrel, bright nickel plating, 6 shot, lanyard ring, one-piece checkered wood grip, smooth cylinder with rear ratchet stops, Adams type ejector rod with mushroom head, angled grip, WEBLEY'S PATENT and winged bullet on left side of frame.
Retailer: J.BRADDELL & SON. BELFAST

Roger G. Michaud collection

Except for the ejector rod finial and ivory grips, this is the first observed example of what we believe is a typically configured large caliber RIC No 2. This example was made in the late 1870s.

Webley RIC No. 2
SN 9852 .442CF, 3 3/4" ramped barrel, 6 shot, nickel plated, one piece smooth ivory grip, smooth cylinder with rear ratchet stops, Adams type ejector rod with unusual thick head and side knurling, angled grip bottom, lanyard ring, WEBLEY'S PATENT and RIC No. 2 on left side of frame, cased and retailed by Agnew & Son.
Retailer: AGNEW & SON 68 SOUTH ST EXETER

Webley RIC No.2
SN 10168 .442CF, 3 3/4" barrel, 6 shot, one-piece checkered wood grip, ramped barrel, raised top strap, smooth cylinder with rear ratchet stops, mushroom headed ejector rod, lanyard ring. Retailer: P. WEBLEY & SON LONDON & BIRMINGHAM

Courtesy of Peter Smith

Webley RIC No.2
SN 10526 .442CF, 3 3/4" barrel, 6 shot, one-piece checkered wood grip, ramped barrel, raised top strap, smooth cylinder with rear ratchet stops, mushroom headed ejector rod, lanyard ring.
Retailer: C. COWLES SYDNEY NSW

Joseph L. Davis collection

Webley RIC No. 2
SN 10337 .44CF LONG, 3 3/4" screwed in ramped barrel, bright nickel, 6 shot, one-piece checkered wood grip, smooth cylinder with rear ratchet stops, Adams type ejector rod with mushroom head, angled butt plate, lanyard ring, cased.
Retailer: P. WEBLEY & SON LONDON & BIRMINGHAM

One of two RIC Nº 2 models known in this caliber (44 Russian); it required an elongated frame and cylinder.
Joel Black collection

Webley RIC No. 2
SN 10555 .450CF, 3 3/4" barrel, 6 shot, one-piece checkered wood grip, ramped barrel, raised top strap, smooth cylinder with rear ratchet stops, elongated acorn headed ejector rod, lanyard ring.
Retailer: not marked

Frank & Jean Pycha collection

Joel Black collection

Webley RIC No. 2
SN 10864 .442CF, 3 3/4" barrel, 6 shot, one-piece checkered wood grip, ramped barrel, raised top strap, smooth cylinder with rear ratchet stops, mushroom headed ejector rod, lanyard ring, angled grip base.
Retailer: P. WEBLEY & SON LONDON & BIRMINGHAM

Webley RIC No. 2
SN 11065 .450CF, 3 3/4" barrel, 6 shot, one-piece checkered wood grip, ramped barrel, raised top strap, smooth cylinder with rear ratchet stops, mushroom headed ejector rod, lanyard ring.
Retailer: P. WEBLEY & SON LONDON & BIRMINGHAM

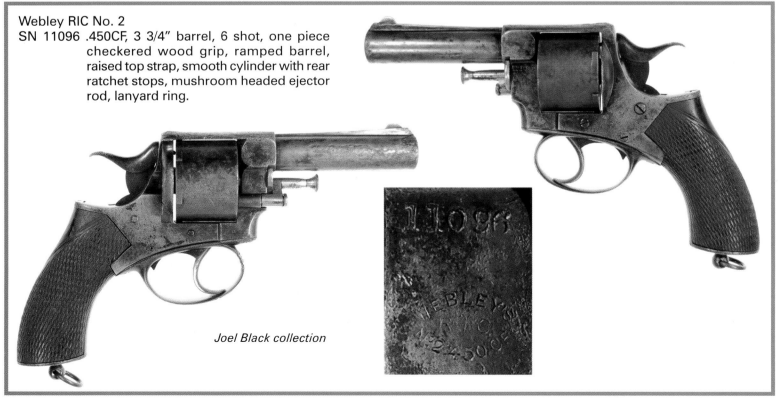

Webley RIC No. 2
SN 11096 .450CF, 3 3/4" barrel, 6 shot, one piece checkered wood grip, ramped barrel, raised top strap, smooth cylinder with rear ratchet stops, mushroom headed ejector rod, lanyard ring.

Joel Black collection

Webley RIC No. 2
SN 11287   .450CF, 3 3/4" barrel, 6 shot, one-piece checkered wood grip, ramped barrel, raised top strap, smooth cylinder with rear ratchet stops, mushroom headed ejector rod, lanyard ring, 5 notches in grip.
Retailer: G. H. DAW & CO 57 THREAD-NEEDLE S^T LONDON

Joseph L. Davis collection

Roger G. Michaud collection

Webley RIC No. 2
SN 11389 .450CF, 3 3/4" barrel, 6 shot, one-piece checkered wood grip, smooth cylinder with rear
ratchet stops, mushroom headed ejector rod,
lanyard ring.
Retailer: G.H. DAW & Co. 57 THREADNEEDLE
S^T. LONDON

Webley Pre-RIC No. 2
SN 20429 .380CF, 3 1/2" barrel, blue, 6 shot, smooth cylinder with rear ratchet stops, two-piece checkered wood grips with diamond escutcheons and flat base, flat head ejector rod, in reproduction case.
Retailer: GEORGE GIBBS 29 CORN ST BRISTOL

Dowell inexplicably described this revolver as an RIC No 1.

Courtesy of Hermann Historica. http://www.hermann-historica-ohg.de/gb/index.htm

Webley RIC No. 2
SN 54679 .380CF, 2 7/8" barrel, nickel, 5 shot, smooth cylinder with rear stops, 2 piece grips
with flat base, flat head ejector
Retailer: J. V. NEEDHAM TEMPLE ST   BIRMINGHAM

Joel Black collection

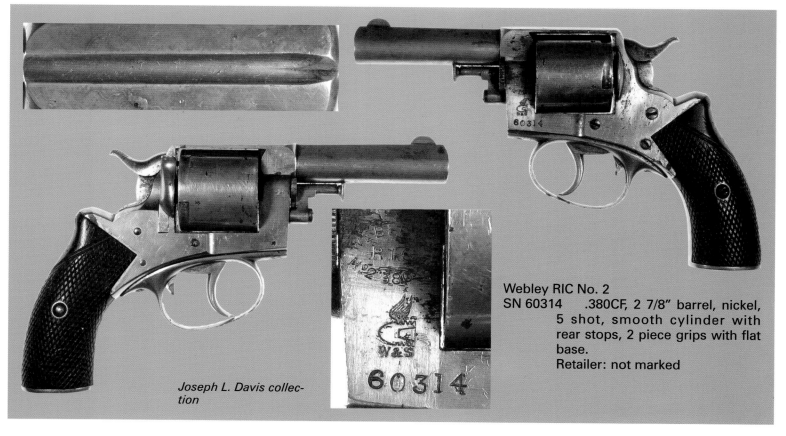

Joseph L. Davis collection

Webley RIC No. 2
SN 60314   .380CF, 2 7/8" barrel, nickel, 5 shot, smooth cylinder with rear stops, 2 piece grips with flat base.
Retailer: not marked

163

Webley RIC No. 2
SN 71361 .450CF, 4 1/2" barrel, 6 shot, blue, acutely slanted grip design with one-piece checkered wood, acorn head ejector rod, conventional cylinder flutes, lanyard ring.
Retailer: no marking

This one of a kind sample (not 1 of 12 as suggested by W. C. Dowell) was made up for Montenegro. The strange grip replicates that of the large knife or handgun ever present in the sash of most male Montenegrins at the time as mandated by King Nikola pictured here. The "WEBLEY'S Nº 2" model stamp is in error. This would suggest a Bull Dog frame, but those could only accept a 5 shot cylinder. In truth, this revolver belongs with the short cylinder RIC New Models.

Joseph L. Davis collection

RIC NO. 3

As with previous RIC models, the No. 3 had many iterations. Two prominent identifying features were a left side lever cylinder axis pin release and lack of a pivoting ejector rod. In most cases, the ejector rod screwed into the bottom of the grip. Otherwise, the cylinder pin would serve this purpose.

The cylinder axis pin lever release was patented by William Tranter on July 19, 1862. It was British Patent No. 2067. Webley made use of it after the patent expiration date.

Courtesy of Ken Hallock

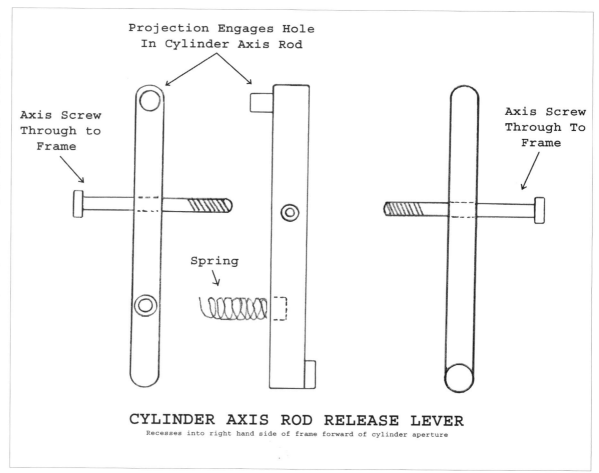

Projection Engages Hole
In Cylinder Axis Rod

Axis Screw
Through to
Frame

Axis Screw
Through To
Frame

Spring

CYLINDER AXIS ROD RELEASE LEVER
Recesses into right hand side of frame forward of cylinder aperture

Hill (Webley?) Pre-RIC No. 3
SN 1160 .442CF, 4" ovate barrel, 6 shot, smooth cylinder with rear projecting ratchet stops, friction brake acts on mid-point of the cylinder, checkered wood grips with tear drop shaped escutcheons, no hole for ejector rod, cylinder pin spring catch on left side, no frame proof mark.
Retailer: not marked

Courtesy of Rock Island Auction Company
http://www.rockislandauction.com/

We suspect that Hill designed this predecessor of the Webley RIC No. 3. He probably had most of the parts made in Belgium. He then assembled and had them proved in England. The upswept hammer and tear drop escutcheons are indicators of Belgium origins, although the exposed sear is British. All of the following Pre-RIC No. 3s are pre-1868. In all likelihood Webley obtained the design from Hill, which resulted in the later relationship, whereby Hill sold Webleys to British police organizations.

Webley Pre-RIC No. 3
SN 37 .442CF, 4" ovate barrel, 6 shot, smooth cylinder with rear projecting ratchet stops, friction brake acts on mid-point of the cylinder, checkered wood grips with diamond shaped escutcheons, hole for ejector rod is plugged, small casting flaw on flat top strap, cylinder pin is held to the frame by a spring catch on left side, an insert is fitted to the floor of the cylinder cut out, WEBLEY'S PATENT marked in oval on left side of frame, winged bullet logo on right, no retailer name.

Roger G. Michaud collection

The friction brake and the insert in the floor of the cylinder cut out are seen in this view.

Webley Pre-RIC No. 3
SN 59 .442RF, 3" round barrel, 6 shot, blue, checkered wood grips with diamond shaped escutcheons, smooth cylinder with rear projecting stops, cylinder pin serves as ejector, RIC No. 3 style push lever cylinder pin release, WEBLEY'S PATENT on left side of frame.
Retailer: not marked

Note the early flat firing pin.

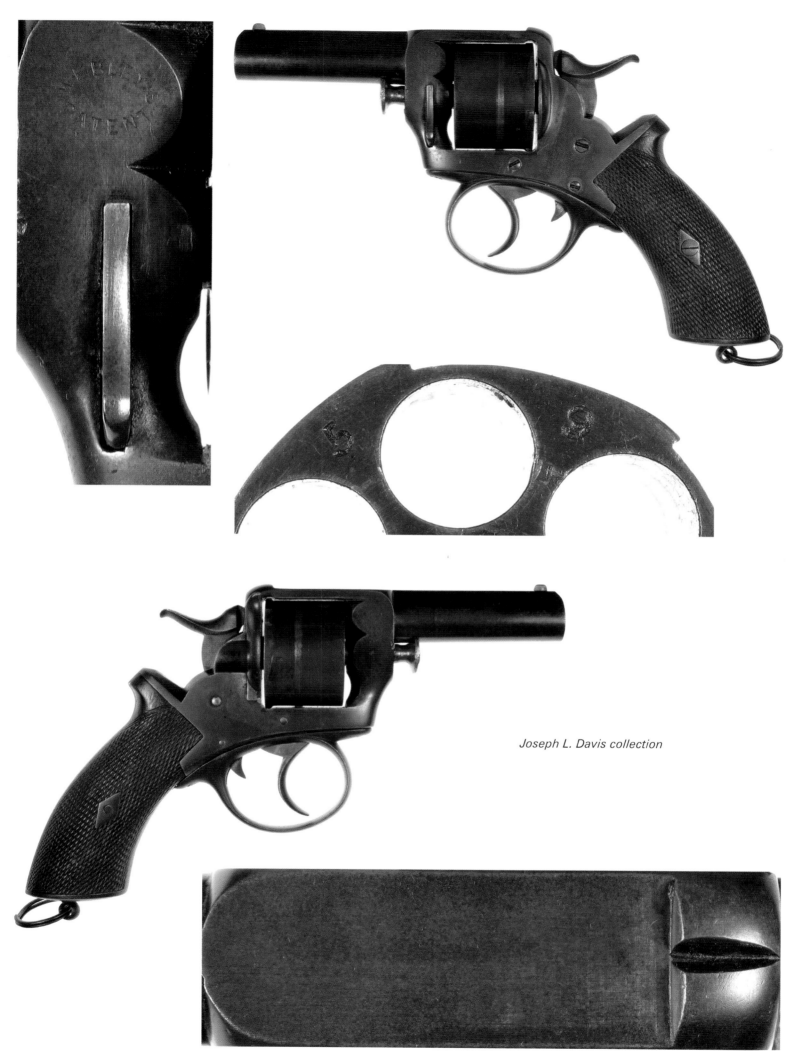

Joseph L. Davis collection

Webley Pre-RIC No. 3
SN 70   .442CF, 3" round barrel, 6 shot, checkered wood grips with diamond shaped escutcheons, smooth cylinder with rear projecting stops, ejector housed in butt plate, push lever cylinder pin release, winged (flying) bullet trademark on right side of frame, flat top.
Retailer: not marked

Joseph L. Davis collection

168

Webley Pre-RIC No. 3

SN 77   .442CF, 3" round barrel, 6 shot, checkered wood grips with diamond shaped escutcheons, smooth cylinder with rear projecting stops, push lever cylinder pin release, winged ("flying") bullet logo on right side of frame, flat top, Rigby registration number 124 is on left side.
Retailer: JOHN RIGBY & Cᵒ DUBLIN

Joseph L. Davis collection

Webley RIC No. 3 Factory Cut Away
SN 5990   .442CF, 2 1/2" barrel, 6 shot, blue, smooth cylinder with front locking recesses, cylinder pin is held by a spring catch on the left side, no ejector rod in base plate, bead front sight.

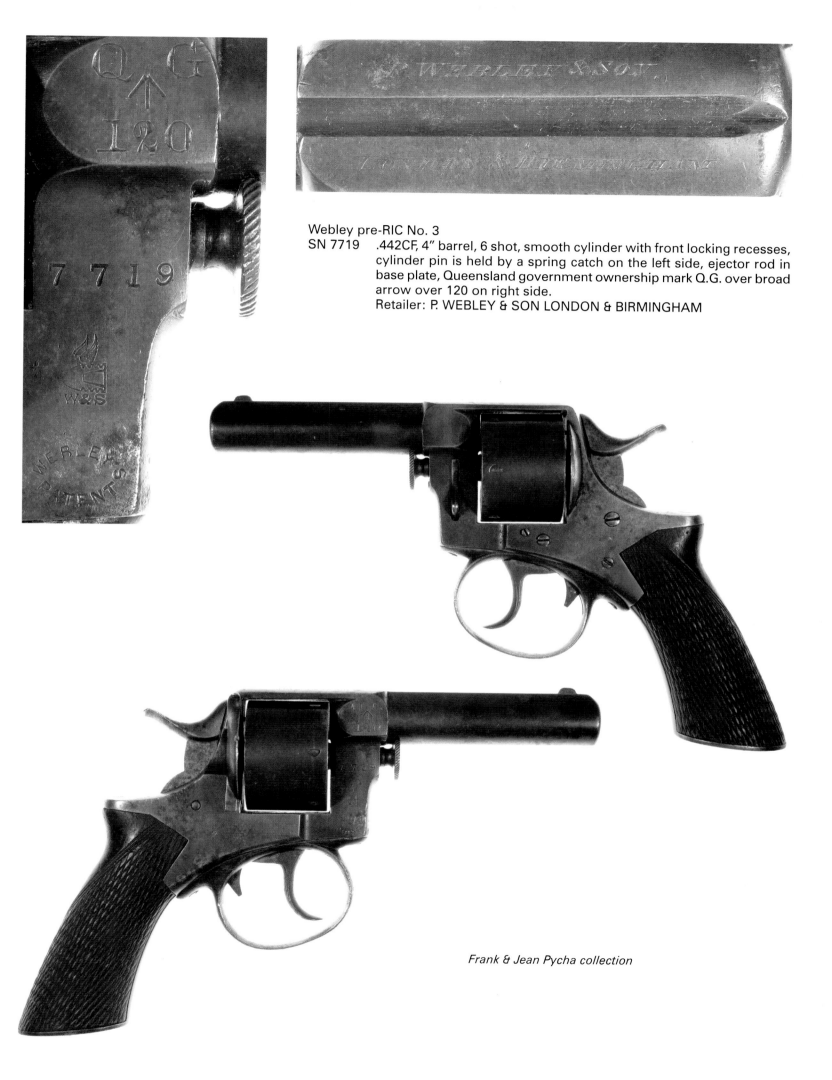

Webley pre-RIC No. 3
SN 7719 .442CF, 4" barrel, 6 shot, smooth cylinder with front locking recesses, cylinder pin is held by a spring catch on the left side, ejector rod in base plate, Queensland government ownership mark Q.G. over broad arrow over 120 on right side.
Retailer: P. WEBLEY & SON LONDON & BIRMINGHAM

Frank & Jean Pycha collection

Webley RIC No. 3
SN 15390 .442CF, 2 1/2" barrel, 6 shot, blue, smooth cylinder with front locking recesses, cylinder pin is held by a spring catch on the left side, lanyard ring rather than ejector rod in base plate.
Retailer: TRULOCK & HARRISS 9 DAWSON S^T DUBLIN

Joseph L. Davis collection

Webley RIC No. 3
SN 16346 .442CF, 4" barrel, 6 shot, smooth cylinder with front locking recesses, cylinder pin is held by a spring catch on the left side, lanyard ring, rather than an ejector rod in base plate, Queensland government ownership mark Q^G over 432 on right side.
Retailer: P. WEBLEY & SON LONDON & BIRMINGHAM

Joseph L. Davis collection

Webley RIC No. 3
NVSN   .442CF, 4" barrel, 6 shot, blue, smooth cylinder with elongated rear locking recesses, cylinder pin is held by a spring catch on the left side, ejector rod in base plate, cased.
Retailer: P. WEBLEY & SON BIRMINGHAM

Joel Black collection

Webley RIC No. 3
SN 31028 .442CF, 4" barrel, 6 shot, smooth cylinder with elongated rear locking recesses, cylinder pin is held by a spring catch on the left side, ejector rod in base plate missing, rounded front sight, Broad-arrow / Q.G on front of left frame (Queensland Government ownership mark).
Retailer: P. WEBLEY & SON BIRMINGHAM

Courtesy of Kerry Guerin

Roger G. Michaud collection

Webley RIC No. 3
SN 34283 .442CF, 4" barrel, 6 shot, one-piece checkered wood grip, smooth cylinder with elongated rear locking recesses, cylinder pin is held by a spring catch on the left side, ejector rod in base plate, rounded front sight, Q.G. over broad arrow on left frame (Queensland Government ownership mark), winged bullet logo on right frame.
Retailer: P. WEBLEY & SON BIRMINGHAM

Webley RIC No. 3
SN 34295 .442CF, 4" barrel, 6 shot, smooth cylinder with elongated rear locking recesses, cylinder pin is held by a spring catch on the left side, ejector rod in base plate, rounded front sight, Q.G. under broad arrow on left frame (Queensland Government ownership mark).
Retailer: P. WEBLEY & SON BIRMINGHAM

Courtesy of Hermann Historica. http://www.hermann-historica-ohg.de/gb/index.htm

Frank & Jean Pycha collection

Webley RIC No. 3
SN 70732 .442CF, 4" barrel, 6 shot, smooth cylinder with elongated rear locking recesses, cylinder pin is held by a spring catch on the left side, ejector rod in base plate, rounded front sight, Q. ^ G. on left frame (Queensland Government ownership mark), rack number 567 engraved on right side.
Retailer: P. WEBLEY & SON BIRMINGHAM

RIC Model/83

The early RIC Model/83 was essentially the No. 2 British Bull Dog with a truncated thickened grip. Unlike Webley's British Bulldog, the later RIC Model/83s were made with a longer cylinder. The Model/83 is a 5 shot revolver. Caliber offerings were in .44 Russian, .450, .455, and 45ACP. Despite the 1884 A&N C.S.L. price list seen here, none have been observed in .320 or .380, although in A&N C.S.L. lists 8 .320s being sold in 1891. This Model was kept in the line longer than any other solid frame revolver. The very last one was chambered for .45ACP.

WEBLEY'S R. I. C. MODEL /83,				·450,	5 Shot,	plain	1	17	6
"	"	"	"	"	"	nickel plated	2	3	6
"	"	"	"	·380,	"	plain	1	17	6
"	"	"	"	"	"	nickel plated	2	3	6
"	"	"	"	·320,	"	plain	1	17	6
"	"	"	"	"	"	nickel plated	2	3	6

Courtesy of Gordon Bruce

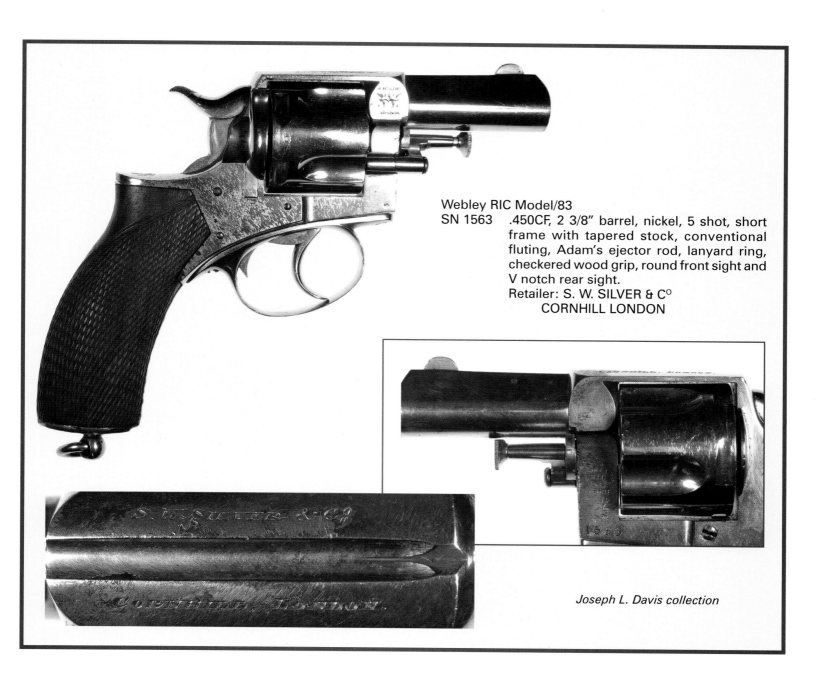

Webley RIC Model/83
SN 1563 .450CF, 2 3/8" barrel, nickel, 5 shot, short frame with tapered stock, conventional fluting, Adam's ejector rod, lanyard ring, checkered wood grip, round front sight and V notch rear sight.
Retailer: S. W. SILVER & Cº
CORNHILL LONDON

Joseph L. Davis collection

SN 4812 .450CF, 2 3/8" barrel, nickel, 5 shot, short frame with tapered stock, conventional fluting, Adam's ejector rod, checkered wood grip, lanyard ring, round front sight and V notch rear sight.
Retailer: ARMY&NAVY C.S.L.

Used with permission of Glasgow University. http://www.gla.ac.uk/archives/

This model was sold to a Mr. Morris October 1886. A study of the A&N C.S.L. records demonstrates that by this time most of the solid frame revolvers were put into the same pool of new serial numbers.

Joseph L. Davis collection

Webley RIC Model/83
SN 60476 .450CF, 2 3/8" barrel, nickel, cased, 5 shot, short frame with tapered stock, conventional fluting, Adam's ejector rod, checkered wood grip, lanyard ring, has S.W. Silver logo, round front sight and V notch rear sight.
Retailer: S. W. SILVER & C°
CORNHILL LONDON

Joel Black collection

S.W. SILVER & C°
CORNHILL LONDON

S.W. SILVER & C°
CORNHILL, LONDON

TRADE MARK

60476

Webley RIC Model/83
SN 61951 .450CF, 2 3/8" barrel, blue, 5 shot, short frame with tapered stock, conventional fluting, Adam's ejector rod, checkered wood grip, lanyard ring, round front sight and V notch rear sight.
Retailer: BOSS &Co. 73.S^T JAMES'S S^T. LONDON.

Roger G. Michaud collection

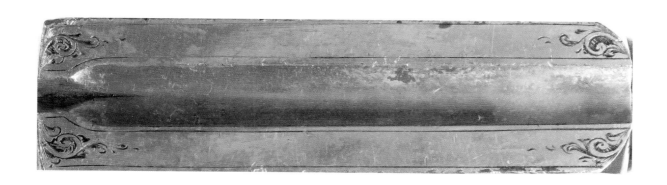

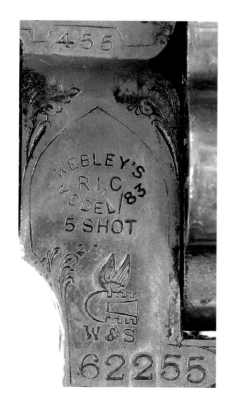

Roger G. Michaud collection

Webley RIC Model/83
SN 62255 .455CF, 2 3/4" barrel, nickel plated, 5 shot, engraved, long frame with broad stock, lanyard ring, church steeple fluting, Adam's style ejector rod, one-piece checkered wood grip, round front sight and V-notch rear sight, was in the Webley factory collection until 1997.
Retailer: P. WEBLEY & SON LONDON & BIRMINGHAM

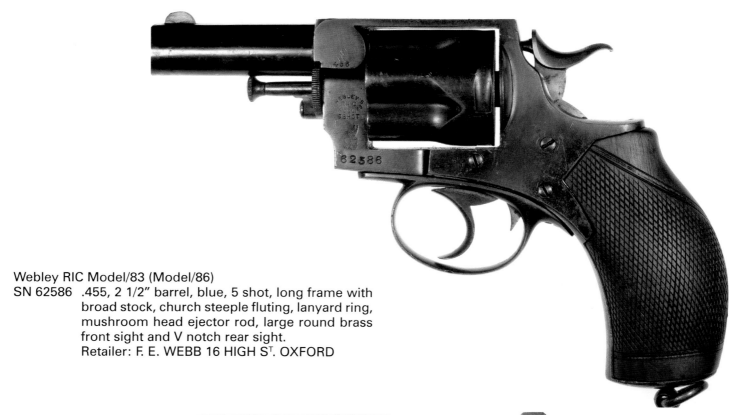

Webley RIC Model/83 (Model/86)
SN 62586 .455, 2 1/2" barrel, blue, 5 shot, long frame with
broad stock, church steeple fluting, lanyard ring,
mushroom head ejector rod, large round brass
front sight and V notch rear sight.
Retailer: F. E. WEBB 16 HIGH S^T. OXFORD

Joseph L. Davis collection

A few other model RIC/83s have been observed
with this RIC/86 marking. It is possible that Webley
changed the model designation to coincide with
lengthening the cylinder and chambering these
revolvers for the .455. As we shall see, Webley did
not continue the "86".

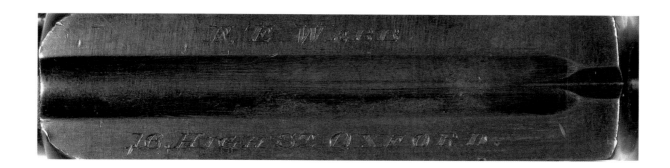

Webley RIC Model/83
SN 67303 .455, 2 1/2" barrel, blue, 5 shot, long frame with broad
stock, church steeple fluting, lanyard ring, mushroom
head ejector rod, large round brass front sight and V
notch rear sight.
Retailer: J. WOODWARD & SONS
64 S^T JAMES'S S^T LONDON SW

Frank & Jean Pycha collection

183

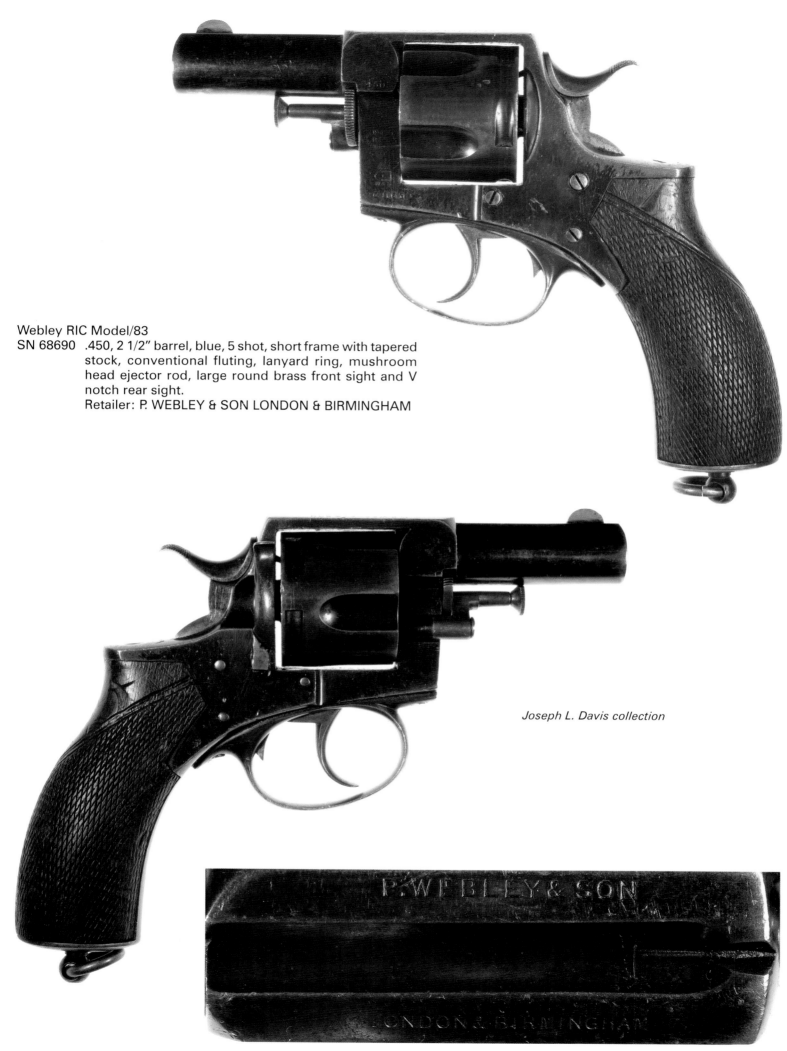

Webley RIC Model/83
SN 68690   .450, 2 1/2" barrel, blue, 5 shot, short frame with tapered stock, conventional fluting, lanyard ring, mushroom head ejector rod, large round brass front sight and V notch rear sight.
Retailer: P. WEBLEY & SON LONDON & BIRMINGHAM

Joseph L. Davis collection

Roger G. Michaud collection

Webley RIC Model/83 (Model/86)
SN 72033 .455CF, dull nickel, 5 shot, church steeple fluting, lanyard ring one-piece checkered wood
grip Watson Bros. registration number 2614
on butt.
Retailer: WATSON BRO[S].
29 OLD BOND S[T] LONDON.

Webley RIC Model/83
SN 74086 .455, 2 1/2" barrel, blue, 5 shot, long frame with broad
stock, church steeple fluting, lanyard ring, mushroom
head ejector rod, large round brass front sight and
V notch rear sight, unusual engraving "P. WEBLEY &
SON L & BIRMINGHAM" on top strap (only observed
example with this marking).
Retailer: SOLD BY J. F. KING DURBAN

Frank & Jean Pycha collection

Joseph L. Davis collection

Webley RIC Model/83
SN 74535 .455, 2 1/2" barrel, blue, 5 shot, long
frame with broad stock, conventional
fluting, lanyard ring, mushroom head
ejector rod, large round brass front
sight and V notch rear sight.
Retailer: WM POWELL & SONS
CARRS LANE BIRMINGHAM

Webley RIC Model/83
SN 77093 .44 RM (Russian), 2 1/2" barrel, blue, 5 shot, one piece wood grip, long frame, broad stock, church steeple fluting, lanyard ring, flat top ejector rod, round steel front sight and V notch rear sight.
Retailer: P. WEBLEY & SON BIRMINGHAM

This is one of very few Webley solid frame revolvers known in this caliber.

Ian Lawrance collection

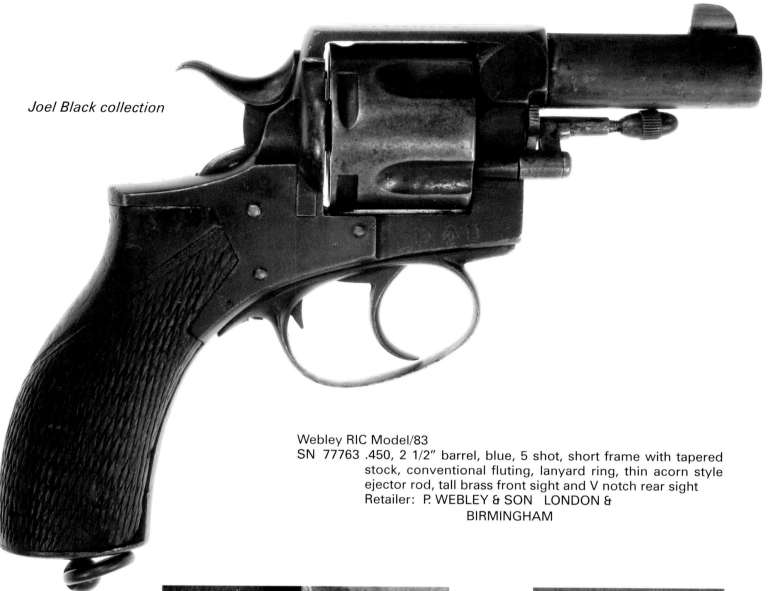

Joel Black collection

Webley RIC Model/83
SN 77763 .450, 2 1/2" barrel, blue, 5 shot, short frame with tapered stock, conventional fluting, lanyard ring, thin acorn style ejector rod, tall brass front sight and V notch rear sight
Retailer: P. WEBLEY & SON   LONDON &
                                                    BIRMINGHAM

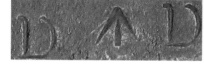

This is an extremely rare RIC/83 that saw military service in Australia as evidenced by the D ^ D marking.

Webley RIC Model/83
SN 79947   .450, 2 1/2" barrel, blue, 5 shot, short frame with tapered stock, conventional fluting, lanyard ring, thin acorn style ejector rod, tall brass front sight and V notch rear sight.
Retailer: P. WEBLEY & SON LONDON & BIRMINGHAM

Frank Pycha & Jean collection

Webley RIC Model/83
SN 80030 .450CF, 2 1/2" barrel, blue, 5 shot, short frame with tapered stock, conventional fluting, lanyard ring, thin acorn style ejector rod, tall brass front sight and V notch rear sight, Australian Government D^D mark on right side (likely from WW II).
Retailer: P. WEBLEY & SON LONDON & BIRMINGHAM

Frank & Jean Pycha collection

191

Webley RIC Model/83
SN 80436 .450, 2 1/2" barrel, blue, 5 shot, short frame with tapered stock, conventional fluting, lanyard ring, thin acorn style ejector rod, tall brass front sight and V notch rear sight.
Retailer: P. WEBLEY & SON LONDON & BIRMINGHAM

Joseph L. Davis collection

Webley RIC Model/83
SN 80688 .455, 2 1/2" barrel, blue, 5 shot, short frame with tapered stock, conventional fluting, lanyard ring, thin acorn style ejector rod, large round steel front sight and V notch rear sight, 3 / 171 and broad-arrow (military) mark on right side.
Retailer: P. WEBLEY & SON LONDON & BIRMINGHAM

Broad arrow and marking are unusual (probably Australia 3rd military district).
Joseph L. Davis collection

Webley RIC Model/83
SN 95367 .455, 2 1/2" barrel, blue, 5 shot, long frame with broad stock, conventional fluting, lanyard ring, thin acorn style ejector rod, tall brass front sight and V notch rear sight.
Retailer: P. WEBLEY & SON
LONDON & BIRMINGHAM

Joseph L. Davis collection

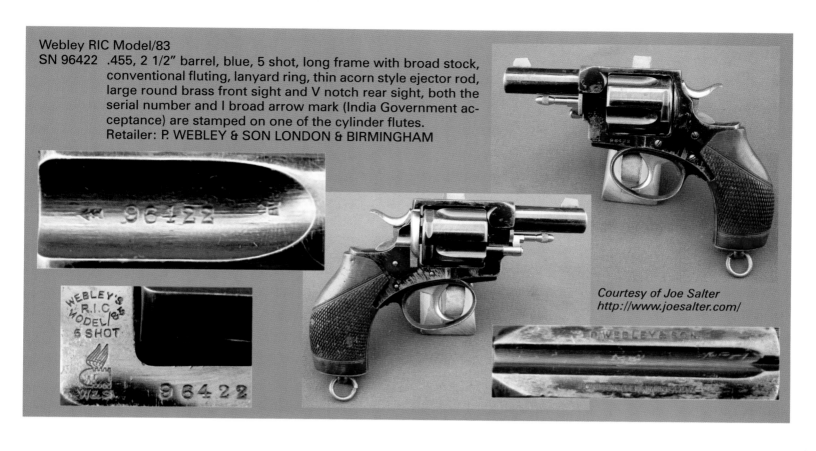

Webley RIC Model/83

SN 96422 .455, 2 1/2" barrel, blue, 5 shot, long frame with broad stock, conventional fluting, lanyard ring, thin acorn style ejector rod, large round brass front sight and V notch rear sight, both the serial number and I broad arrow mark (India Government acceptance) are stamped on one of the cylinder flutes.
Retailer: P. WEBLEY & SON LONDON & BIRMINGHAM

Courtesy of Joe Salter
http://www.joesalter.com/

Webley RIC Model/83

SN 96638 .455, 2 1/2" barrel, blue, 5 shot, long frame with broad stock, conventional fluting, lanyard ring, thin acorn style ejector rod, large round brass front sight and V notch rear sight, both the serial number and I broad arrow mark (India Government acceptance) are stamped on one of the cylinder flutes, radius corner to bottom front frame.
Retailer: P. WEBLEY & SON LONDON & BIRMINGHAM

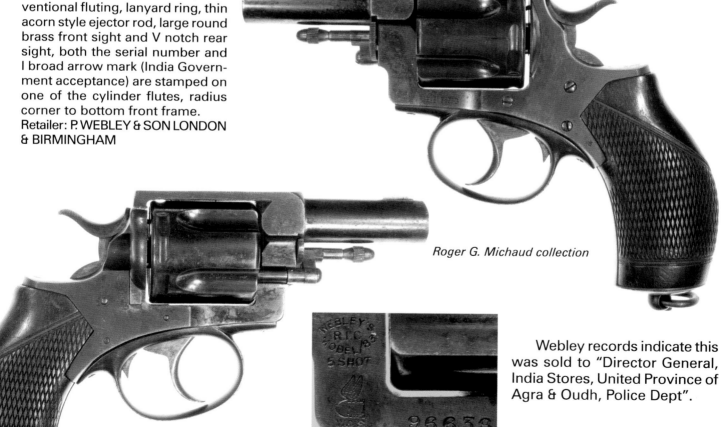

Roger G. Michaud collection

Webley records indicate this was sold to "Director General, India Stores, United Province of Agra & Oudh, Police Dept".

195

Webley RIC Model/83
SN 96648 .455, 2 1/2" barrel, blue, 5 shot, long frame with broad stock, conventional fluting, lanyard ring, thin acorn style ejector rod, large round brass front sight and V notch rear sight, both the serial number and I broad arrow mark (India Government acceptance) are stamped on one of the cylinder flutes.
Retailer: P. WEBLEY & SON LONDON & BIRMINGHAM

Frank & Jean Pycha collection

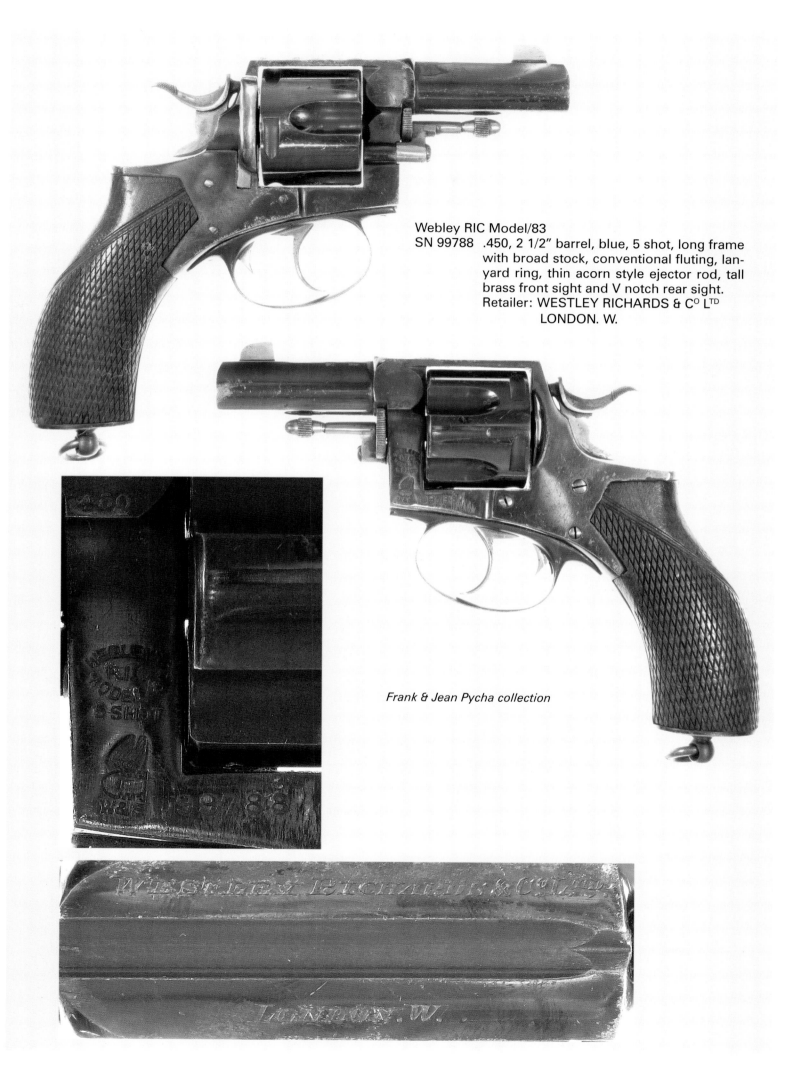

Webley RIC Model/83
SN 99788 .450, 2 1/2" barrel, blue, 5 shot, long frame
with broad stock, conventional fluting, lanyard ring, thin acorn style ejector rod, tall
brass front sight and V notch rear sight.
Retailer: WESTLEY RICHARDS & C⁰ L^TD
    LONDON. W.

Frank & Jean Pycha collection

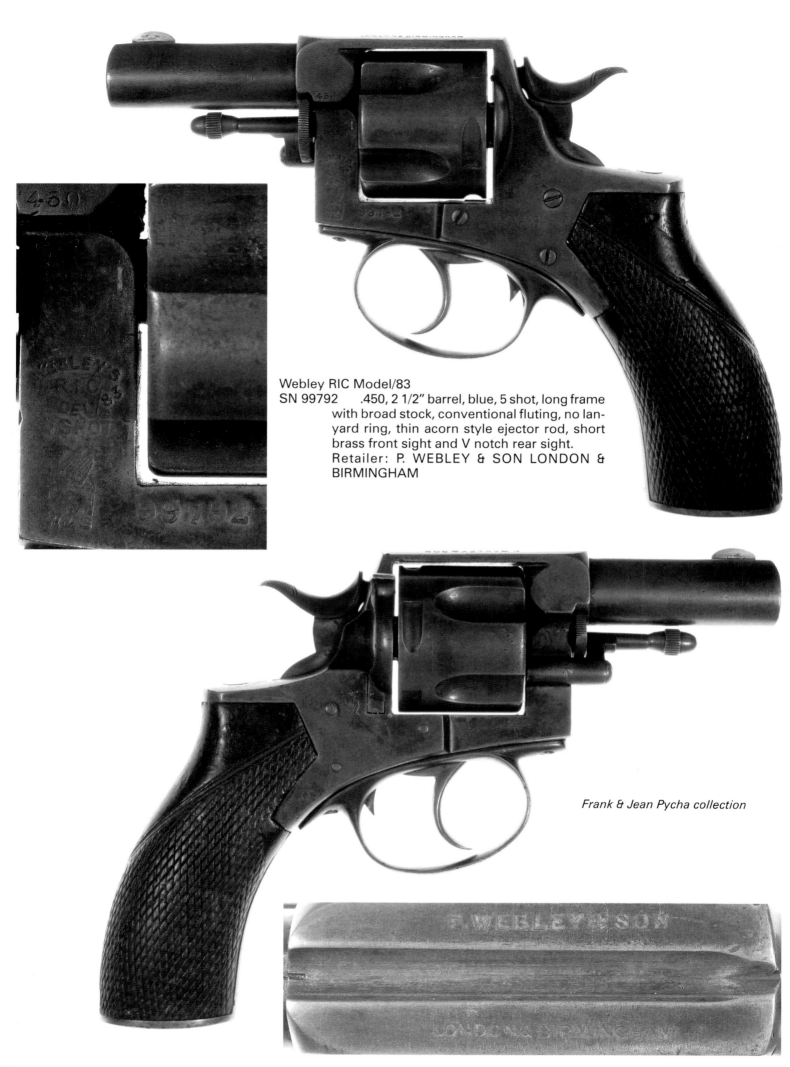

Webley RIC Model/83
SN 99792   .450, 2 1/2" barrel, blue, 5 shot, long frame with broad stock, conventional fluting, no lanyard ring, thin acorn style ejector rod, short brass front sight and V notch rear sight.
Retailer: P. WEBLEY & SON LONDON & BIRMINGHAM

Frank & Jean Pycha collection

Roger G. Michaud collection

Webley RIC Model/83
SN 101527 .455CF, shortened 1 3/4" barrel, blue, 5 shot, larger frame
with broader stock, SN also stamped in one flute, thin
acorn style ejector rod with flat tip to match barrel length,
has bobbed hammer spur, conventional flutes, round
front sight, lanyard ring removed and replaced by metal
plug, later factory modifications done at the behest of the
owner.
Retailer: P. WEBLEY & SON LONDON & BIRMINGHAM

Webley RIC Model/83
SN 102063 .455, 2 1/2" barrel, blue, 5 shot, long frame
with broad stock, conventional fluting, lanyard ring, thin acorn style ejector rod, large
round front sight and V notch rear sight.
Retailer: P. WEBLEY & SON LONDON &
BIRMINGHAM

These solid frame Webleys were assembled
well into the twentieth century but still used this
obsolete marking.

Joel Black collection

Webley RIC Model/83
SN 102490 .455CF, 2 1/2" barrel, high luster blue, 5 shot, larger frame with broader stock, elongated acorn style ejector rod, conventional flutes, lanyard ring, nitro proved, serial number is also stamped on one cylinder flute. Retailer: WEBLEY & SCOTT L^{TD} BIRMINGHAM & LONDON

Only the last few hundred solid frame Webleys were marked WEBLEY & SCOTT L^{TD}. All others bore the old P. Webley name even 35 years after their amalgamation in 1897 as a limited company that included W. C. Scott and Richard Ellis.

Roger G. Michaud collection

84   A. F. STOEGER, Inc., 5

WEBLEY & SCOTT .455

Solid Frame
"BULL DOG"
Five Shot

2¼ inch barrel. Weight 1 lb. 5 oz. 5 shot. Used extensively by the Irish Constabulary.

Price $40.00

With advertisements like this in a 1928 Stoegers catalog, it is no wonder that many of today's collectors incorrectly identify all short barreled Webleys as Bull Dogs.

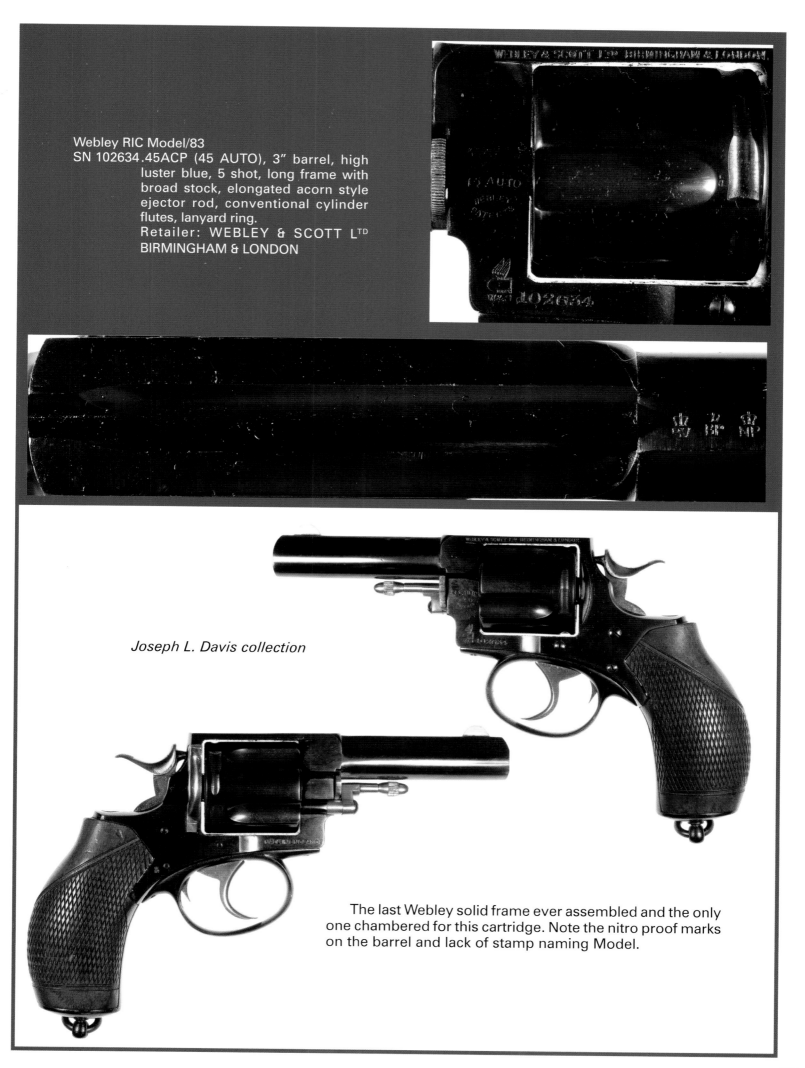

Webley RIC Model/83
SN 102634.45ACP (45 AUTO), 3" barrel, high
luster blue, 5 shot, long frame with
broad stock, elongated acorn style
ejector rod, conventional cylinder
flutes, lanyard ring.
Retailer: WEBLEY & SCOTT L^TD
BIRMINGHAM & LONDON

Joseph L. Davis collection

The last Webley solid frame ever assembled and the only
one chambered for this cartridge. Note the nitro proof marks
on the barrel and lack of stamp naming Model.

RIC Copies

Probably nothing about Webley solid frames is more controversial than the origin of the many copies found in the UK and the rest of the world. It is likely that many of these revolvers were made entirely outside of England. Top-notch Belgium companies like Francotte and Dumoulin could turn out revolvers that were easily the equal of Webleys, while others made poor copies. Many British retailers would import parts from Belgium, finish them, and then have proof testing at either the Birmingham or London Proof House.

This retailer's catalog page *(right)* was unusually honest.

(Below) The top right revolver is by Bland, the bottom right British and the bottom ones on the left were probably made in Belgium.

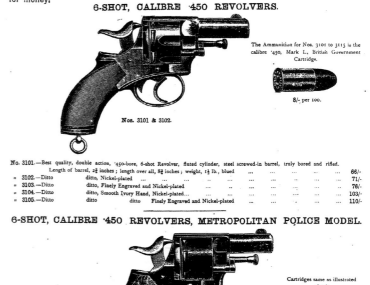

BEST SOLID-BODY REVOLVERS.

The following Revolvers (Nos. 3101 to 3145) are excellent weapons, and are recommended to buyers requiring Solid Body Revolvers of really first quality. They are entirely ENGLISH-MADE, and bear the English Proof-Mark, and are warranted to give satisfaction.

They are vastly superior in safety, accuracy, action, and wearing qualities to the low-priced Continental-made weapons, and, although higher in price, they are better value for money.

6-SHOT, CALIBRE ·450 REVOLVERS.

The Ammunition for Nos. 3101 to 3115 is the calibre ·450, Mark L., British Government Cartridge.

8/- per 100.

Nos. 3101 & 3102.

No. 3101.—Best quality, double action, ·450-bore, 6-shot Revolver, fluted cylinder, steel screwed-in barrel, truly bored and rifled. Length of barrel, 2¾ inches ; length over all, 8¾ inches ; weight, 1½ lb., blued 66/-
" 3102.—Ditto ditto, Nickel-plated 71/-
" 3103.—Ditto ditto, Finely Engraved and Nickel-plated 76/-
" 3104.—Ditto ditto, Smooth Ivory Hand, Nickel-plated... ... ... 103/-
" 3105.—Ditto ditto ditto Finely Engraved and Nickel-plated 110/-

6-SHOT, CALIBRE ·450 REVOLVERS, METROPOLITAN POLICE MODEL.

Cartridges same as illustrated above,
8/- per 100.

Nos. 3106 & 3107.

REVOLVERS OF BEST ENGLISH FINISH—*continued.*

26 & 27.
28 & 29.

Trade No.
26. Reduced Bulldog, the smallest 320 central fire revolver made, blued £0 12 6
27. " " " " nickled £0 13 0
320 380 450
28. Bulldog, long chequered walnut grip, fine weapon, blued ... ... 15/- 16/- . . . ..
29. " " " nickled ... ... 16/- 17/- . . . ..

31.
82.

81. Army Pattern, chequered grip, blued finished ... ... — — 22/- —
82. Army Cavalry Pattern, ring stock, one of the best made ... ... — — 38/6 —
SPECIAL.—The foregoing English finished Revolvers are English prooved, and can be named to suit customers, without extra cost.

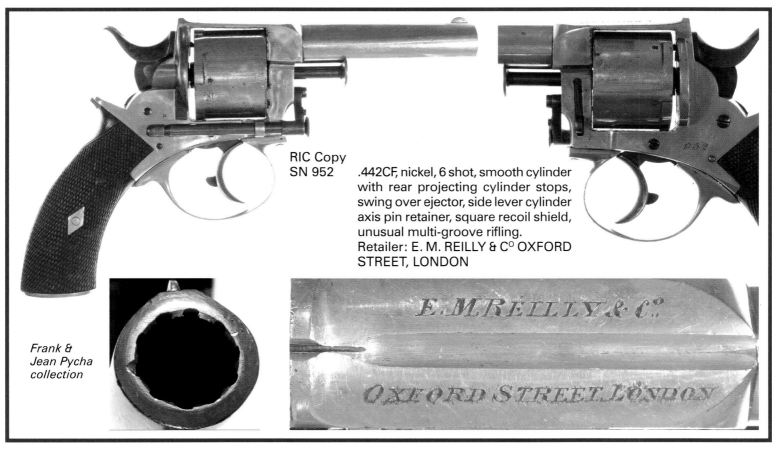

RIC Copy
SN 952

.442CF, nickel, 6 shot, smooth cylinder with rear projecting cylinder stops, swing over ejector, side lever cylinder axis pin retainer, square recoil shield, unusual multi-groove rifling.
Retailer: E. M. REILLY & Cº OXFORD STREET, LONDON

Frank & Jean Pycha collection

E. M. REILLY & Cº
OXFORD STREET LONDON

RIC Copy
NVSN   .442CF, 6 shot, blued, smooth cylinder with rear projecting cylinder stops, square recoil shield, swing over ejector, unusual multi-groove rifling, side lever cylinder axis pin retainer, from the same maker as the previous E. M. Reilly retailed revolver.
Retailer: LEMON & SONS ENNISKILLEN

Apparently the bank manager must have encouraged his employees to practice with this revolver.

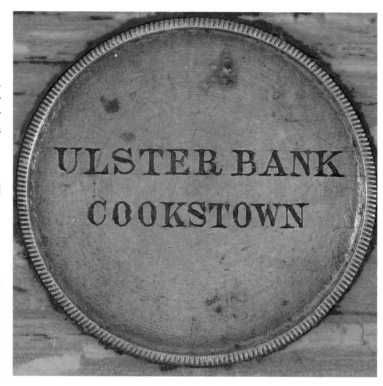

Frank & Jean Pycha collection

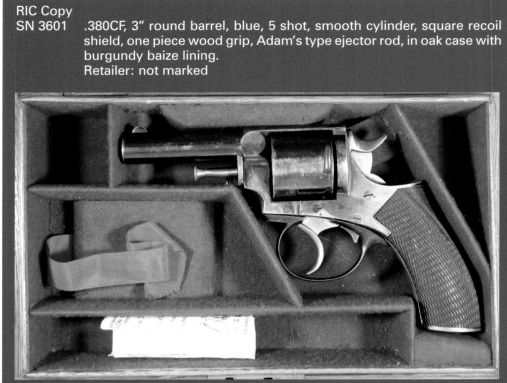

RIC Copy
SN 3601   .380CF, 3" round barrel, blue, 5 shot, smooth cylinder, square recoil shield, one piece wood grip, Adam's type ejector rod, in oak case with burgundy baize lining.
Retailer: not marked

Frank & Jean Pycha collection

RIC Copy
SN 50922   .450CF, blue, 5 shot, square recoil shield, lanyard ring 3" round barrel, smooth cylinder with rear locking recesses.
Retailer: BLISSETT & SON LIVERPOOL

RIC Copy
SN 9029

.450CF, nickel, 6 shot, smooth cylinder, square recoil shield, Tranter style loading gate, Webley Wing Brand trademark (in the 1880s, a Webley internal memo refer to the winged bullet as such) on right.

This is a rare example of an RIC that was outsourced by Webley. Besides the recoil shield and loading gate, another clue is the sculptured trigger. The triggers on Webley RICs were flat sided.

Courtesy of Richard Milner
http://www.armsresearch.co.uk/

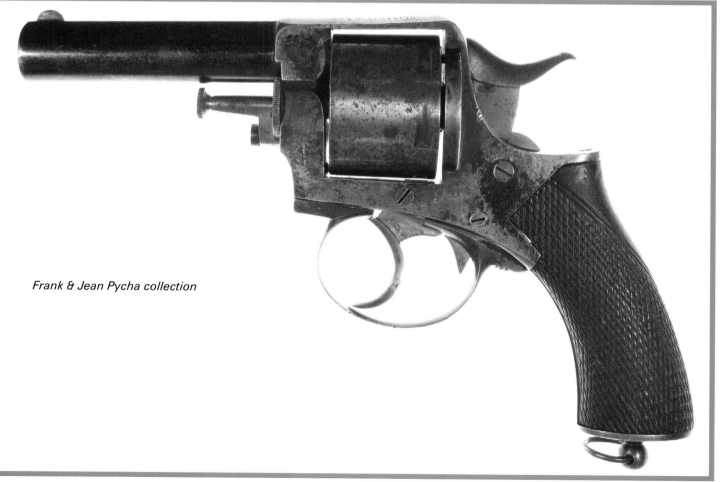

Frank & Jean Pycha collection

RIC Copy
SN 31615 .450CF, nickel, 6 shot, smooth cylinder with rear locking recesses, 4" octagonal barrel, extensive engraving, square recoil shield, P. WEBLEY & SON stamped in groove of top strap.
Retailer: BLISSETT & SON LIVERPOOL

The wide trigger, elongated sear, and octagonal barrel are clues to this revolver having been outsourced by Webley and supplied to Blissett as the genuine article.

Frank & Jean Pycha collection

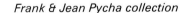

Engraved on barrel:

*"PRESENTED TO
ALFRED HAMARD
BY THE CADETS OF THE CONWAY
AS A TOKEN OF THEIR
GREAT ESTEEM & REGARD"*

Roger G. Michaud collection

RIC Copy
SN 3592 .450CF, nickel plated, 6 shot, one-piece checkered wood grip, smooth cylinder with rear locking recesses, ramped barrel, square recoil shield, squared loading gate, maker unknown.
Retailer: E.FLETCHER GLOUCESTER

Square recoil shield

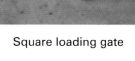

Square loading gate

RIC Copy No. 5 (RIC MODEL/83 style)
SN 258   .450CF, 2 5/8" barrel, nickel finish, 5 shot, conventional fluted cylinder with rear locking recesses, lanyard ring, one-piece checkered wood grip.
Retailer: W.W.GREENER 68 HAY-MARKET LONDON.

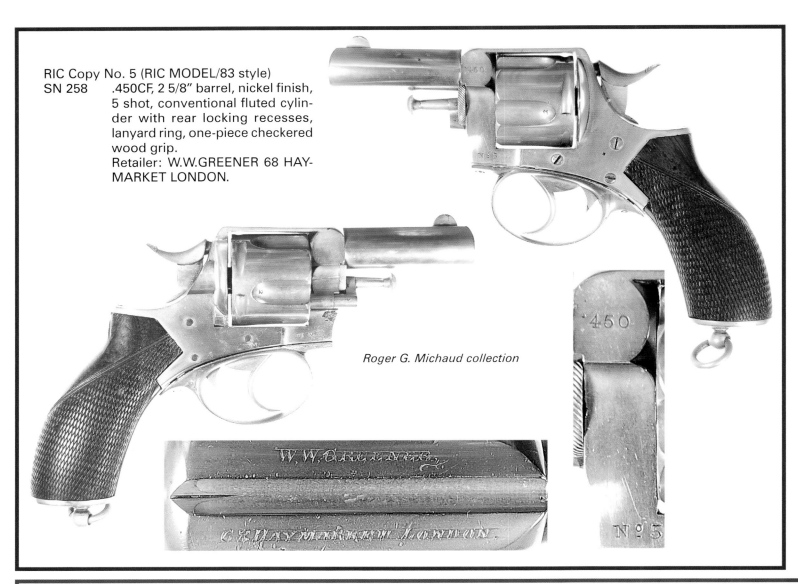

Roger G. Michaud collection

RIC Copy No. 2 (made by Thomas Bland)
SN 1900   .297/230CF (rook), 3" barrel, blue, 6 shot, conventional cylinder flutes, Adams style ejector rod, octagonal barrel.
Retailer: CHARLES ROSSON 4 MARKET HEAD DERRY

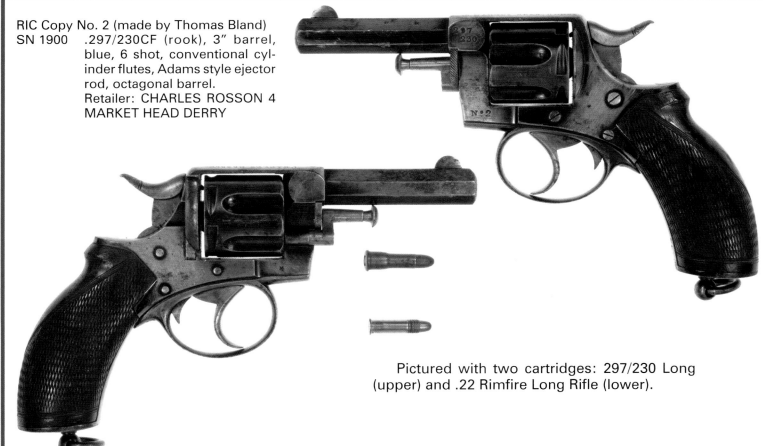

Pictured with two cartridges: 297/230 Long (upper) and .22 Rimfire Long Rifle (lower).

RIC Copy No. 6 1/2
SN 3115   .300CF (rook), 3" barrel, blue, 6 shot, Adams style ejector rod,
octagonal barrel, conventional cylinder flutes, lanyard ring.
Retailer: not marked

Frank & Jean Pycha collection

This looks like some RIC copies retailed by Greener, but we have not discovered who made them for Greener, although we know some were made by Bland.

Joel Black collection

RIC Copy No. 9 1/2 (Bland)
SN 1520   .320CF, 3" round barrel, blue, 6 shot, one-piece checkered wood grip, Adams style ejector rod, conventional cylinder flutes, lanyard ring.
Retailer: W.W.GREENER 68 HAY-MARKET LONDON.

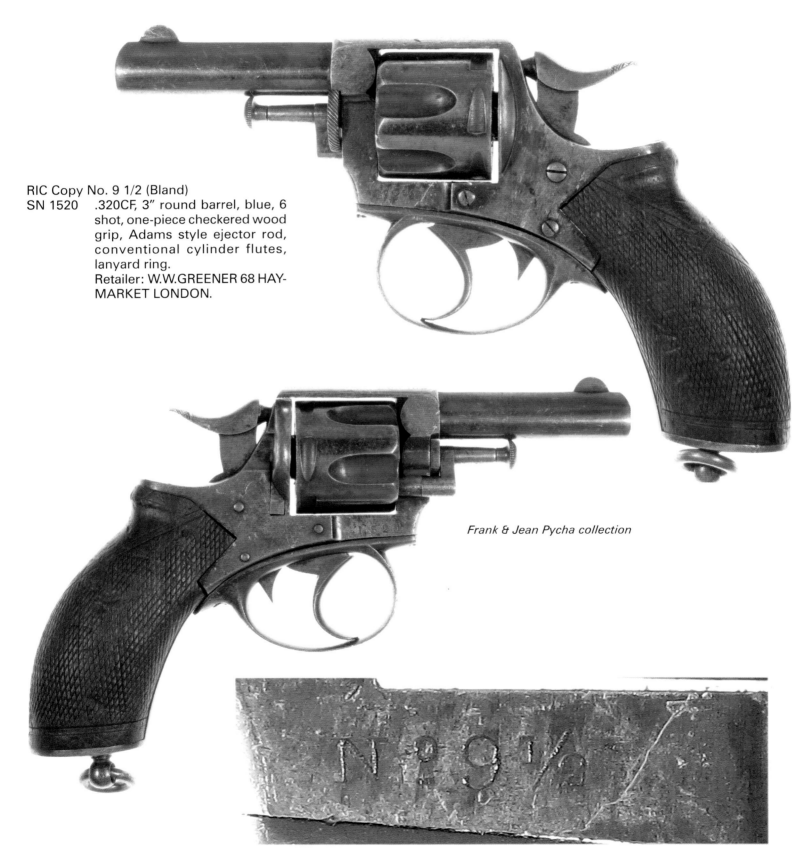

Frank & Jean Pycha collection

Roger G. Michaud collection

RIC Copy (Bland)
SN 590   .450CF, 3 1/2" barrel, blue, 6 shot, one piece wood grip, birdshead butt, no lanyard ring, commercial British proofs, conventional cylinder flutes, retailer's registration number 590 is on bottom of the trigger guard.
Retailer: C. W. ANDREWS L^TD LONDON

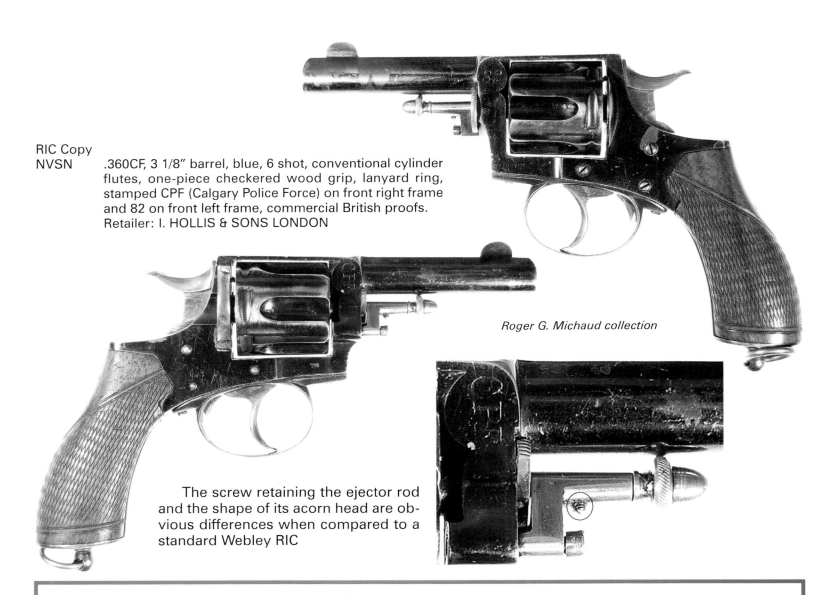

RIC Copy
NVSN   .360CF, 3 1/8" barrel, blue, 6 shot, conventional cylinder flutes, one-piece checkered wood grip, lanyard ring, stamped CPF (Calgary Police Force) on front right frame and 82 on front left frame, commercial British proofs.
Retailer: I. HOLLIS & SONS LONDON

Roger G. Michaud collection

The screw retaining the ejector rod and the shape of its acorn head are obvious differences when compared to a standard Webley RIC

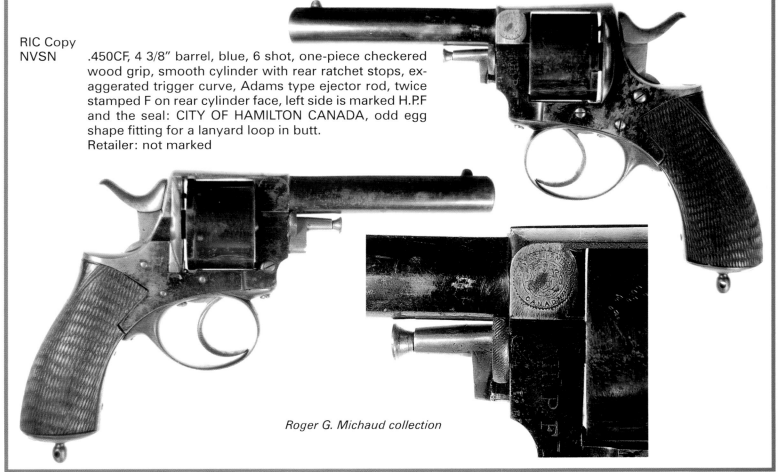

RIC Copy
NVSN   .450CF, 4 3/8" barrel, blue, 6 shot, one-piece checkered wood grip, smooth cylinder with rear ratchet stops, exaggerated trigger curve, Adams type ejector rod, twice stamped F on rear cylinder face, left side is marked H.P.F and the seal: CITY OF HAMILTON CANADA, odd egg shape fitting for a lanyard loop in butt.
Retailer: not marked

Roger G. Michaud collection

212

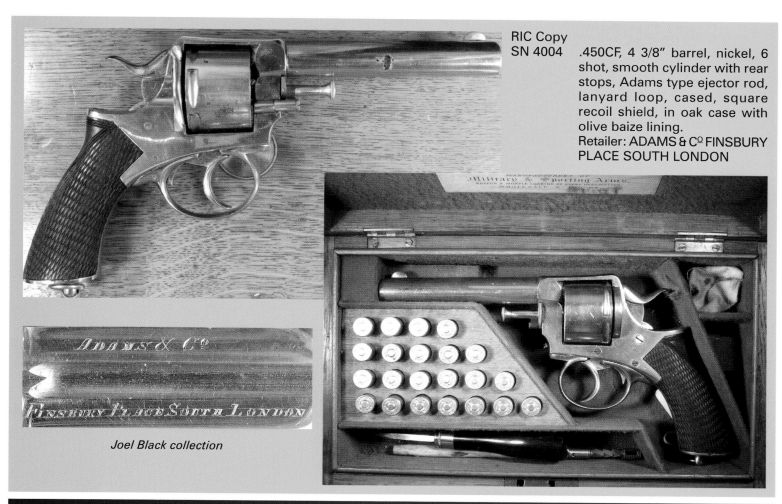

RIC Copy
SN 4004

.450CF, 4 3/8" barrel, nickel, 6 shot, smooth cylinder with rear stops, Adams type ejector rod, lanyard loop, cased, square recoil shield, in oak case with olive baize lining.
Retailer: ADAMS & C° FINSBURY PLACE SOUTH LONDON

Joel Black collection

RIC Copy
NVSN

.450CF, 4 3/8" barrel, blue, 6 shot, smooth cylinder with rear stops, Adams type ejector rod, lanyard loop, square recoil shield, cased.
Retailer: J. BLANCH & SON. 29 GRACECHURCH S^T LONDON

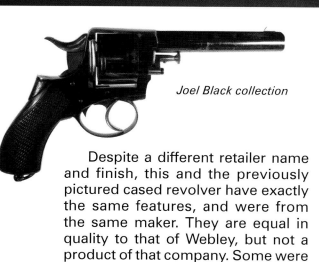

Joel Black collection

Despite a different retailer name and finish, this and the previously pictured cased revolver have exactly the same features, and were from the same maker. They are equal in quality to that of Webley, but not a product of that company. Some were undoubtedly also produced by the same maker for Webley.

Pryse RIC Copy
SN 6479   .450CF, 4 3/8" barrel, nickel plated, 6 shot, smooth cylinder with rear stops, raised rear top strap, Adams type ejector rod, lanyard loop, cased, square recoil shield, cylinder marked "STEEL", left frame stamped PRYSE'S RIC
Retailer: ARMY & NAVY C.S.L. LONDON.

Frank & Jean Pycha collection

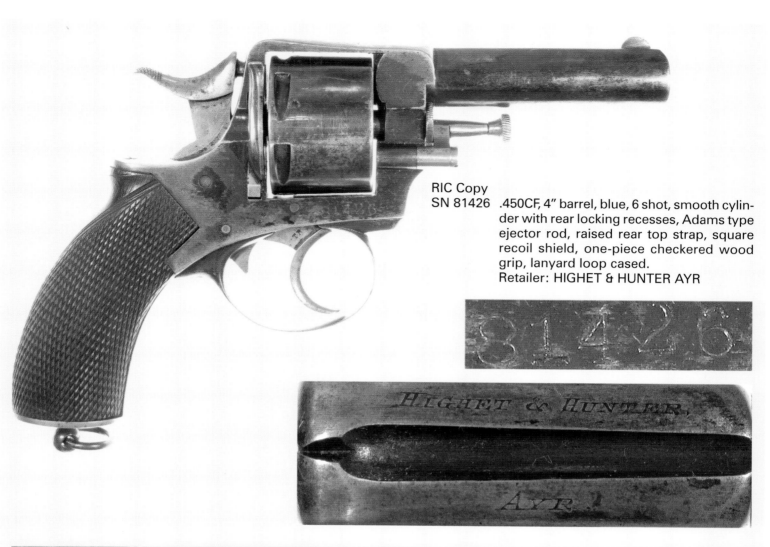

RIC Copy
SN 81426   .450CF, 4" barrel, blue, 6 shot, smooth cylinder with rear locking recesses, Adams type ejector rod, raised rear top strap, square recoil shield, one-piece checkered wood grip, lanyard loop cased.
Retailer: HIGHET & HUNTER AYR

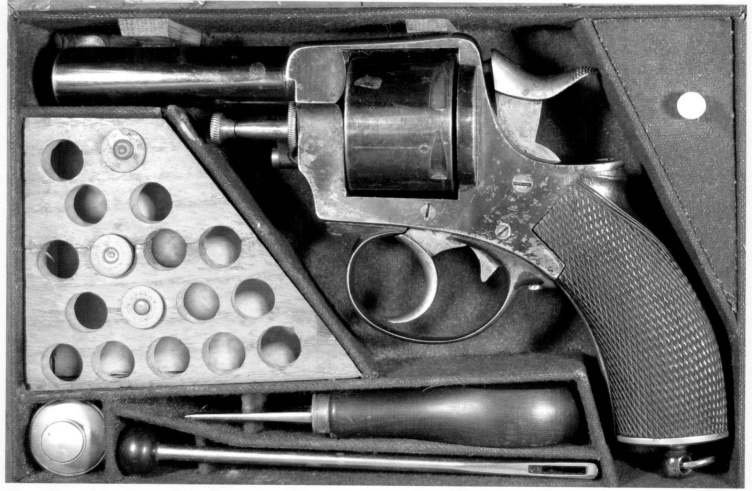

215

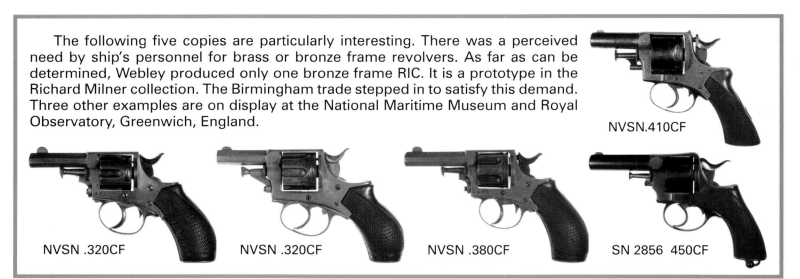

The following five copies are particularly interesting. There was a perceived need by ship's personnel for brass or bronze frame revolvers. As far as can be determined, Webley produced only one bronze frame RIC. It is a prototype in the Richard Milner collection. The Birmingham trade stepped in to satisfy this demand. Three other examples are on display at the National Maritime Museum and Royal Observatory, Greenwich, England.

NVSN.410CF

NVSN .320CF   NVSN .320CF   NVSN .380CF   SN 2856 450CF

RIC Copy
NVSN   .320CF, 2 5/8" octagonal barrel, brass frame, 6 shot, conventional cylinder flutes, one-piece checkered wood grip. Retailer: not marked

Leroy Thompson collection

216

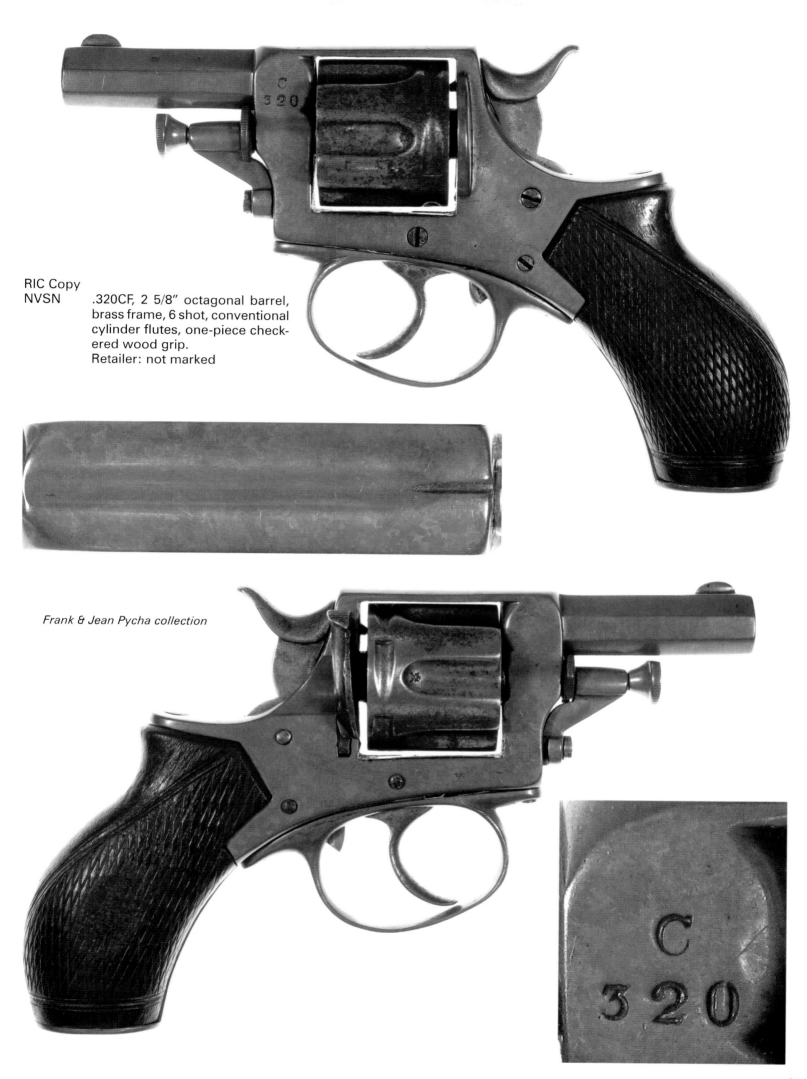

RIC Copy
NVSN .320CF, 2 5/8" octagonal barrel, brass frame, 6 shot, conventional cylinder flutes, one-piece checkered wood grip.
Retailer: not marked

Frank & Jean Pycha collection

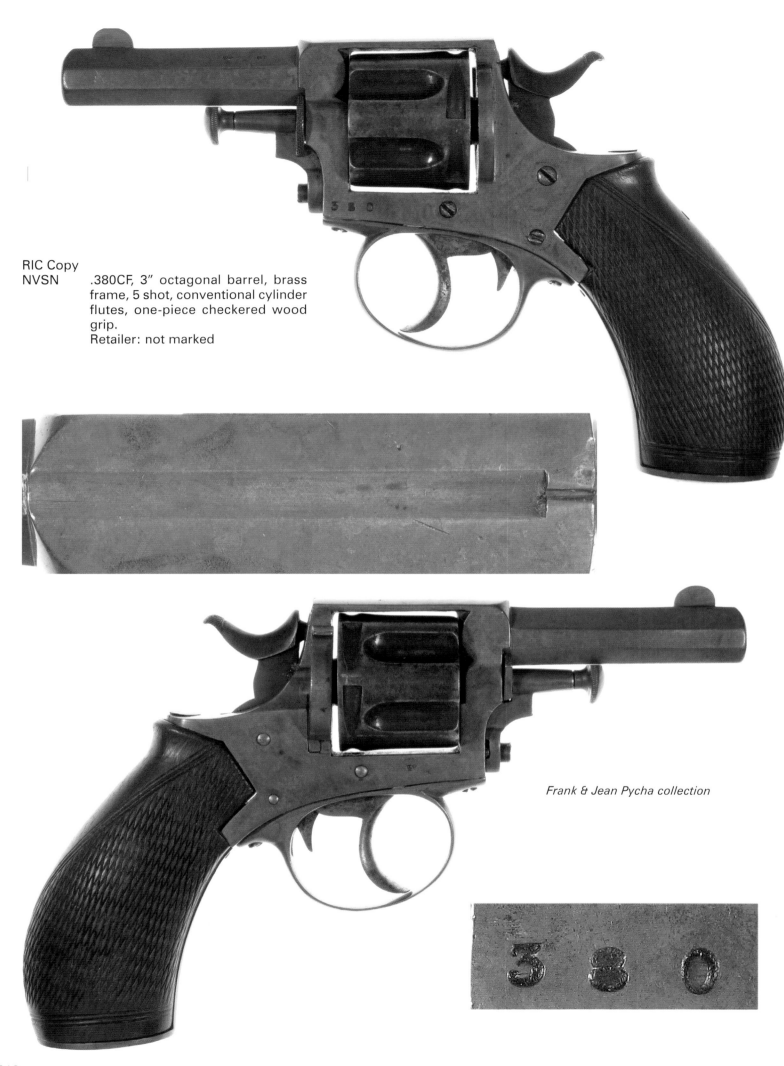

RIC Copy
NVSN   .380CF, 3" octagonal barrel, brass frame, 5 shot, conventional cylinder flutes, one-piece checkered wood grip.
Retailer: not marked

Frank & Jean Pycha collection

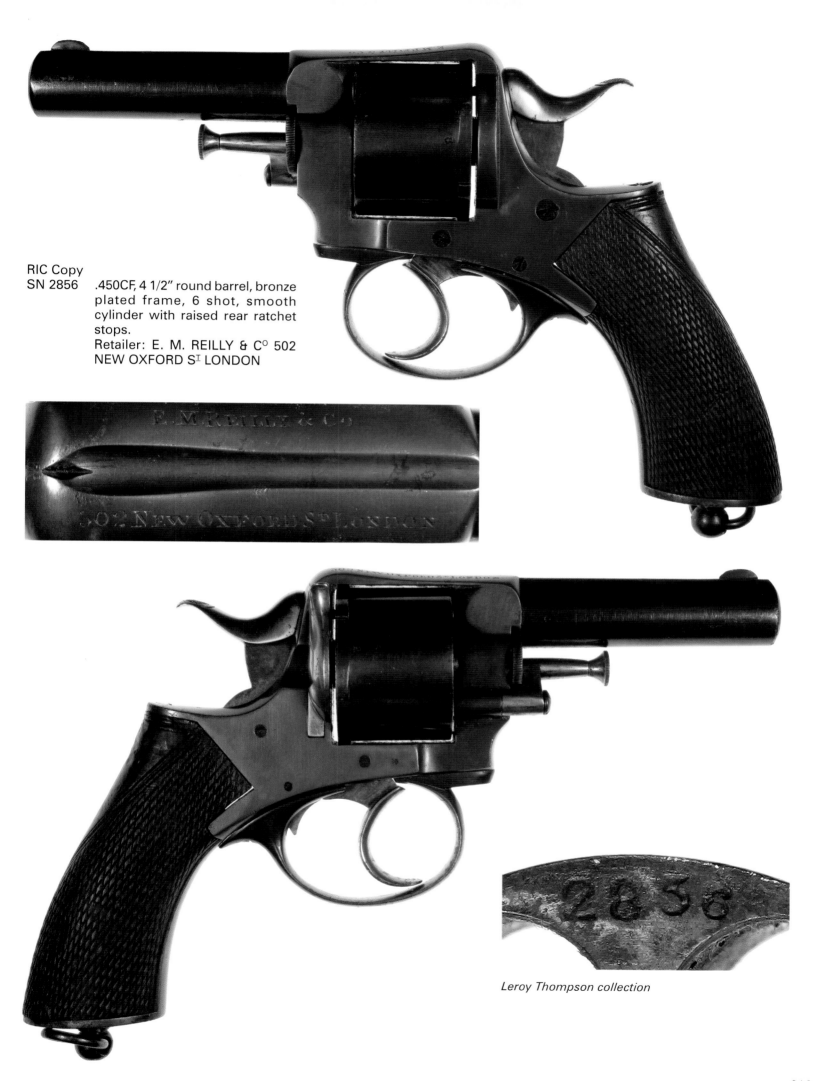

RIC Copy
SN 2856   .450CF, 4 1/2" round barrel, bronze plated frame, 6 shot, smooth cylinder with raised rear ratchet stops.
Retailer: E. M. REILLY & C° 502 NEW OXFORD S^I LONDON

Leroy Thompson collection

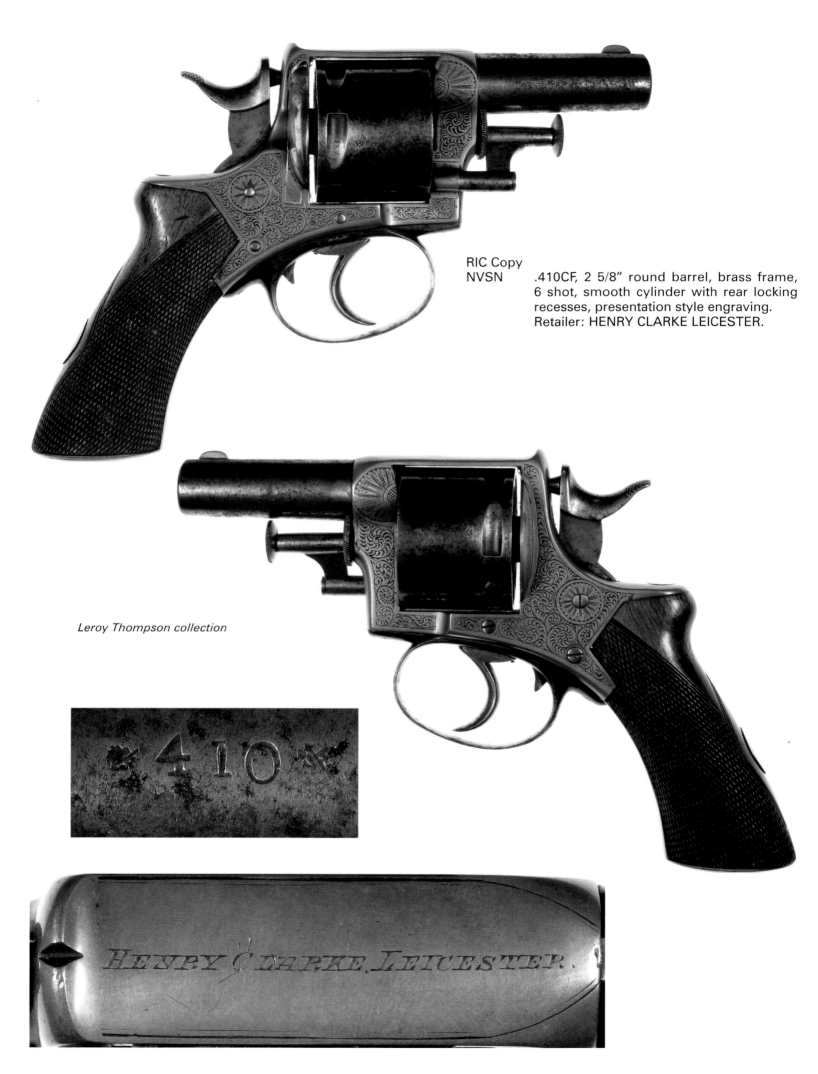

RIC Copy
NVSN

.410CF, 2 5/8" round barrel, brass frame, 6 shot, smooth cylinder with rear locking recesses, presentation style engraving. Retailer: HENRY CLARKE LEICESTER.

Leroy Thompson collection

Webley RIC No. 5 Army Express

This model designation is arbitrary. In essence, these very scarce revolvers represent an evolution from the RIC No. 1 New Model to the No. 5 New Army Express. The frame is a standard New Model RIC which has been fitted with a Colt style ejector and housing. The Webley sales book entry notation is ".455 RIC 6 inch with side rod".

Webley RIC No. 5 Army Express
SN 77375 .450 and .455CF, lanyard ring, one-piece checkered wood grip, cylinder axis pin is retained by lever on left, conventional flutes, Abadie loading system: disconnects the hammer when the loading gate is open to allow each pull on the trigger to rotate the cylinder one chamber at a time in order to load the chamber, rebounding hammer, commercial British proofs (no military proof mark).
Retailer: P.WEBLEY & SON LONDON & BIRMINGHAM

Roger G. Michaud collection

221

Webley RIC No. 5 Army Express
SN 77417 .450 and .455CF, lanyard ring, one-piece checkered wood grip, cylinder axis pin retained by lever on left, conventional flutes, Abadie loading system.
Retailer: P. WEBLEY & SON LONDON & BIRMINGHAM

Frank & Jean Pycha collection

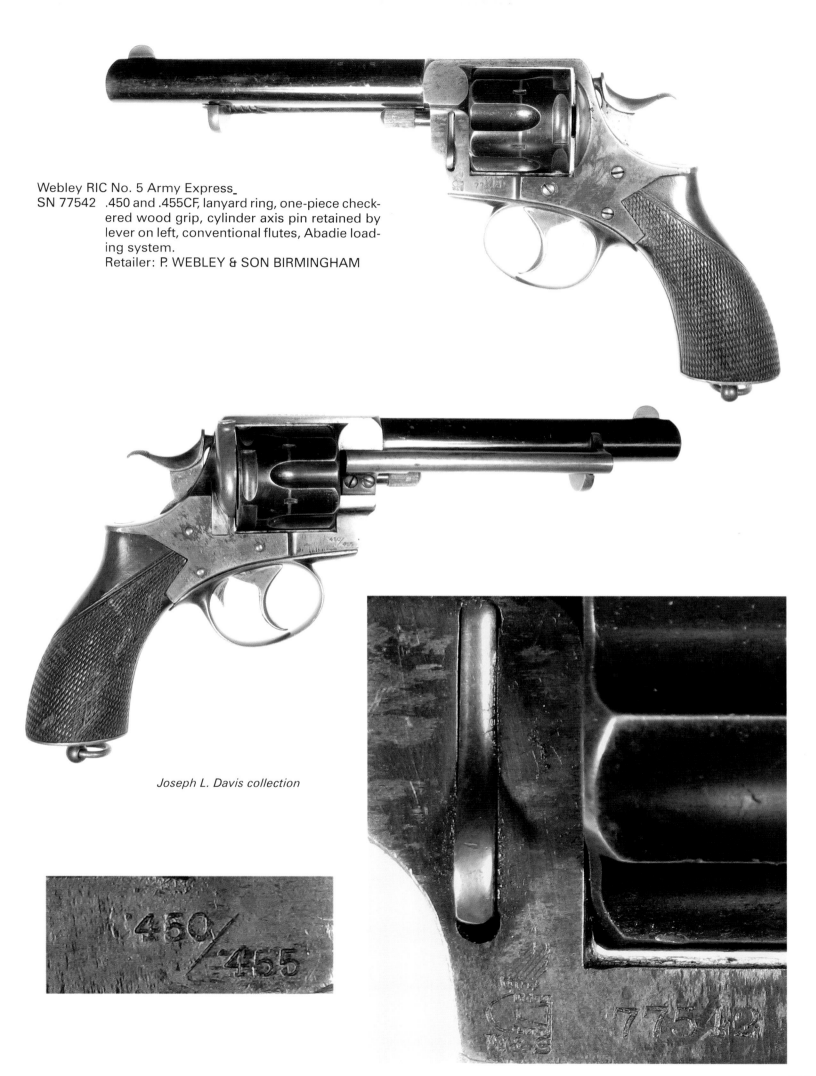

Webley RIC No. 5 Army Express
SN 77542 .450 and .455CF, lanyard ring, one-piece checkered wood grip, cylinder axis pin retained by
lever on left, conventional flutes, Abadie loading system.
Retailer: P. WEBLEY & SON BIRMINGHAM

Joseph L. Davis collection

No. 5 New Model Army Express

All Webley No.5 New Model Army Express revolvers are solid frame, 6 shot, and have conventional cylinder flutes. The grips are two-piece checkered wood. A lanyard ring, smooth (non-serrated) trigger, serrated tip hammer spur, and V notch rear sight are also standard. A front end spring catch retains the cylinder pin. This handgun model was intended to compete with the Colt Model 1878 double action revolver. Calibers available were 38/40, 44/40, .450, .455, .45 LONG (45 Colt), and .476.

Courtesy of Gordon Bruce.
Copied from a January 1886 Army & Navy C.S.L. price list.

WEBLEY'S No. 5 ARMY REVOLVER.
AS ADOPTED BY THE TRANSVAAL GOVERNMENT.

This Revolver, of all the modern double-action type, is acknowledged to be the strongest, best sighted, and most accurately shooting Pistol in the market, and is constructed to shoot point blank at 25 yards.

6-shot. 5½in. Barrel. Double action. Made to take Cartridges described below.

No. 3038—Blued ...	...	...	...	...	**£4 15 6**	
No. 3039—Nickel-plated	...	...	...	...	**£5 7 0**	

Size "No. 5 '476" is adapted to shoot the Regulation Service Cartridges, '455 (Enfield Mark II.), and '476 (Enfield Mark III.), to be obtained from the Stores of an Army in the Field. It will also shoot the '450 (Enfield Mark I.) The same Revolver will also fire the American '45 U.S. Cavalry Cartridges.

U.S. '45 Cavalry Cartridges,	'476 and '455 Cartridges,	'450 Cartridges,
14/- per 100.	10/3 per 100.	8/- per 100.

Size "No. 5 '44 W|" is designed to shoot the '44 Winchester Magazine Rifle Cartridge, which contains 40 grains powder, and a bullet of 200 grains.

Price of Cartridges, 12/- per 100.

Suitable Cases 14/- or 19/6 each.   Cleaning Implements 3/9 per set.

Best Quality Leather Waist Belt, with Revolver Holster and Ammunition Pouch, 18/-; strong serviceable quality, 10/6 per set.

Webley No.5 New Model Army Express
SN 579   .450, 5 1/2" barrel, blue, squared uppermost backstrap, Colt style ejector, Lesotho (South Africa) mark on bottom of barrel.
Retailer: V & R BLAKEMORE LONDON

Courtesy of Peter Sheaf

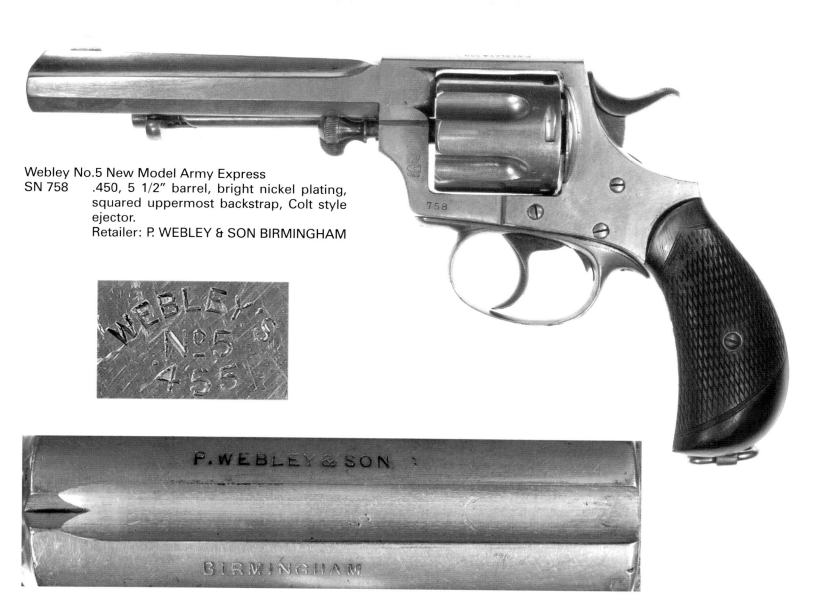

Webley No.5 New Model Army Express
SN 758   .450, 5 1/2" barrel, bright nickel plating, squared uppermost backstrap, Colt style ejector.
Retailer: P. WEBLEY & SON BIRMINGHAM

Roger G. Michaud collection

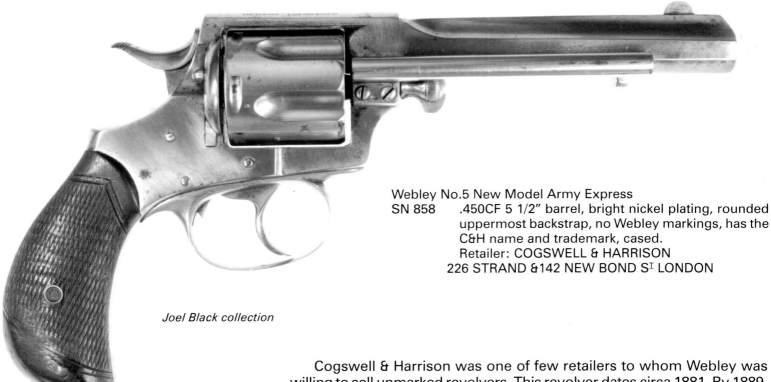

Webley No.5 New Model Army Express
SN 858   .450CF 5 1/2" barrel, bright nickel plating, rounded uppermost backstrap, no Webley markings, has the C&H name and trademark, cased.
Retailer: COGSWELL & HARRISON
226 STRAND &142 NEW BOND S^T LONDON

Joel Black collection

Cogswell & Harrison was one of few retailers to whom Webley was willing to sell unmarked revolvers. This revolver dates circa 1881. By 1889, Webley's "minutes book" indicates a decision was made to henceforth mark all (rather than some) of their revolvers with the "Wing Brand" (flying bullet) and "WEBLEY'S PATENT" trademarks. This was a reaction to a newspaper account of an incident attributed to a poorly made revolver that was erroneously described as made by Webley.

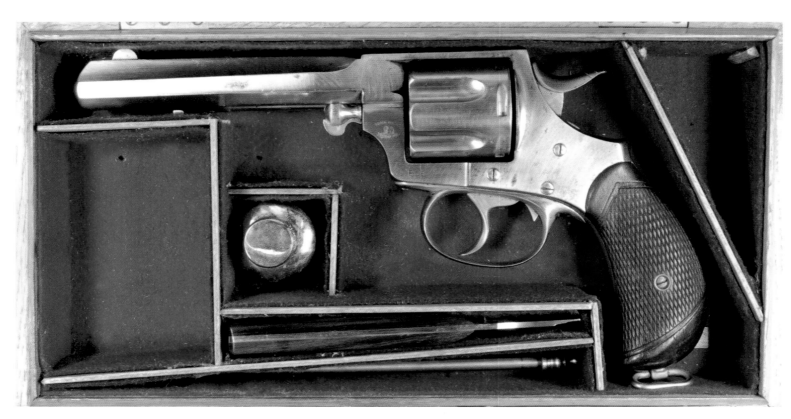

Webley No.5 New Model Army Express
SN 910   .450, 5 1/2" barrel, blue, squared upper-
most backstrap, Colt style ejector.
Retailer: not marked

Frank & Jean Pycha collection

*John Gailey collection. Photos courtesy of
http://www.collectorsfirearms.com/*

Webley No.5 New Model Army Express
SN 1159   .455CF 5 1/2" barrel, blue, rounded uppermost
backstrap, sold to a Clarke Esq. December 1883
Retailer: ARMY & NAVY C.S.L. EXPRESS

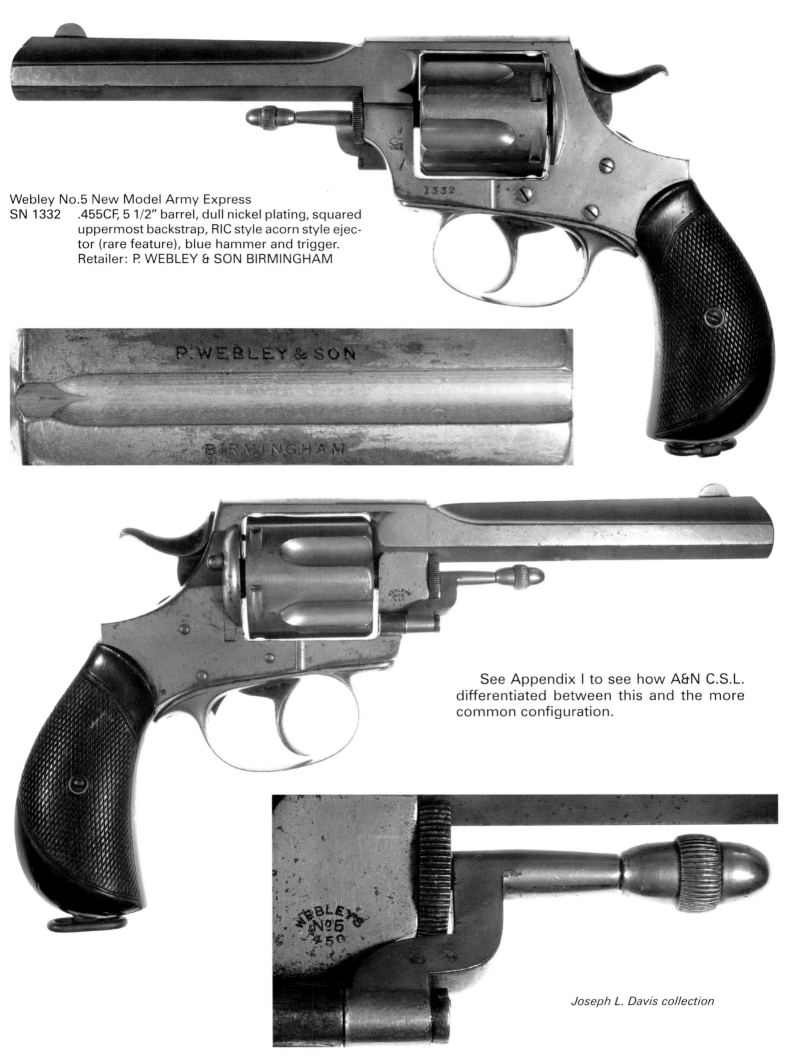

Webley No.5 New Model Army Express
SN 1332   .455CF, 5 1/2" barrel, dull nickel plating, squared uppermost backstrap, RIC style acorn style ejector (rare feature), blue hammer and trigger.
Retailer: P. WEBLEY & SON BIRMINGHAM

See Appendix I to see how A&N C.S.L. differentiated between this and the more common configuration.

Joseph L. Davis collection

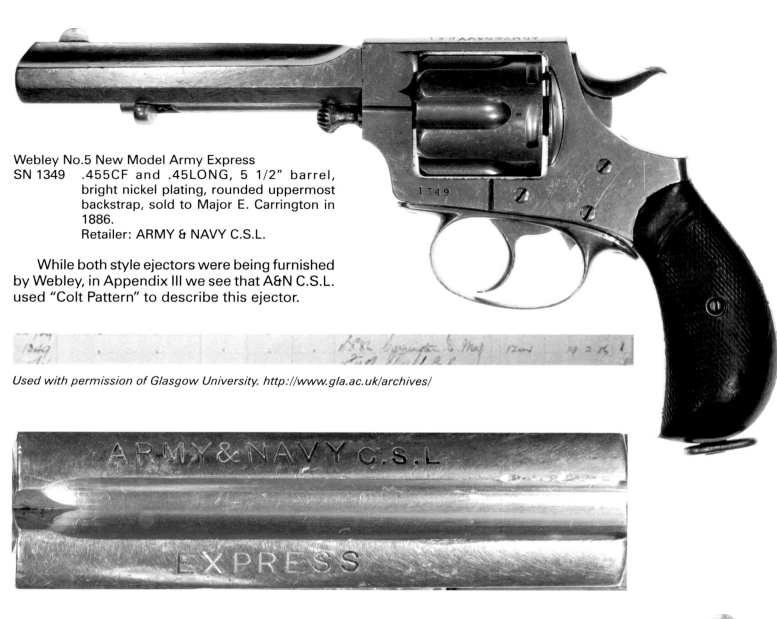

Webley No.5 New Model Army Express
SN 1349   .455CF and .45LONG, 5 1/2" barrel,
      bright nickel plating, rounded uppermost
      backstrap, sold to Major E. Carrington in
      1886.
      Retailer: ARMY & NAVY C.S.L.

   While both style ejectors were being furnished
by Webley, in Appendix III we see that A&N C.S.L.
used "Colt Pattern" to describe this ejector.

Used with permission of Glasgow University. http://www.gla.ac.uk/archives/

*Roger G. Michaud
collection*

Webley No.5 New Model Army Express (unmarked)
SN 1374   .450, 5 1/2" barrel, blue, Cogswell & Harrison
TRADEMARK of a lion atop the banner VENI-
VIDIVICI, rounded uppermost backstrap, no
"Webley" logo.
Retailer: COGSWELL & HARRISON
226 STRAND & 142 NEW BOND S^T LONDON

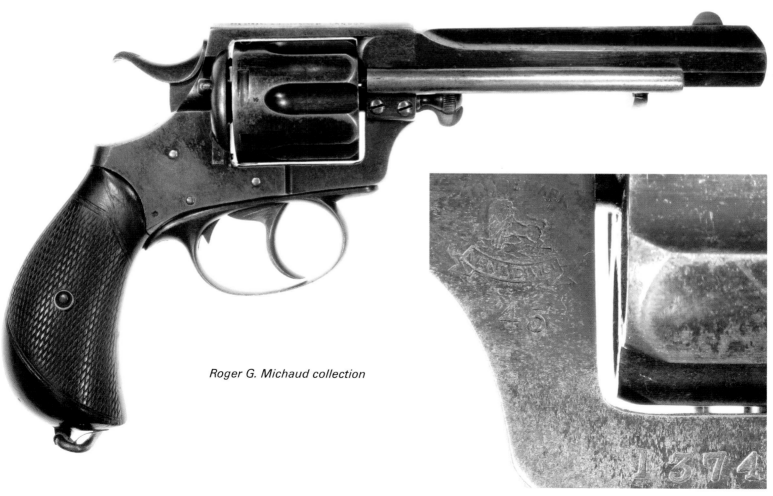

Roger G. Michaud collection

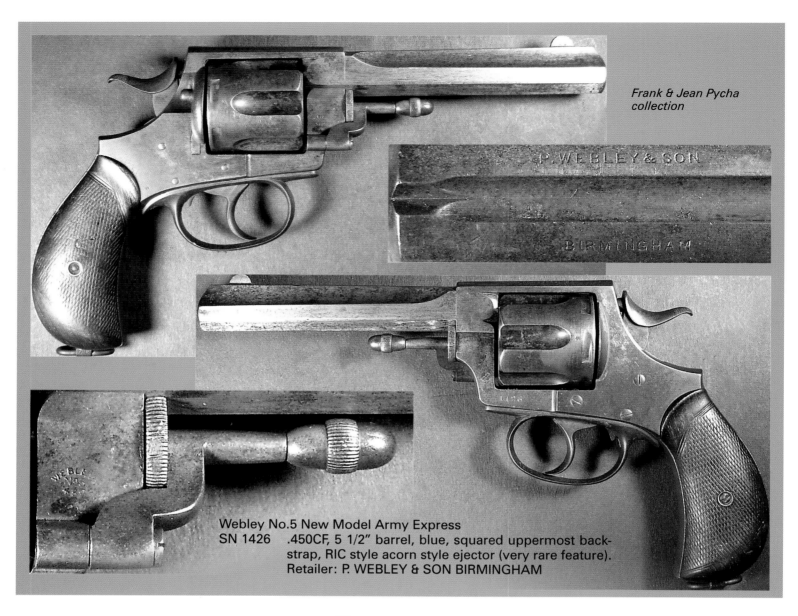

Frank & Jean Pycha collection

Webley No.5 New Model Army Express
SN 1426 .450CF, 5 1/2" barrel, blue, squared uppermost back-
strap, RIC style acorn style ejector (very rare feature).
Retailer: P. WEBLEY & SON BIRMINGHAM

Frank & Jean Pycha collection

Webley No.5 New Model Army Express
SN 4253 .450, 5 1/2" barrel, nickel plated, squared upper-
most backstrap, Colt style ejector.
Retailer: P. WEBLEY & SON BIRMINGHAM

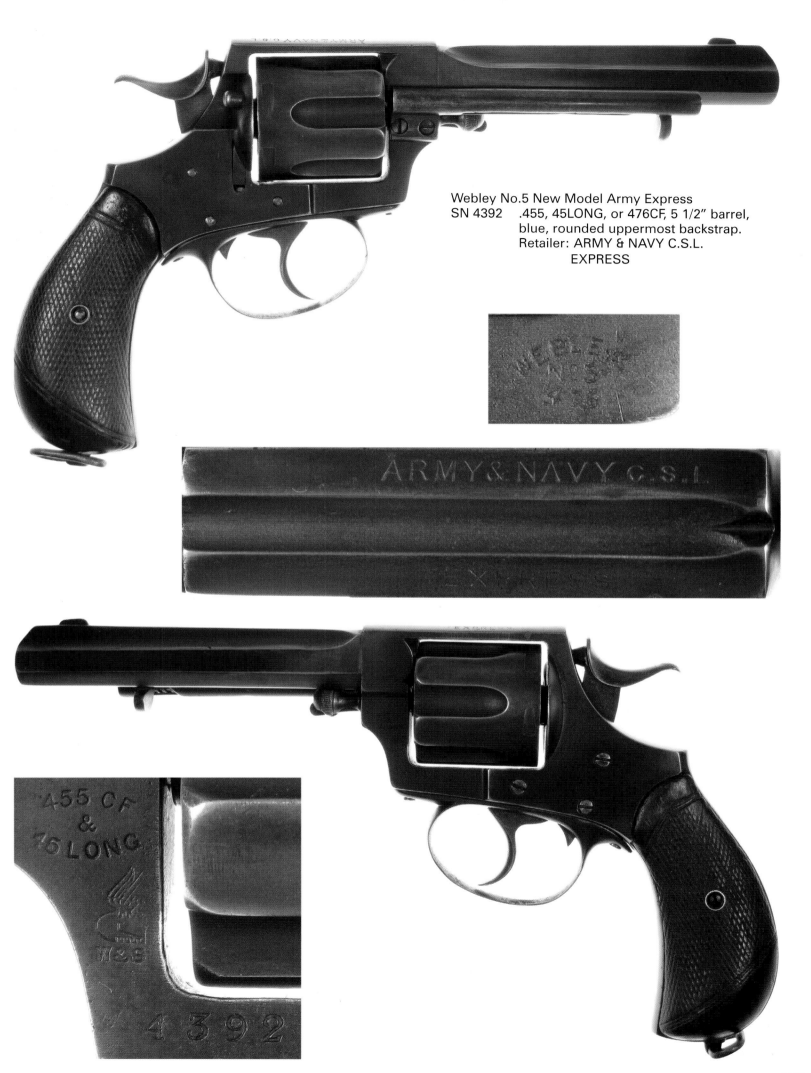

Webley No.5 New Model Army Express
SN 4392   .455, 45LONG, or 476CF, 5 1/2" barrel,
blue, rounded uppermost backstrap.
Retailer: ARMY & NAVY C.S.L.
EXPRESS

Webley No.5 New Model Army Express
SN 4856   .450CF, 5 1/2" barrel, nickel squared uppermost backstrap, RIC style acorn style ejector (rare feature), blue hammer and trigger.
Retailer: P. WEBLEY & SON BIRMINGHAM

WEBLEY'S
Nº5
.450

Courtesy of http://www.collectorsfirearms.com/

P. WEBLEY & SON

BIRMINGHAM

Webley No.5 New Model Army Express
SN 4935 .450CF, 5 1/2" barrel, blue, squared
uppermost backstrap.
Retailer: not marked

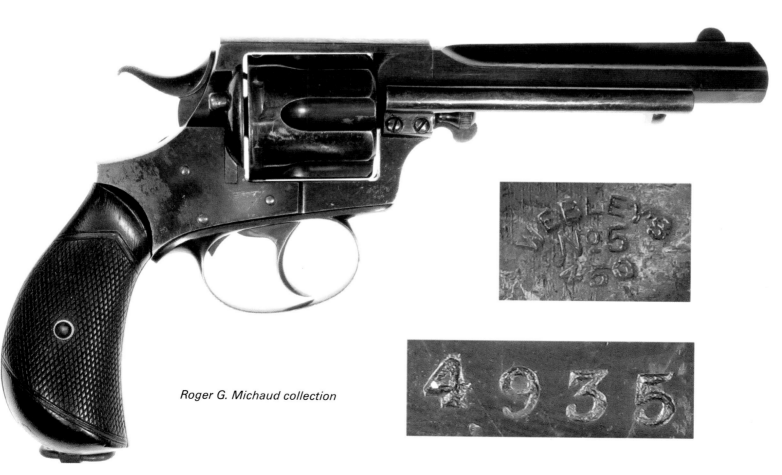

Roger G. Michaud collection

Webley No.5 New Model Army Express
SN 4976   .476CF and .45 LONG, 5 1/2" barrel, rounded
           uppermost backstrap.
    Retailer: ARMY & NAVY C.S.L.
              EXPRESS

The caliber markings are very strange. A revolver chambered for these cartridges could also handle a .455 and was usually so marked.

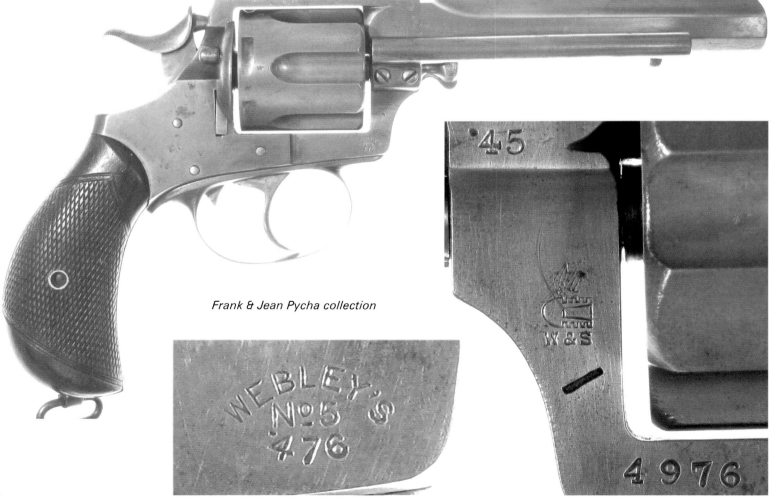

Frank & Jean Pycha collection

Webley No.5 New Model Army Express
SN 5018   .455, 476, and .45 Long, 5 1/2" barrel, squared uppermost backstrap.
Retailer: THO^S. TURNER 19 BROOK S^T, BOND S^T LONDON.

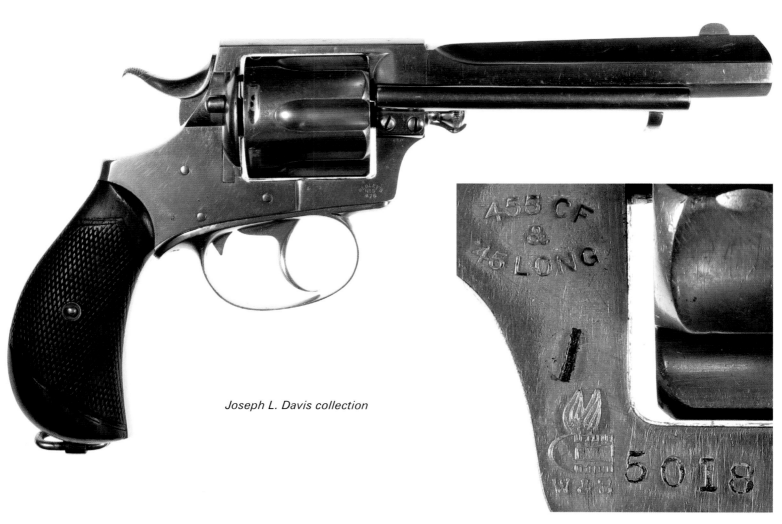

Joseph L. Davis collection

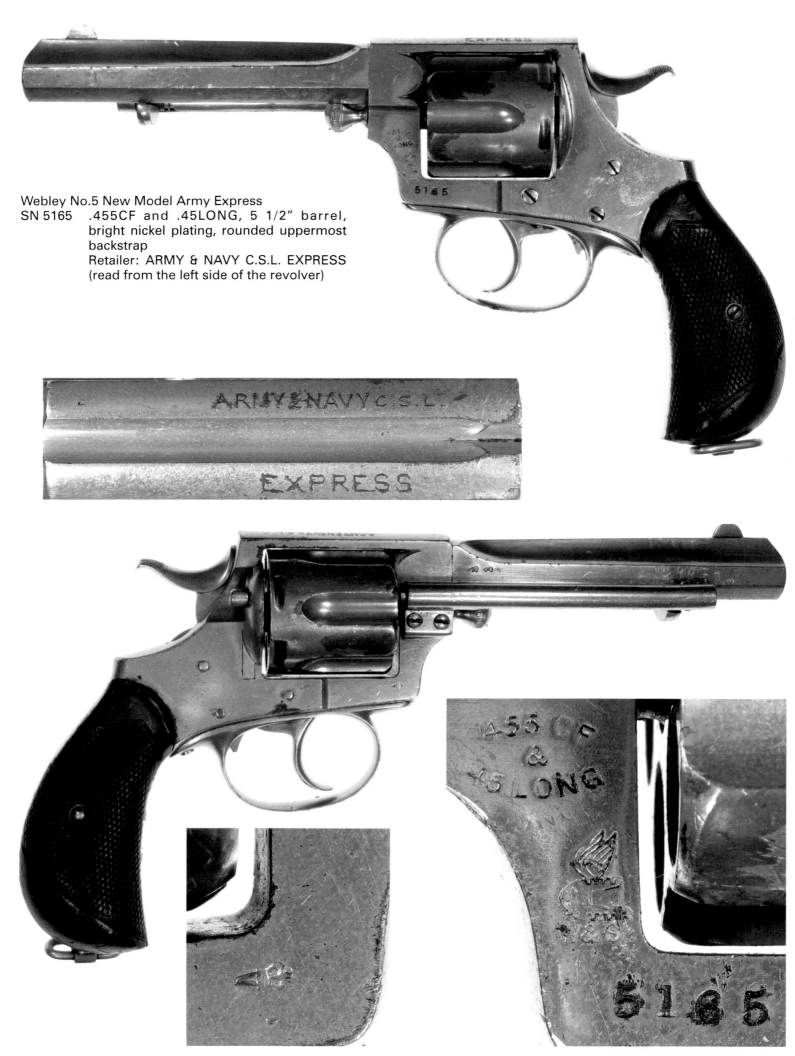

Webley No.5 New Model Army Express
SN 5165   .455CF and .45LONG, 5 1/2" barrel,
bright nickel plating, rounded uppermost
backstrap
Retailer: ARMY & NAVY C.S.L. EXPRESS
(read from the left side of the revolver)

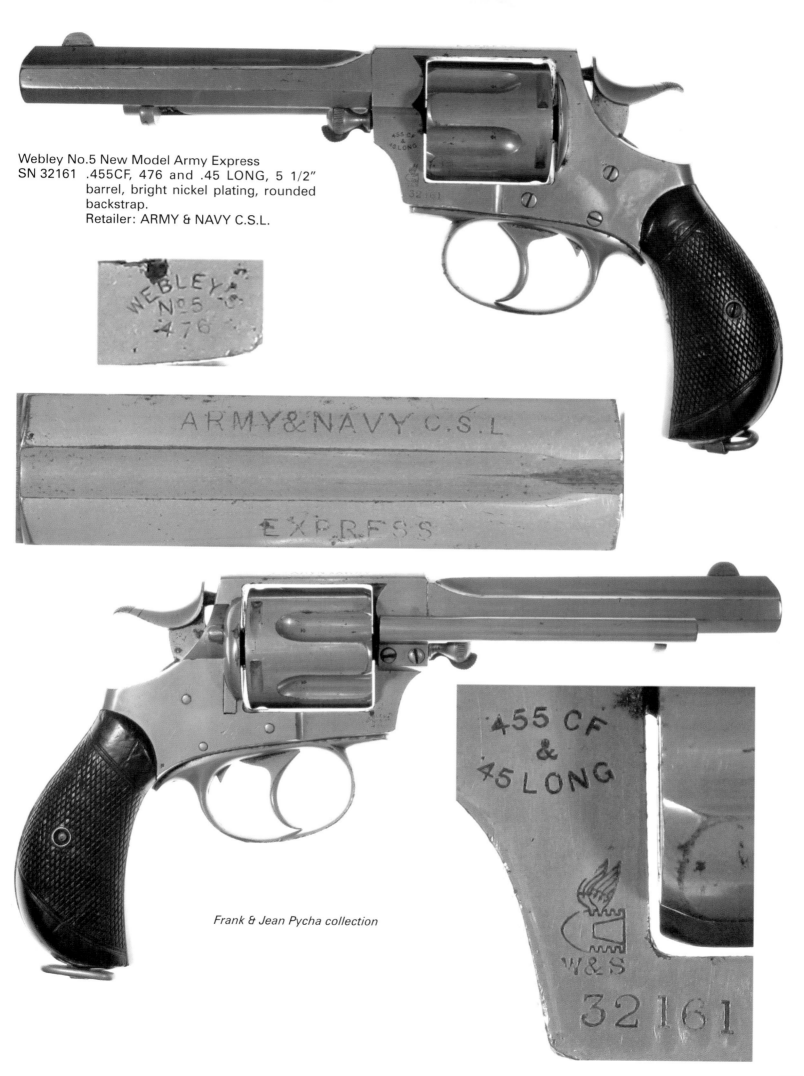

Webley No.5 New Model Army Express
SN 32161 .455CF, 476 and .45 LONG, 5 1/2"
barrel, bright nickel plating, rounded
backstrap.
Retailer: ARMY & NAVY C.S.L.

Frank & Jean Pycha collection

239

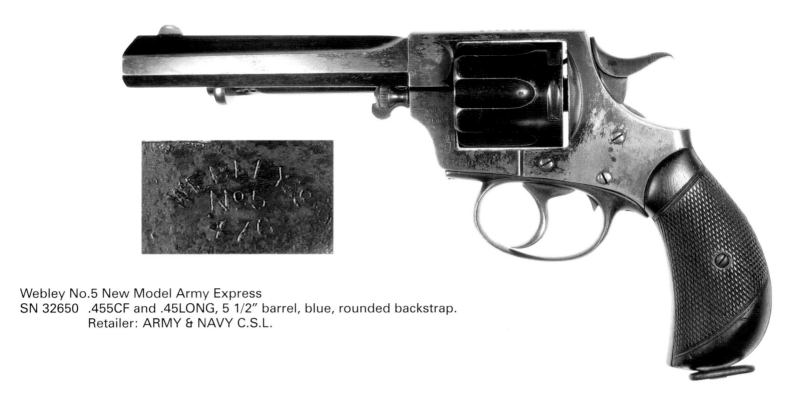

Webley No.5 New Model Army Express
SN 32650 .455CF and .45LONG, 5 1/2" barrel, blue, rounded backstrap.
Retailer: ARMY & NAVY C.S.L.

Joseph L. Davis collection

Webley No.5 New Model Army Express
SN 32777 .455CF and .45LONG, .476 5 1/2" barrel,
bright nickel plating, rounded uppermost
backstrap, has extra screw in gripstrap
behind trigger guard (page 96 Webley Revolvers by Bruce and Reinhart).
Retailer: ARMY & NAVY C.S.L.

Roger G. Michaud collection

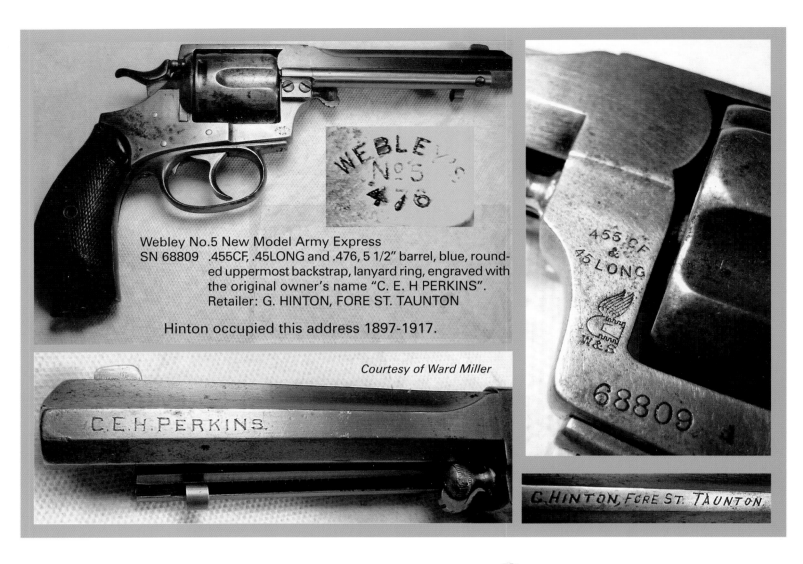

Webley No.5 New Model Army Express
SN 68809 .455CF, .45LONG and .476, 5 1/2" barrel, blue, rounded uppermost backstrap, lanyard ring, engraved with the original owner's name "C. E. H PERKINS".
Retailer: G. HINTON, FORE ST. TAUNTON

Hinton occupied this address 1897-1917.

Courtesy of Ward Miller

Webley No.5 New Model Army Express
SN 68837 .455CF, .45LONG and .476, 5 1/2" barrel, blue, rounded uppermost backstrap, lanyard ring.
Retailer: P. WEBLEY & SON LONDON & BIRMINGHAM

Mark Oijen collection

Webley No.5 New Model Army Express
SN 95332 .450CF, 5 1/2" barrel, blue, rounded
uppermost backstrap.
Retailer: V&R. BLAKEMORE LONDON

Joseph L. Davis collection

Lesotho Mounted Police
(South Africa) mark

Top of grip strap

Front of frame

Webley No.5 New Model Army Express
SN 95524 .450CF, blue, black powder proofs CP (Cape Police) mark on right
        frame, U broad-arrow marked (post-1911 South African Govern-
        ment ownership mark) on front of frame and upper gripstrap.
        Retailer: V&R. BLAKEMORE LONDON

Roger G. Michaud collection

244

No. 5 .360 Express

All Webley No.5 .360 Express revolvers have six chambers, a one-piece checkered wood grip, lanyard ring, and an ovate barrel. The rear sight is V-notched and the front sight is rounded. Many No. 5 Express revolvers are found with so-called "church steeple" cylinder fluting. As evidenced by the following examples, we cannot determine a serial number range exclusive to this feature. These were offered as pocket revolvers to the civilian market. The No. 5 .360 express employs the same frame as the RIC/83. It gave the buyer the opportunity to acquire a 6 shot pocket revolver that used a relatively powerful cartridge. A few examples were long-barreled to take advantage of the new "Any Revolver" Class to compete at the British National Rifle Association "Imperial Meeting" in 1892.

WEBLEY'S No. 5 '360 EXPRESS REVOLVER.

DOUBLE ACTION.

Six Shot. 3in. or 4½in. Barrel.

No. 3048—Blued	...	...	**68/6**
" 3049—Nickel-Plated	...	**77/6**

Cartridge 8/9 per 100.

This Revolver has been specially designed to meet the wants of Travellers, Householders, and others requiring a powerful and accurate weapon, in which are also combined lightness and rapidity of action.

It is made specially to shoot the No. 5 '360 Rook Rifle Cartridge, but will shoot also the ordinary '380 Revolver (7/3 per 100) and Rook Rifle (8/- per 100) Cartridges.

At twelve yards these Revolvers will put every shot into a 3in. circle.

R.I.C. No. 2 '320 (Double Action). Six Shot Revolver.

No. 3050—Blued	...	**66/-**	No. 3051—Nickel-Plated	...	**73/-**

Suitable cases, 14/- or 19/6 each.   Cleaning Implements, 3/9 per set.

From an original 1888 Bland catalog

However, this competition class was discontinued prior to the (British) National Rifle Association's 1897 Bisley "Imperial Meeting".

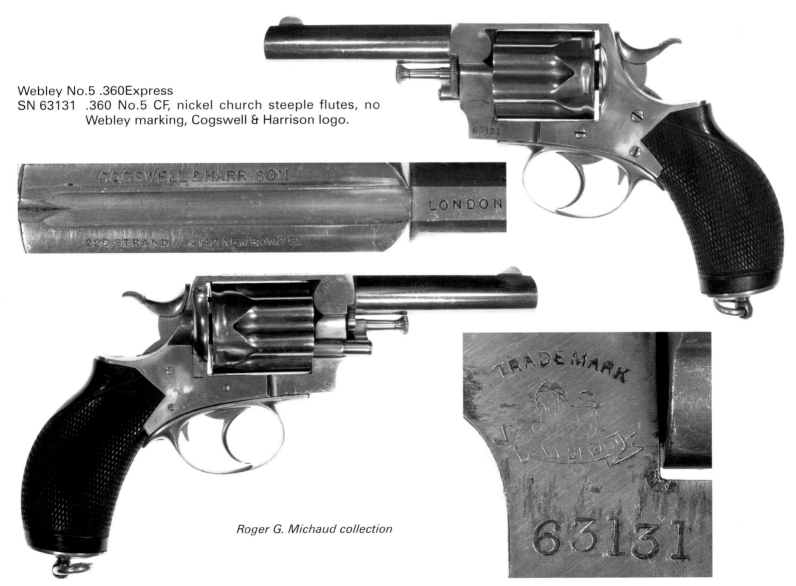

Webley No.5 .360Express
SN 63131 .360 No.5 CF, nickel church steeple flutes, no Webley marking, Cogswell & Harrison logo.

Roger G. Michaud collection

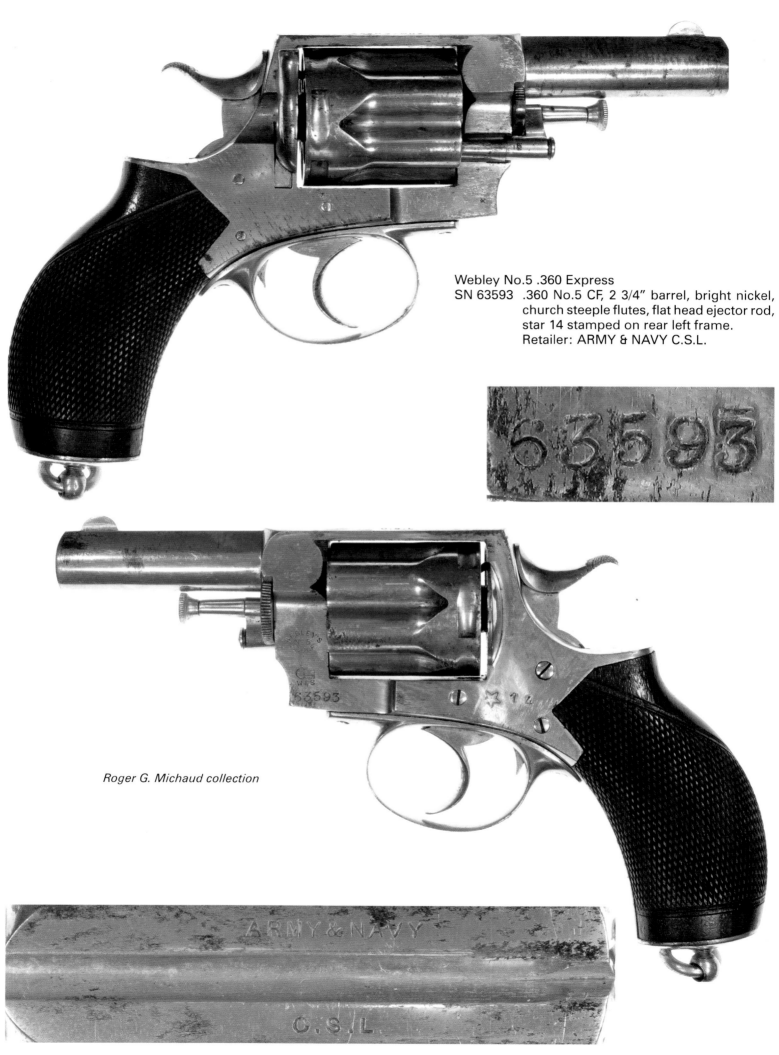

Webley No.5 .360 Express
SN 63593 .360 No.5 CF, 2 3/4" barrel, bright nickel,
church steeple flutes, flat head ejector rod,
star 14 stamped on rear left frame.
Retailer: ARMY & NAVY C.S.L.

Roger G. Michaud collection

Webley No.5 .360 Express
SN 63573 .360 No.5 CF, 2 3/4" barrel, blue, church
    steeple flutes, flat head ejector rod.
    Retailer: J. HARTWELL TRURO

Frank & Jean Pycha collection

247

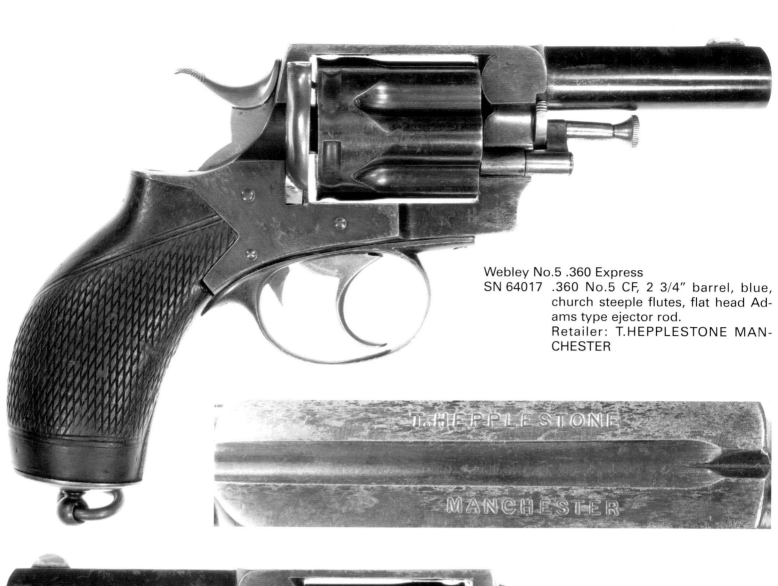

Webley No.5 .360 Express
SN 64017 .360 No.5 CF, 2 3/4" barrel, blue, church steeple flutes, flat head Adams type ejector rod.
Retailer: T.HEPPLESTONE MANCHESTER

Roger G. Michaud collection

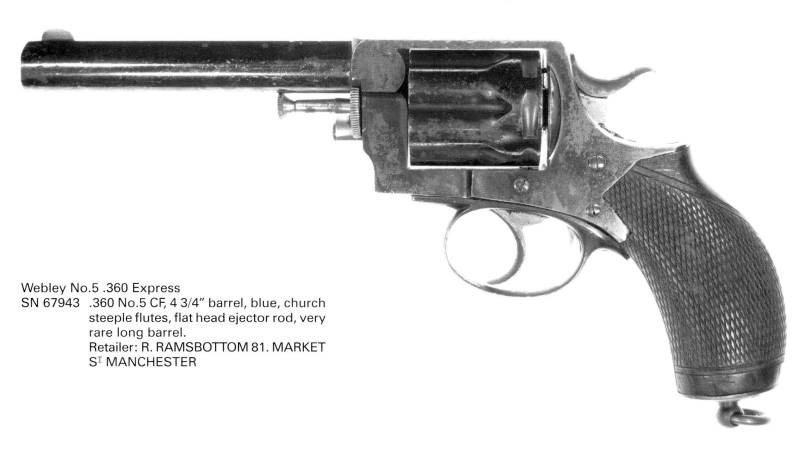

Webley No.5 .360 Express
SN 67943 .360 No.5 CF, 4 3/4" barrel, blue, church
steeple flutes, flat head ejector rod, very
rare long barrel.
Retailer: R. RAMSBOTTOM 81. MARKET
S^T MANCHESTER

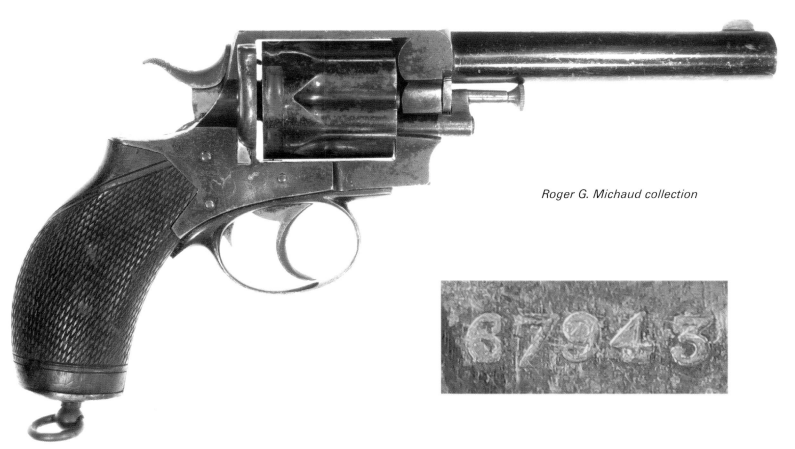

Roger G. Michaud collection

Webley No.5 .360 Express
SN 67993 .360 No.5 CF, 7" barrel, blue, church steeple flutes, flat head ejector rod, very rare long barrel.
Retailer: HOLLAND & HOLLAND 98 NEW BOND S^T LONDON

P WEBLEY & SON, R.I.C. NO 5 .360 EXPRESS. with a special made 7 inch target barrel. It was retailed, and is marked on the cylinder strap "HOLLAND & HOLLAND 9 NEW BOND ST LONDON". <u>This combination of barrel and calibre is so rare that this is probably the only one of this combination ever manufactured.</u> This revolver is pictured in "THE WEBLEY STORY" (35A) and was written about on page 71, it was previously owned by William Chipchase Dowell, the author of that book. It is also pictured in "WEBLEY REVOLVERS" by Bruce & Reinhart. This is an early version with a fluted (church steeple) cylinder, and a flat ejector knob. It is shown in its original case, with a letter from Holland & Holland.
.360 Express (Rook Rifle) CF BP   S/N 65993

Frank & Jean Pycha collection

Frank & Jean Pycha collection

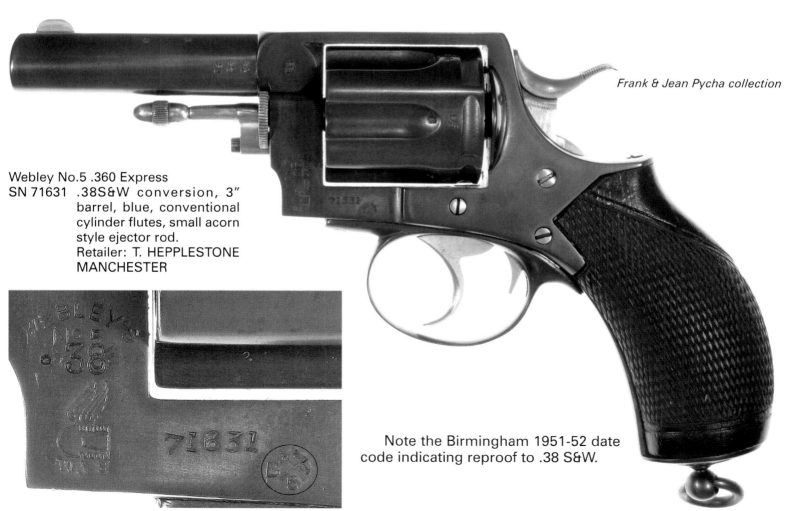

Webley No.5 .360 Express
SN 71631 .38S&W conversion, 3"
barrel, blue, conventional
cylinder flutes, small acorn
style ejector rod.
Retailer: T. HEPPLESTONE
MANCHESTER

Note the Birmingham 1951-52 date
code indicating reproof to .38 S&W.

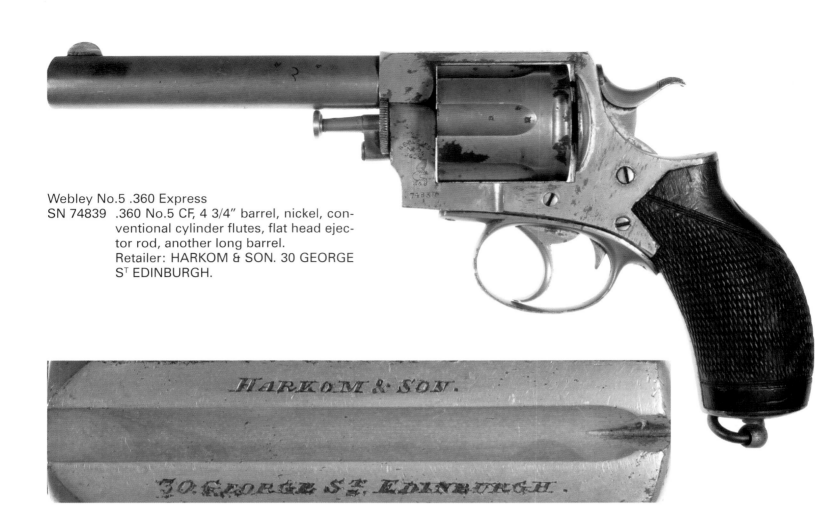

Webley No.5 .360 Express
SN 74839 .360 No.5 CF, 4 3/4" barrel, nickel, conventional cylinder flutes, flat head ejector rod, another long barrel.
Retailer: HARKOM & SON. 30 GEORGE S^T EDINBURGH.

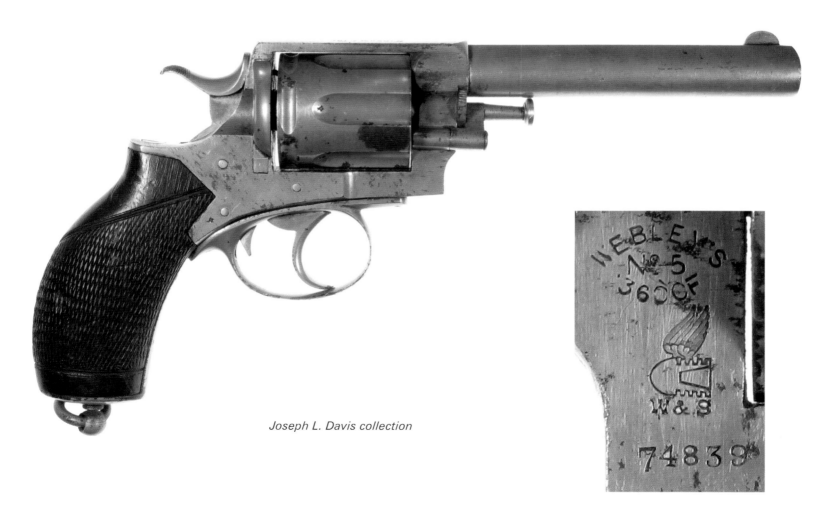

Joseph L. Davis collection

Webley No.5 .360 Express
SN 74912 .360 No.5 CF, 3" barrel, blue, conventional cylinder flutes, small acorn style ejector rod.
Retailer: P. WEBLEY & SON LONDON & BIRMINGHAM

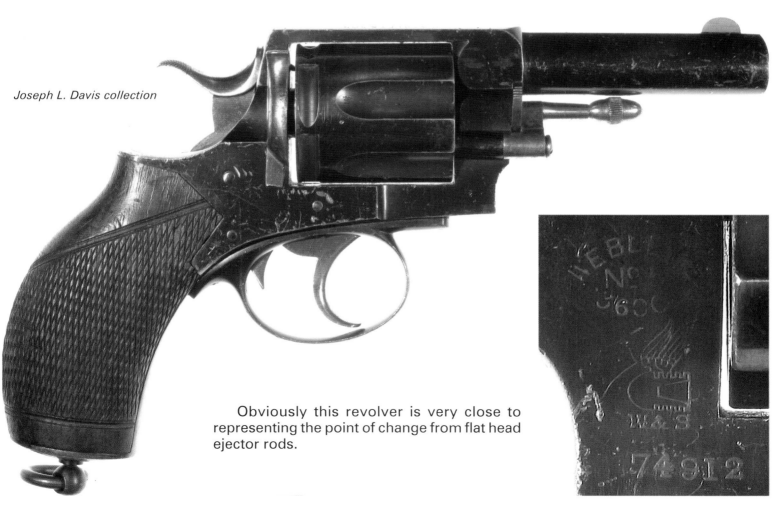

Joseph L. Davis collection

Obviously this revolver is very close to representing the point of change from flat head ejector rods.

Webley No.5 .360 Express
SN 81645 .38S&W conversion, 3" barrel, blue, conventional cylinder flutes, small acorn style ejector rod, one-piece checkered wood grip, original black powder proofing and later nitro-proofs, lanyard ring, lower left frame has a post WWI inspector view mark.
Retailer: ARMY & NAVY C.S.L.

Roger G. Michaud collection

Webley No.5 .360 Express
SN 83393 .360 No.5 CF, 3 1/4" barrel, dull nickel plating, church steeple flutes, flat head ejector rod, cased with accessories.
Retailer: not marked

Joel Black collection

A close up of a church steeple flute. This is late in the serial range for this style cylinder flute.

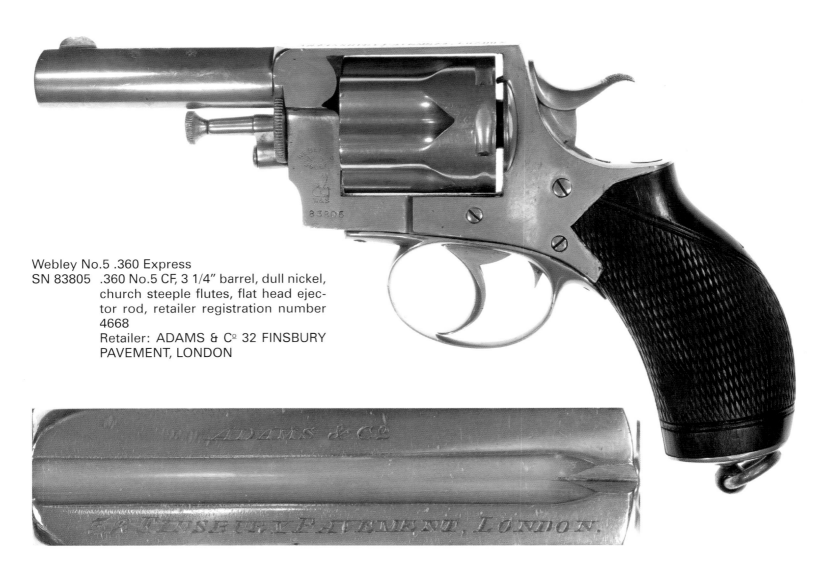

Webley No.5 .360 Express
SN 83805   .360 No.5 CF, 3 1/4" barrel, dull nickel, church steeple flutes, flat head ejector rod, retailer registration number 4668
Retailer: ADAMS & Cº 32 FINSBURY PAVEMENT, LONDON

Roger G. Michaud collection

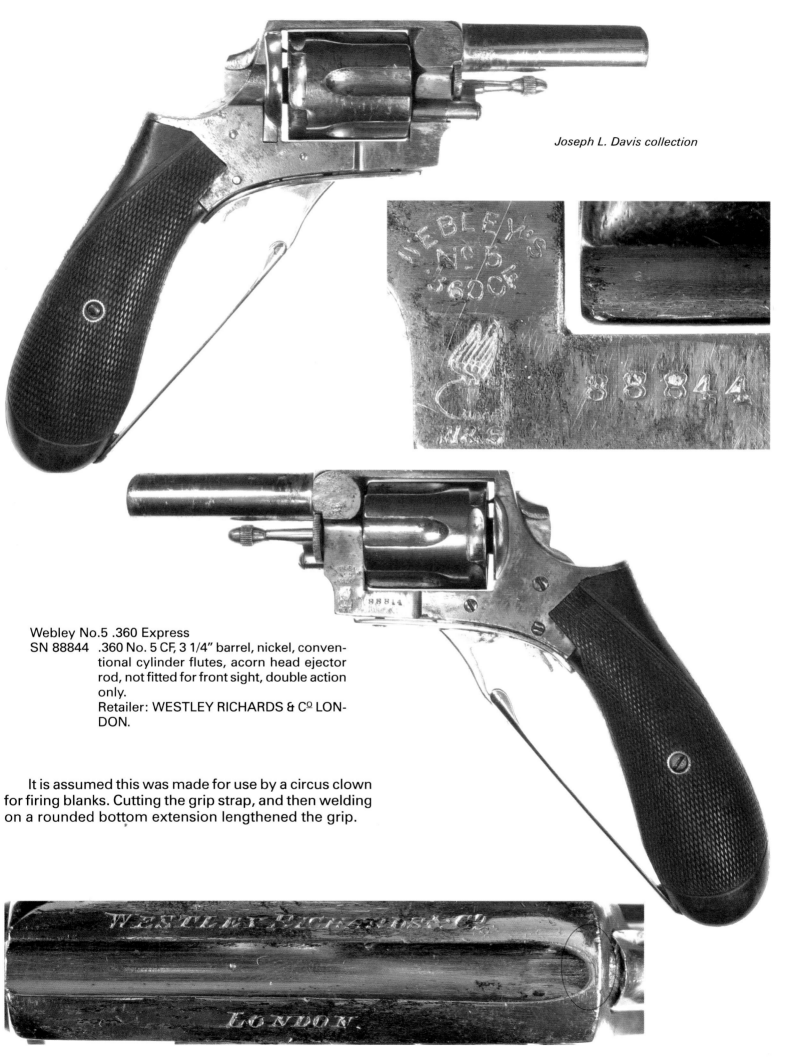

Joseph L. Davis collection

Webley No.5 .360 Express
SN 88844 .360 No. 5 CF, 3 1/4" barrel, nickel, conventional cylinder flutes, acorn head ejector rod, not fitted for front sight, double action only.
Retailer: WESTLEY RICHARDS & Cº LONDON.

It is assumed this was made for use by a circus clown for firing blanks. Cutting the grip strap, and then welding on a rounded bottom extension lengthened the grip.

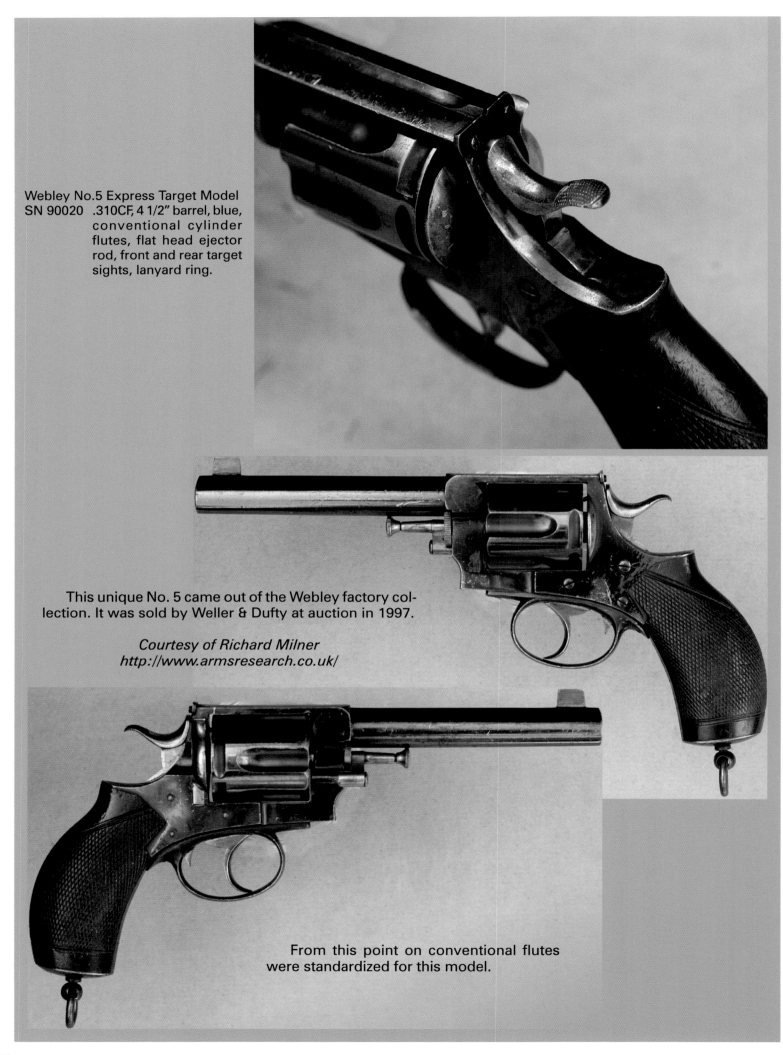

Webley No.5 Express Target Model SN 90020 .310CF, 4 1/2" barrel, blue, conventional cylinder flutes, flat head ejector rod, front and rear target sights, lanyard ring.

This unique No. 5 came out of the Webley factory collection. It was sold by Weller & Dufty at auction in 1997.

Courtesy of Richard Milner
http://www.armsresearch.co.uk/

From this point on conventional flutes were standardized for this model.

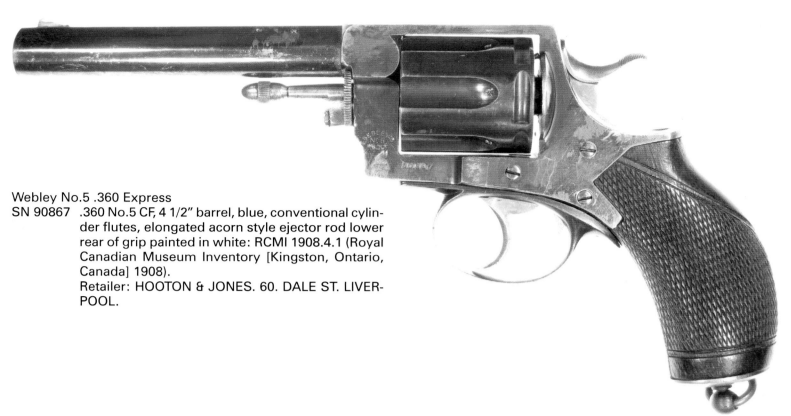

Webley No.5 .360 Express
SN 90867 .360 No.5 CF, 4 1/2" barrel, blue, conventional cylinder flutes, elongated acorn style ejector rod lower rear of grip painted in white: RCMI 1908.4.1 (Royal Canadian Museum Inventory [Kingston, Ontario, Canada] 1908).
Retailer: HOOTON & JONES. 60. DALE ST. LIVERPOOL.

Roger G. Michaud collection

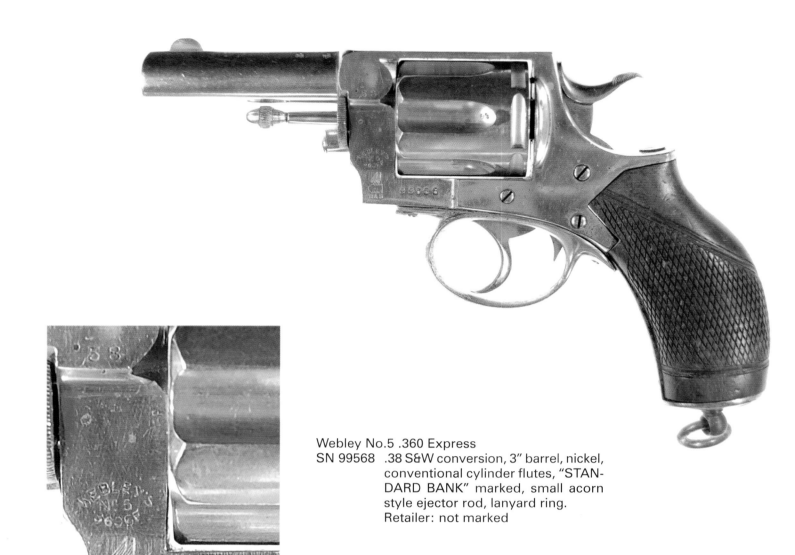

Webley No.5 .360 Express
SN 99568   .38 S&W conversion, 3" barrel, nickel, conventional cylinder flutes, "STANDARD BANK" marked, small acorn style ejector rod, lanyard ring.
Retailer: not marked

Standard Bank of South Africa.
Greg Reddick collection

Miscellaneous Solid Frame Webleys

Webley Sheath (Spur) trigger
SN 77   32RF, 3" barrel, blue, smooth cylinder with front locking recess, curved spring pushes in from left to release cylinder axis pin.
Retailer: not marked.

This revolver was mistakenly reported by Dowell as a .30RF.

The majority of parts used in this revolver were furnished by Tranter.

Joseph L. Davis collection

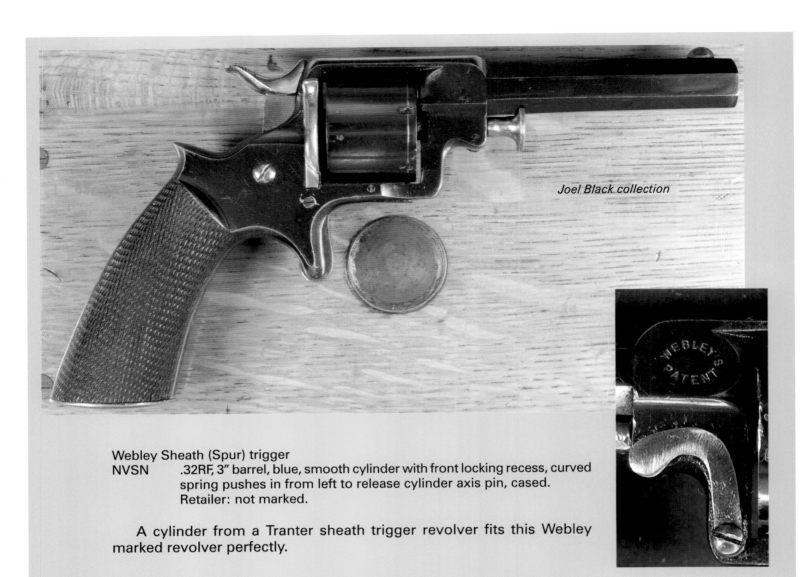

Joel Black collection

Webley Sheath (Spur) trigger
NVSN   .32RF, 3" barrel, blue, smooth cylinder with front locking recess, curved
         spring pushes in from left to release cylinder axis pin, cased.
         Retailer: not marked.

A cylinder from a Tranter sheath trigger revolver fits this Webley marked revolver perfectly.

ARMY.

RETURN showing Number and Cost of Small Arms, Sword-Bayonets, Machine Guns, &c., manufactured in the Royal Small Arms Factories at Enfield and Birmingham, and by the Trade, during the past ten years. Also the Number of Men Employed in the two Government Factories for the same Period, and their Wages.

Presented to Parliament by Command of His Majesty.

LONDON:
PRINTED FOR HIS MAJESTY'S STATIONERY OFFICE,
BY HARRISON AND SONS, ST. MARTIN'S LANE,
PRINTERS IN ORDINARY TO HIS MAJESTY.

And to be purchased, either directly or through any Bookseller, from
WYMAN AND SONS, LTD., FETTER LANE, E.C.; and
32, ABINGDON STREET, WESTMINSTER, S.W.; or
OLIVER AND BOYD, EDINBURGH; or
E. PONSONBY, 116, GRAFTON STREET, DUBLIN.

[Cd. 2431.]   *Price 3d.*

TABLE XVIII.

STATEMENT showing the Numbers of Pistols ordered from the Trade during the years 1886 to 1904 (with average prices).

(*There were no orders for Pistols to the Trade from 1880–85 inclusive.*)

Description	1886-87 No.	1886-87 Price each. (s. d.)	1887-88 No.	1887-88 Price each. (s. d.)	1888-89 No.	1888-89 Price each. (s. d.)	1889-90 No.	1889-90 Price each. (s. d.)	1890-91 No.	1890-91 Price each. (s. d.)	1891-92 No.	1891-92 Price each. (s. d.)	1892-93 No.	1892-93 Price each. (s. d.)
Pistols:—														
R.I.C Revolver	—	35 0	—	—	100	35 0	100	35 0	312	35 0	160	35 0	249	35 0
Webley	—	57 0	10,000 Mk. I.	61 0	—	—	11,385 Mk. I.	58 6	—	—	1,594 Mk. I.	58 6	3,495 Mk. I.	58 6

Description	1893-94 No.	1893-94 Price each. (s. d.)	1894-95 No.	1894-95 Price each. (s. d.)	1895-96 No.	1895-96 Price each. (s. d.)	1896-97 No.	1896-97 Price each. (s. d.)	1897-98 No.	1897-98 Price each. (s. d.)	1898-99 No.	1898-99 Price each. (s. d.)	1899-1900 No.	1899-1900 Price each. (s. d.)
Pistols:—														
R.I.C. Revolver	100	35 0	24	35 0	—	—	—	—	14	35 0	—	—	—	—
Webley	5,000 Mk. I.	57 0	5,207 Mk. I.	57 0	5,000 Mk. II.	60 0	15,621 Mk. II.	56 0	2,190 Mk. II.; 1,230 Mk. III.	56 0 } 58 6	2,101 Mk. III.	58 6	510 Mk. III.; 13,374 Mk. IV.	58 6 } 61 0

Description	1900-01 No.	1900-01 Price each. (s. d.)	1901-02 No.	1901-02 Price each. (s. d.)	1902-03 No.	1902-03 Price each. (s. d.)	1903-04 No.	1903-04 Price each. (s. d.)	1904-05 No.	1904-05 Price each. (s. d.)
Pistols:—										
R.I.C. Revolver	—	—	—	—	—	—	—	—	—	—
Webley	9,227 Mk. IV.	61 0	5,395 Mk. IV.	61 0	8,760 Mk. IV.	61 0	—	—	—	—

By Command of the Army Council,

[signature]

WAR OFFICE,
1st *April*, 1905.

Loading Tools

When work began on this book, none of the authors had observed many loading tools for English cartridge revolvers. Cased British percussion revolvers were usually sold with a plethora of loading tools and molds. Except for dual cylinder convertible revolvers, no cased Webley solid frame cartridge revolver has been observed with loading tools.

To explain this, one must understand cartridge handgun ownership in England. Generally, most cartridge handguns were owned by military officers stationed in colonies. They were armed with privately bought side arms chambered for military cartridges. Even in the furthest Colonial outpost, the officer would have access to an armory full of cartridges. When officers returned to England, those who retained their service revolver would shoot at the available ranges (except for Dr. Watson, of course). Still, Dixon did produce some handgun cartridge loading tools.

Dixon .455 Loading Tool

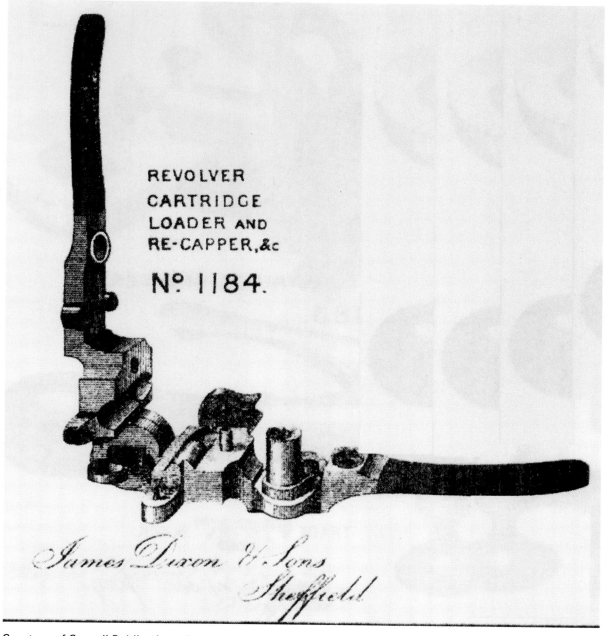

REVOLVER CARTRIDGE LOADER AND RE-CAPPER, &c

Nº 1184.

James Dixon & Sons
Sheffield

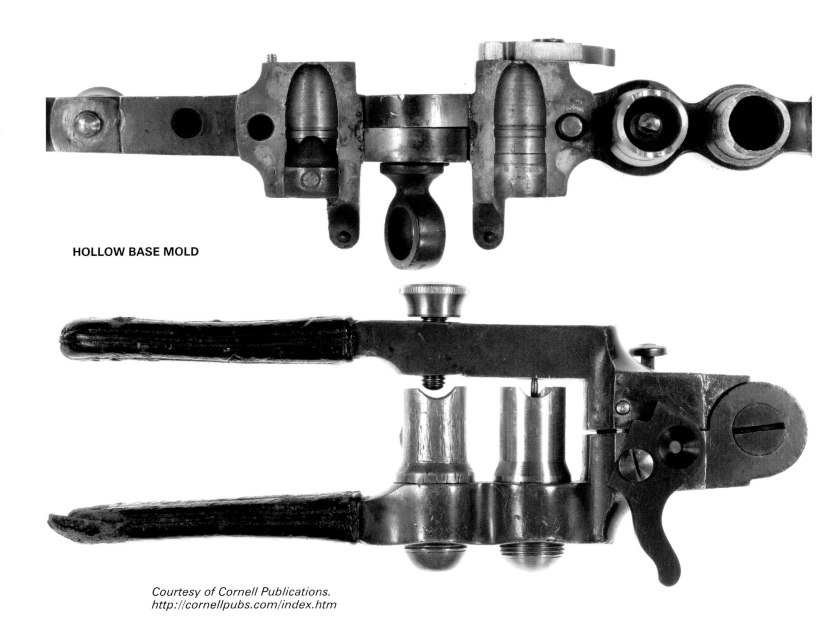

HOLLOW BASE MOLD

Courtesy of Cornell Publications.
http://cornellpubs.com/index.htm

CRIMPPER

DECAPPER SEATER RE-CAPPER

IDEAL MANUFACTURING CO., NEW HAVEN, CONN., U. S. A. 83

SPECIAL LIST.

NO. 8 IDEAL TOOL.

INSIDE LUBRICATION

SECTION NEW NAVY REVOLVER.

COLT'S 38

C—Re-Capper. A—Opening Mouth of Shell. D—Loading Chamber. F—Cavity Former. E—Bullet Sizing Die B—Bullet Mould.

32 LONG RIFLE INSIDE LUBRICATION

This tool is made especially for cartridges having bullets with a deep cavity at the base. It has our patent non detachable cavity former and bullet sizer. It is made especially for the new .38 long Colt's and .41 long Colt's, *inside lubrication*. We also make it for the cartridges, .450 and .455 *British, as supplied to H. M. War Department*. Adapted to the New Service Webley, Mark I. Revolvers, Colt's, Smith & Wesson and other Double Action Pistols and for Target Pistols. The Shells as made by Messrs. Eley Bros, of London, or The Union Metallic Cartridge Co., of Bridgeport, Conn., U. S. A., may be used. We find the shells made by the U. M. C. CO., to be better for reloading purposes and we recommend them. This tool will not reload the *Old Outside Lubricated* .38 long or 41 long Colt.*

Joel Black collection

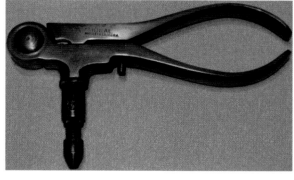

Courtesy of Thomas Quigley

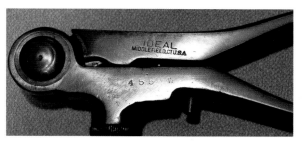

The arrival of these photos of a No. 3 Ideal loading tool with a hand stamped marking for the .455 Webley started a search through a collection of old catalogs. Until this page was found, it was assumed someone had altered a .45 Colt tool.

Joel Black collection

Frank & Jean Pycha collection

Webley Solid Frame Revolver Cartridges

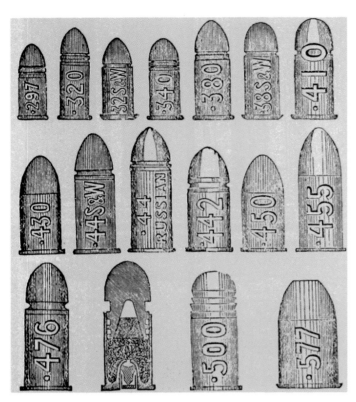

From a reprint of a 1905 Eley catalog.
Used with permission of Cornell Publications.
http://cornellpubs.com/index.htm

Courtesy of Ray Giles.
http://www.rtgammo.com/

LOS REVOLVERS DE WEBLEY SON ADAPTADOS A LOS SIGUIENTES CARTUCHOS.

Mark IV, pagina 5
W.G. ,, ... 7, 8. 15
W. & S. ,, ... 6
R.I.C. /No. 1 ·450/455... ... 17
R.I.C. /83 ·455 18

Estes Cartuchos pueden ser cargados
tambien con Cordite.

Calibro ·455 ... 7 granos Cordite.
,, ·450 ... 5 ,, ,,

Un grano Ingles equivale á 0·648 decigramos.

Webley Fosbery Automatico
pagina 9, 10.

Este modelo especialmente construido
para tomar el Cartucho reglamentario
·455 cargado con 7 granos de Cordite
y bala de 265 granos, pero en caso
de necesidad puedese utilizar los
siguientes cartuchos.

Devese observar que estes siendo
cargados con polvora negra, l'elevacion
no será como cuando se usa Cordite.

El W. F. ·38 Automatico es
construido solamente para tomar
Cartuchos ·38 cal.
Automatic Colt Pistol,
o Ingléses o Americanos.

El Mark III, pagina 11, 12, 16.

o construido especialmente para

Estes Cartuchos pueden ser cargados
con 4 granos de Cordite.
R.I.C./83 ·450, pagina ... 18
No. 2 ·450 ,, ... 20
M.P. ·450 ,, ... 21

Los modelos
R I.C. ·450/455, pagina 17
R.I.C. /83 ,, 18
pueden ser construidos para recibir
los Cartuchos ·44 R.M. sin augmen-
tacion de precio.

Mark III, pagina ... 11, 12, 16
W.P. sin perillo (Hammerless)
pagina 14
W.P. con perillo 13
R.I.C./No. 2 ·320 19
No. 2 ·320 20

o especialmente construido para

Estes Cartuchos pueden ser cargados
con 2 granos de Cordite.
El No. 5 ·360 Express es especialmente construido para tomar los
Cartuchos No. 5 ·360 Carabina para
conejas

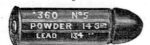

peró puede ser construido para tomar
cualquier de los Cartuchos de ·38

1

LOS PRECIOS SON EN FRANCOS ORO.

Courtesy of Richard Milner http://www.armsresearch.co.uk/   http://www.armsresearch.co.uk/

Cartridge Boxes

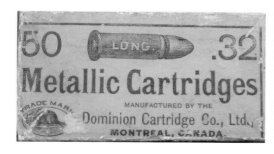

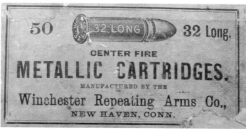

Courtesy of Joe Salter.
http://www.joesalter.com/

Joel Black collection

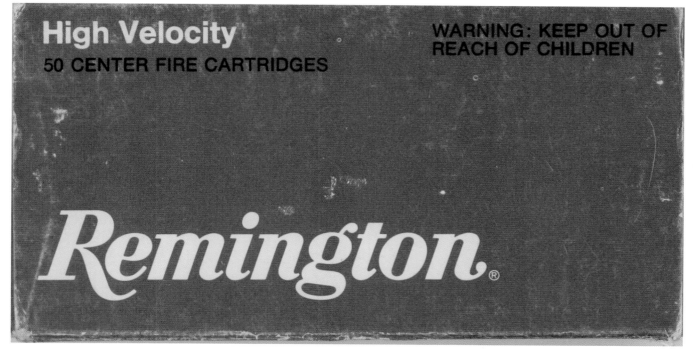

Joel Black collection

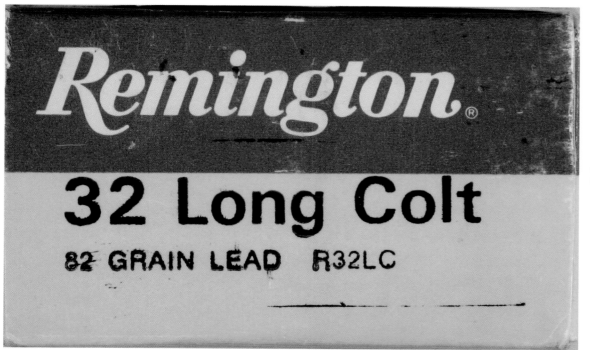

Joel Black collection

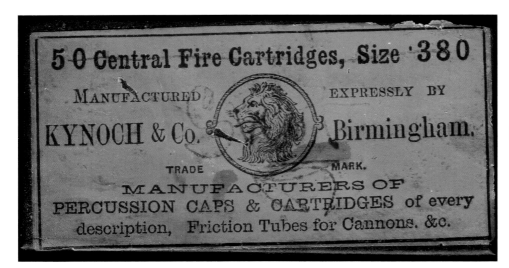

Rare Tin Box

Courtesy of Ray Giles
http://www.rtgammo.com/

These tin boxes were intended for use in humid or tropical climates.
Courtesy of Ray Giles
http://www.rtgammo.com/

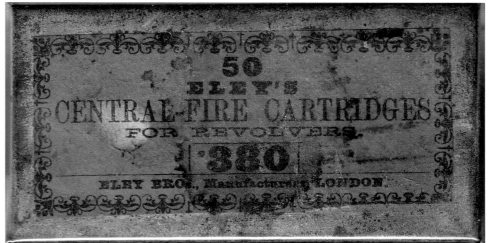

"BOXER" is blacked out.
Courtesy of Ray Giles
http://www.rtgammo.com/

Courtesy of
Frank Michaels

50

ELEYS' PATENT CENTRAL-FIRE

CARTRIDGES

FOR REVOLVERS.

·442

ELEY BROs. Limited, Manufacturers, LONDON.

50, CAL. 44,

Russian Central Fire Cartridges

—FOR THE—

S. & W. PISTOL,

Made with Great Care for Target Pistol Shooting by the

U. S. CARTRIDGE CO., LOWELL, MASS.

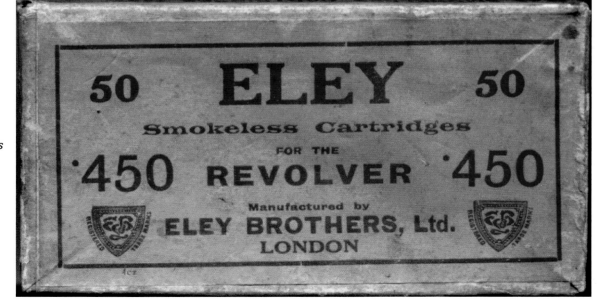

50 ELEY 50

Smokeless Cartridges

FOR THE

·450 REVOLVER ·450

Manufactured by

ELEY BROTHERS, Ltd.

LONDON

Tin Box. *Courtesy of Ray Giles*
http://www.rtgammo.com/

Homer Ficken collection

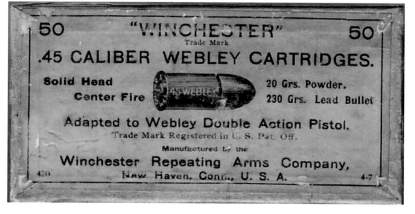

Courtesy of Ray Giles
http://www.rtgammo.com/

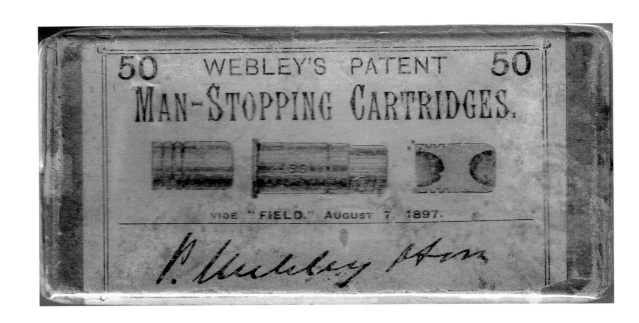

Courtesy of Ray Giles
http://www.rtgammo.com/

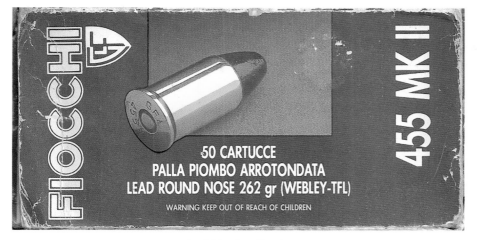

Joel Black collection

Joel Black collection

This was a very short-lived label.

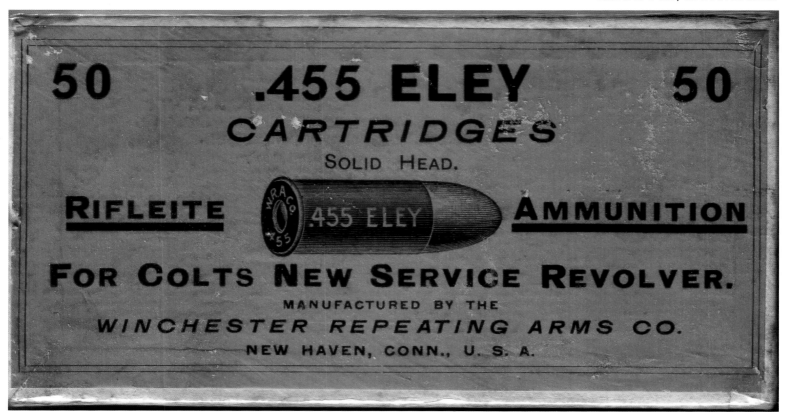

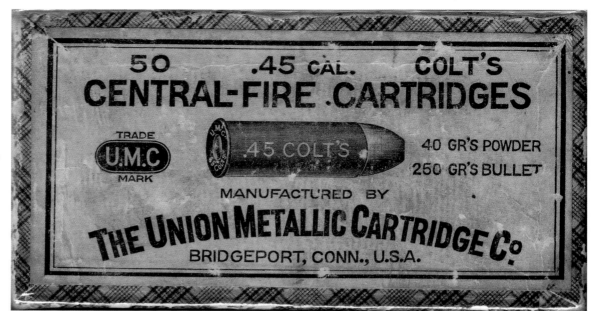

This is a very rare
box known as a
Maltese Cross box
by collectors.

Examples of the .476 cartridge are uncommon. A full
tin box by Eley Brothers.
The bullet is 265 grains.

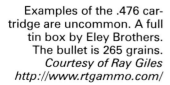

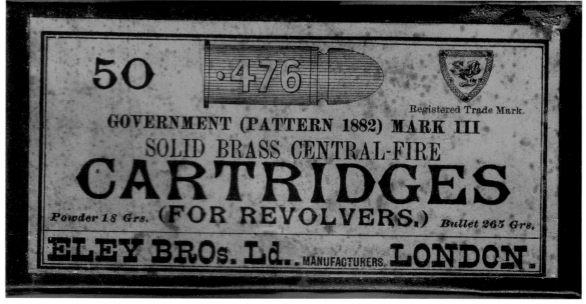

1903 Webley Solid Frame Revolver Catalog

Joel Black collection

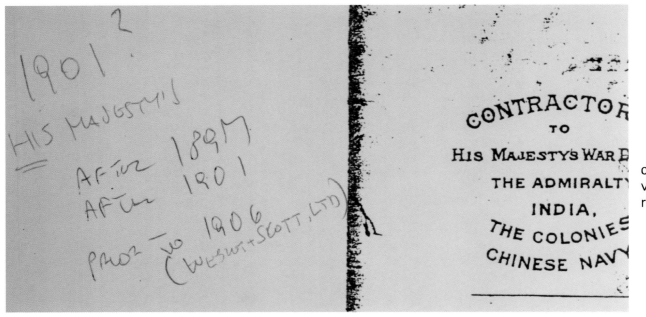

Original Webley catalogs solely devoted to solid frame revolvers are rare.

B
WEBLEY'S REVOLVERS.
NET WHOLESALE PRICES.

EXTRACTORS.

	Blue.	Nickel.
"W.G." (Army Model.) '476/'455 ..	80/-	84/-
Do. Do. Wood Stock	85/-	89/-
(Target Model) '450/'455 Wood Stock	90/-	94/-
MARK IV. (Service Model) '455/'476 ..	70/-	74/-
" " '455/'476 6 in. Barrel	75/-	79/-
" III. '38, 3 or 4 in. Barrel	48/-	48/-
" " '38, 6 in. Barrel	53/-	53/-
" " '38, Target Model, Wood Stock ..	70/-	70/-
" " '320 or '32	48/-	48/-
"W.P." Hammerless, '320 or '32	48/-	48/-
WEBLEY-FOSBERY AUTOMATIC, 4 in.	85/-	89/-
" " 6 in. ..	90/-	94/-
" " 7¼in.Target	95/-	99/-

SOLID FRAMES.

	Blue.	Nickel.
R.I.C. No. 1 '476	32/6	36/6
" '44 R.M. ..	32/6	36/6
/83 '455 ..	30/-	33/-
/83 '450 ..	30/-	33/-
No. 2 '320 ..	29/-	32/-
M.P. '450 ..	30/-	33/-
No. 5 '360 ..	30/-	33/-
2 '450 ("British Bull Dog.") ..	29/-	32/-
2 '380 ..	29/-	32/-
2 '320 ..	29/-	32/-

A
WEBLEY'S REVOLVERS.

EXTRACTORS.

	Blue.			Nickel.		
"W.G." (Army Model.) '476/'455 ..	5	0	0	5	5	0
Do. Do. Wood Stock	5	6	0	5	11	0
(Target Model) '450/'455 Wood Stock	5	10	0	5	15	0
MARK IV. (Service Model) '455/'476 ..	4	5	0	4	10	0
" " '455/'476 6 in. Barrel	4	10	0	4	15	0
" III. '38, 3 or 4 in. Barrel	3	0	0	3	0	0
" " '38, 6 in. Barrel	3	10	0	3	10	0
" " '38, Target Model, Wood Stock	4	10	0	4	10	0
" " '320 or '32 ..	3	0	0	3	0	0
"W.P." Hammerless, '320 or '32 ..	3	0	0	3	0	0
WEBLEY-FOSBERY AUTOMATIC, 4 in. ..	5	10	0	5	15	0
" " 6 in. ..	5	10	0	5	15	0
" " 7¼in.Target	5	15	0	6	0	0

SOLID FRAMES.

	Blue.			Nickel.		
R.I.C. No. 1 '476	2	2	0	2	7	0
" '44 R.M.	2	2	0	2	7	0
/83 '455 ..	1	17	6	2	1	6
/83 '450 ..	1	17	6	2	1	6
No. 2 '320 ..	1	15	6	1	19	6
M.P. '450 ..	1	17	6	2	1	6
No. 5 '360 ..	1	17	6	2	1	6
2 '450 ("British Bull Dog.") ..	1	16	6	2	0	6
2 '380 ..	1	16	6	2	0	6
2 '320 ..	1	16	6	2	0	6

This catalog was a present given to Joel Black by noted firearms writer, Paul Lederer. Paul's notations give insight to how catalogs are dated. "After 1897" refers to Webley's merger with Scott. "After 1901" is derived from Queen Victoria's death, resulting in "His Majesty". "Prior to 1906" is deduced from "The Webley & Scott Revolver & Arms Co. Limited" changing to "Webley & Scott Ltd." The only addition Mr. Black would add to this wonderful Sherlock Holmes-like act of deduction is that there is no caliber designation shown for the Fosbery, which suggests a late 1901 date.

This catalog presents many surprises to long-time Webley collectors. In the following pages, we see that after 1900 Webley started offering the RIC No. 1 and RIC Model/83 in .45 Colt and .44 S&W Russian. A .32 S&W was added to the RIC No. 2 line. The Bull Dog (style) No. 2 was now offered in .32 S&W and .38 S&W. All of this further indicates Webley's desperation to make use of frames that had been in inventory since the mid-1890s. Even so, it took until the late 1930s for the last frame to be used. Very few Webleys have been observed in these calibers. Richard Milner's observations from factory records agree that the offering of these popular models had waned. Thus, contracts for the short frame RICs in .442 caliber were sold at a discount to distant police departments. The longer solid frame revolvers in .455 and .476 still found homes with military officers, who could not afford a more expensive hinge frame Webley. Given Britain's constant colonial presence and problems, A&N C.S.L. records reveal several pages of sales of the newer self-extracting WG and Government Service Models.

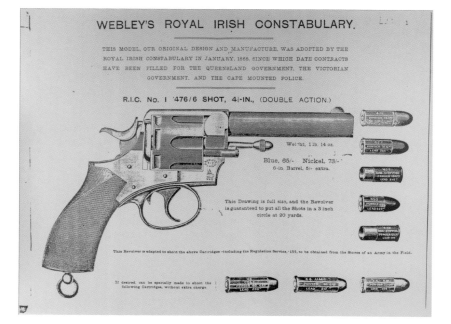

WEBLEY'S No. 5 '360 EXPRESS.

No. 5 '360, 3 OR 4½-IN. (DOUBLE ACTION)

Blue, 60/-
Nickel, 66/-

Weight, 1 lb. 3 oz.

This Revolver has been specially designed to meet the wants of Travellers, Householders, and others requiring a powerful and accurately shooting weapon, combined with lightness and rapidity of action.

It is made specially to shoot the No. 5 '360 Rook Rifle Cartridge, but will shoot all '38 Cartridges.

At twelve yards these Revolvers will put every shot into a 3-inch circle.

R.I.C. No. 2, '320 (DOUBLE ACTION.)

Blue, 58/-
Nickel, 64/-

Weight, 12 oz.

These Drawings are full size, and the Revolvers are guaranteed to put all the Shots in a 3 inch circle at 12 yards.

Can, if desired, be made to shoot the '33 S. & W. instead of the above Cartridges, without extra charge.

Note that while the .45 Colt and .44 UMC were cancelled, the .44 Russian was not.

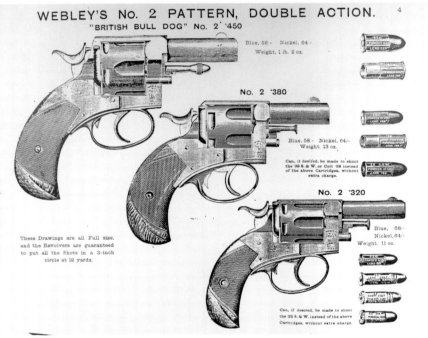

WEBLEY'S No. 2 PATTERN, DOUBLE ACTION.

"BRITISH BULL DOG" No. 2 '450

Blue, 58/- Nickel, 64/-

Weight, 1 lb. 2 oz.

No. 2 '380

Blue, 58/- Nickel, 64/-
Weight, 13 oz.

Can, if desired, be made to shoot the '38 S. & W. or Colt '38 instead of the above Cartridges, without extra charge.

No. 2 '320

Blue, 58/-
Nickel, 64/-

Weight, 11 oz.

These Drawings are all Full size, and the Revolvers are guaranteed to put all the Shots in a 3-inch circle at 12 yards.

Can, if desired, be made to shoot the '33 S. & W. instead of the above Cartridges, without extra charge.

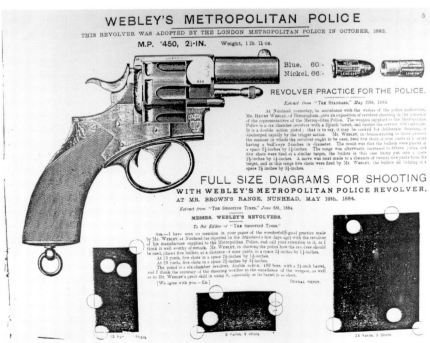

WEBLEY'S METROPOLITAN POLICE

THIS REVOLVER WAS ADOPTED BY THE LONDON METROPOLITAN POLICE IN OCTOBER, 1883.

M.P. '450, 2½-IN.   Weight, 1 lb. 11 oz.

Blue, 60/-
Nickel, 66/-

REVOLVER PRACTICE FOR THE POLICE.

Extract from "THE STANDARD," May 20th, 1884.

At Nunhead yesterday, in accordance with the wishes of the police authorities, Mr. HENRY WEBLEY, of Birmingham, gave an exposition of revolver shooting in the presence of representatives of the Metropolitan Police. The weapon supplied to the Metropolitan Police is a six-chamber revolver with a 2½-inch barrel, and carries the service '450 cartridge. It is a double action pistol; that is to say, it may be cocked for deliberate shooting, or discharged rapidly by the trigger action. Mr. WEBLEY, in demonstrating to those present the manner in which the revolver ought to be used, fired five shots at nine yards at a target having a bull's-eye 2-inches in diameter. The result was that the bullets were placed in a space 2½-inches by 1½-inches. The range was afterwards increased to fifteen yards, and five shots were fired at a similar target, the bullets in this case being put into a space 2½-inches by 1½-inches. A move was next made to a distance of twenty-five yards from the target, and at this range five shots were fired by Mr. WEBLEY, the bullets all lodging in a space 2½ inches by 3½-inches.

FULL SIZE DIAGRAMS FOR SHOOTING

WITH WEBLEY'S METROPOLITAN POLICE REVOLVER,
AT MR. BROWN'S RANGE, NUNHEAD, MAY 19th, 1884.

Extract from "THE SHOOTING TIMES," June 6th, 1884.

MESSRS. WEBLEY'S REVOLVERS.

To the Editor of "THE SHOOTING TIMES."

SIR,—I have seen no mention in your paper of the wonderfully good practice made by Mr. WEBLEY, at Nunhead (as reported in the *Standard* a few days ago) with the revolver of his manufacture supplied to the Metropolitan Police, and call your attention to it, as I think it well worthy of remark. Mr. WEBLEY, in showing the police how the revolver should be used, placed five bullets, at a distance of nine yards, in a space 2½-inches by 1½-inches. At 15 yards, five shots in a space 2½-inches by 3½-inches. At 25 yards, five shots in a space 2½-inches by 3½-inches.

The pistol is a six-chamber revolver, double action, '450 bore, with a 2½-inch barrel, and I think the accuracy of the shooting testifies to the excellence of the weapon, as well as to Mr. WEBLEY'S great skill in using it, especially as its barrel is so short.

[We agree with you.—ED.]

BENGAL SEPOY.

Previously Unknown Caliber Offerings

Besides demonstrating the delivery of non-standard calibers, a glance at the serial numbers in the April 11th 1910 "day book" entries from Richard Milner's collection confirms that few solid frame revolvers were being sold, and frames were being pulled out of existing stock.

On this page we see an invoice for Webley solid frame revolvers in very rare calibers. It is not known if any have survived ravages of time or periodic government round up and destruction that has made all Webley solid frame revolver models uncommon.

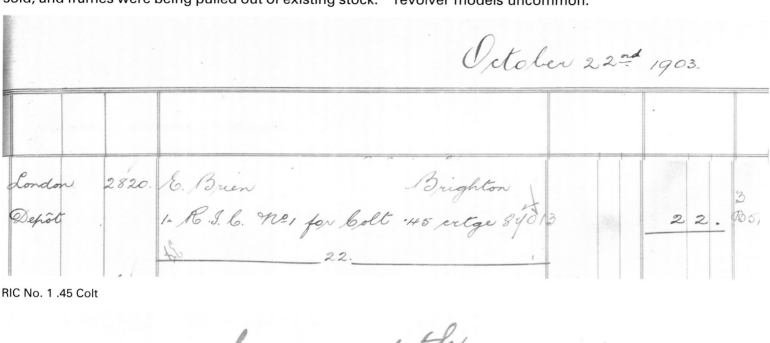

RIC No. 1 .45 Colt

RIC No 1 .44-40

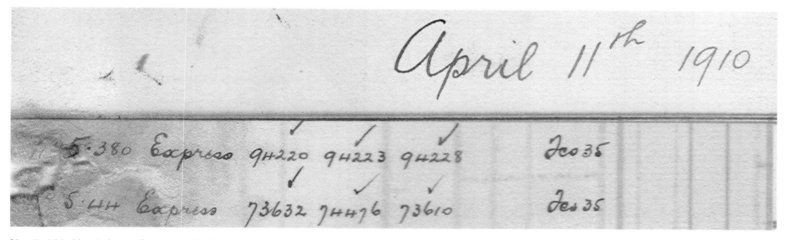

No. 5 .380, No. 5 Army Express .44 Russian

Relative Rarity of Solid Frame Webleys Known to Still Exist

Rarest 5 or Fewer Known	
RIC No. 1 New Model with S&F Patent and wood stock	1 known
RIC with swing out simultaneous ejection	1 known
RIC No. 1 in .44 Russian	1 known
RIC No. 2 in .44 Russian	1 known
No. 5 Express in .310	1 known
RIC/82 (w/model marked)	1 known
RIC/83 in .44 Russian	1 known
RIC No. 1 6 shot in .500 Webley	1 known
RIC No. 2 with elongated grip (Montenegrin)	1 known
RIC No. 1 made up as a short rifle with wood stock	1 known
No. 5 New Model Army Express with 12" barrel	1 known
No. 5 New Model Army Express Chaine Patent	2 known
RIC Model/83 in .45 ACP	1 known
No. 5 .360 Express with 7" barrel	1 known
RIC with bronze frame	1 known
RIC No. 2 with Tranter sear on trigger	1 known
Webley in .577 caliber	1 known
RIC No. 2 with thumb screw safety	2 known
RIC No. 1 with Tranter ejector	2 known
RIC No. 1 Chaine Patent	2 known
RIC No. 1 cut for or furnished with shoulder stock	2 known
MP with rebounding hammer	2 known
No. 5 .360 Express "clown" version	2 known
Sheath Trigger	2 known

Rare: 12 or Fewer Known	
RIC No. 1 5 shot in .500 Webley	5 known
RIC No. 5 Army Express with Abadie Patent	6 known
No. 5 New Model Army Express with swiveling ejector	5 known
RIC by Charles Pryse & Co.	7 known
RIC Model/82	8 known
RIC No. 3	10 known

Scarce: 30 or Fewer Known
RICs sold to any police agency other than Metropolitan Police
RIC with the Silver & Fletcher Patent

Webley Solid Frame Dates of Manufacture

This is an important question faced by the many collectors in those countries that limit firearms ownership depending on the date of manufacture of the frame (receiver, body). The authors agree that Webley bought no frames after 1893, despite assembling solid frame revolvers from old stocks into the twentieth century. We have provided reasons for reaching this conclusion throughout these two volumes, but the most salient point is that the Webley factory records as held by Richard Milner show no purchases of frames after 1893.

For those collectors wishing to know when, and to whom, their Webley or Wilkinson revolver was sold, Mr. Milner can provide that information for many of them at: http://www.armsresearch.co.uk/

Memo Relating to First RIC Purchase

Memo from Dublin Castle dated November 1867: "request of the Treasury to reserve a sum of £632 for purchase of revolvers for use by constabulary".

Memo from Dublin Castle dated February 1868: "requests the proper offices at Birmingham be instructed to have the 1000 pistols manufacturing by Messrs. Webley for the constabulary viewed as suggested by Inspector General Wood".

The original memos of this purchase (*courtesy of Richard Milner http://www.armsresearch.co.uk/*) are in a state that precludes them being reprinted.

M/2

-: May 21st 1912 :-

Messrs. Rice, Lewis & Son.,

Toronto.

May 21st 1912.

SB
35/39   D5598
B1270

37 R.I.C. revs .442 blue 3½" barrel no ring
in butt, wing brand.   24/- ea   44 8 0
marked T.P.F. Nos. 211, 291 & 426 to 460.
211/95664 291/95640 426/95665 427/95644
428/95663 429/95668 430/95639 431/95648
432/95647 433/95667 434/95662 435/95661
436/95641 437/95660 438/95666 439/95669
440/95643 441/?5645 442/95646 443/95649
444/95642 445/99281 446/99285 447/99287
448/99286 449/99289 450/99284 451/99288
452/99280 453/99282 455/99283 454/99295
456/99296 457/99298 458/99291 459/99293
460/99297.

10 R.I.C. revs .442 blue 2½" barrel, no ring
in butt, wing brand.   24/- ea   12 0 0
Marked T.P.F. Nos 70 to 79.
70/99274 71/99275 72/99279 73/99271
74/99272 75/99270 76/99277 77/99273
78/99276 79/99278.

1 Tin lined I.H.S.C. Case.   [W & S Ltd #160 Toronto c/No D5598]   9/6   9 6

Net weight   1-cwt 0-qrs 2-lbs.   56 17
Gross   "   1-cwt 1-qr 22-lbs.

Measurements 29½ - 23¾ - 11.

Per Messrs W. H. Pellow & Co.,

12, Lancelot Hey, Liverpool.

" The above articles have all been made in
England".

Appendix I

4762	Express	Plain	455
865	"	"	"
1234	"	"	"
1070	"	"	"
1007	"	"	"
5085	"	"	"
✓ 1010	"	"	"
4475	"	"	"
4536	"	"	"
4540	"	"	"
4754	"	"	"
4785	"	"	"
4580	"	Ammn. Cole Patn	45.
4390	"	"	"	"	"
✓ 4564	"	"	"	"	"
✓ 4566	"	"	"	"	"
4540	"	"	"	"	"
✓ 4589	"	"	"	"	"
1023	Express	Plain	455

Used with permission of Glasgow University

1912 Purchase of RICs by Toronto Police

M/2

-: May 21st 1912 :-

Messrs. Rice,Lewis & Son.,

Toronto.

May 21st 1912.

SB 35/39 B1270	D5598	37 R.I.C. revs .442 blue 3½" barrel no ring in butt,wing brand. 24/- ea		44	8	0

marked T.P.F. Nos.211,291 & 426 to 460.
211/95664 291/95640 426/95665 427/95644
428/95663 429/95668 430/95639 431/95648
432/95647 433/95667 434/95662 435/95661
436/95641 437/95660 438/95666 439/95669
440/95643 441/?5645 442/95646 443/95649
444/95642 445/99281 446/99285 447/99287
448/99286 449/99289 450/99284 451/99288
452/99280 453/99282 455/99283 454/99295
456/99296 457/99298 458/99291 459/99293
460/99297.

10 R.I.C. revs .442 blue 2½" barrel, no ring
in butt,wing brand.   24/- ea   12   0   0
Marked T.P.F. Nos 70 to 79.
70/99274 71/99275 72/99279 73/99271
74/99272 75/99270 76/99277 77/99273
78/99276 79/99278.

1 Tin lined I.H.S.C. Case.   [diamond: W&S Ltd #160 Toronto o/no D5598]   9/6   9   6

Net weight 1-cwt 0-qrs 2-lbs.   56 17
Gross " 1-cwt 1-qr 22-lbs.
Measurements 29½ - 23¾ - 11.
Per Messrs W. H. Pellow & Co.,
            12, lancelot Hey,Liverpool.
" The above articles have all been made in
England".

Appendix III

This short excerpt from the original Silver & Fletcher patent No. 16078 of 1884 served to settle a friendly difference of opinion between Joel Black and Richard Milner. Mr. Black always thought the automatic ejection aspect of the patent was silly. He assumed that a revolver fitted with one was intended to be fired with the loading gate open thus ejecting the cartridge with each shot. In the terribly frantic conditions of war, this would seem fraught with disaster. Mr. Milner opined that the revolver was meant to be fired with the loading gate closed. After firing all chambers he thought the loading gate would then be opened and the trigger pulled six more times to eject the empty brass. As it turns out both were correct. This

short excerpt from the original Silver & Fletcher patent No. 16078 of 1884 served to settle a friendly difference of opinion between Joel Black and Richard Milner. Mr. Black always thought the automatic ejection aspect of the patent was silly. He assumed that a revolver fitted with one was intended to be fired with the loading gate open thus ejecting the cartridge with each shot. In the terribly frantic conditions of war, this would seem fraught with disaster. Mr. Milner opined that the revolver was meant to be fired with the loading gate closed. After firing all chambers he thought the loading gate would then be opened and the trigger pulled six more times to eject the empty brass. As it turns out both were correct.

> 25 successive firing of a full cartridge by opening the gate M or the empty cartridge cases may be retained within the chamber by closing the gate at the will of the person using the arm, this is with reference to the pistol shown in Figure 1 or if the gate be closed all the cartridges can be fired in succession and then the gate can be opened and all the empty cases extracted in succession.

A.D. 1884. Dec. 6. Nº 16,078.
SILVER & FLETCHER'S Complete Specification.

(1 SHEET)

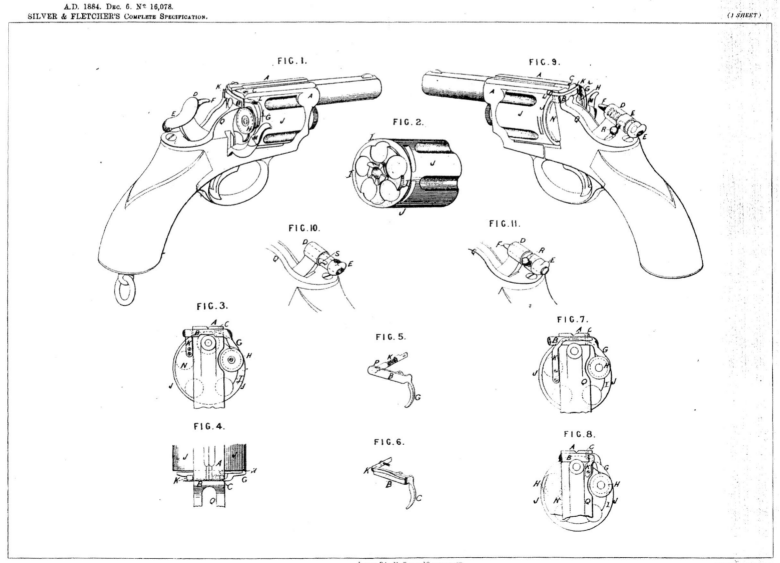

London...Printed by Eyre and Spottiswoode.
Printers to the Queen's most Excellent Majesty. 1885.

Malby & Sons, Photo-Litho.

Appendix IV
Military Purchases of Solid Frame Webleys

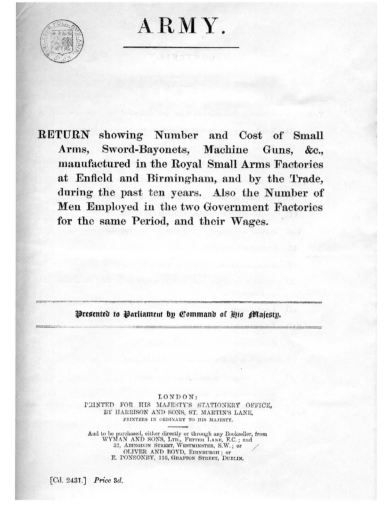

Courtesy of Alan David

ARMY.

RETURN showing Number and Cost of Small Arms, Sword-Bayonets, Machine Guns, &c., manufactured in the Royal Small Arms Factories at Enfield and Birmingham, and by the Trade, during the past ten years. Also the Number of Men Employed in the two Government Factories for the same Period, and their Wages.

Presented to Parliament by Command of His Majesty.

LONDON:
PRINTED FOR HIS MAJESTY'S STATIONERY OFFICE,
BY HARRISON AND SONS, ST. MARTIN'S LANE,
PRINTERS IN ORDINARY TO HIS MAJESTY.

And to be purchased, either directly or through any Bookseller, from
WYMAN AND SONS, LTD., FETTER LANE, E.C.; and
32, ABINGDON STREET, WESTMINSTER, S.W.; or
OLIVER AND BOYD, EDINBURGH; or
E. PONSONBY, 116, GRAFTON STREET, DUBLIN.

[Cd. 2431.] *Price 3d.*

TABLE XVIII.

STATEMENT showing the Numbers of Pistols *ordered* from the Trade during the years 1886 to 1904 (with average prices).
(There were no orders for Pistols to the Trade from 1880–85 inclusive.)

Description	1886–87. No.	Price each.	1887–88. No.	Price each.	1888–89. No.	Price each.	1889–90. No.	Price each.	1890–91. No.	Price each.	1891–92. No.	Price each.	1892–93. No.	Price each.
		s. d.		s. d.		s. d.		s. d.		s. d.		s. d.		s. d.
Pistols:— R.I.C. Revolver	—	—	—	—	100	35 0	100	35 0	312	35 0	160	35 0	249	35 0
Webley	—	—	10,000 Mk. I	61 0	—	—	11,385 Mk. I	58 6	—	—	1,594 Mk. I	58 6	3,495 Mk. I	58 6

Description	1893–94. No.	Price each.	1894–95. No.	Price each.	1895–96. No.	Price each.	1896–97. No.	Price each.	1897–98. No.	Price each.	1898–99. No.	Price each.	1899–1900. No.	Price each.
		s. d.		s. d.		s. d.		s. d.		s. d.		s. d.		s. d.
Pistols:— R.I.C. Revolver	100	35 0	24	35 0	—	—	—	—	14	35 0	—	—	510	58 6
Webley	5,000 Mk. I	57 0	5,207 Mk. I	57 0	5,000 Mk. II	60 0	15,621 Mk. II	56 0	2,190 Mk. II / 1,230 Mk. III	56 0 / 58 6	2,101 Mk. III	58 6	510 Mk. III, 13,374 Mk. IV	61 0

Description	1900–01. No.	Price each.	1901–02. No.	Price each.	1902–03. No.	Price each.	1903–04. No.	Price each.	1904–05. No.	Price each.
		s. d.		s. d.		s. d.		s. d.		s. d.
Pistols:— R.I.C. Revolver	—	—	—	—	—	—	—	—	—	—
Webley	9,227 Mk. IV	61 0	5,395 Mk. IV	61 0	8,760 Mk. IV	61 0	—	—	—	—

WAR OFFICE,
1st April, 1905.

By Command of the Army Council,

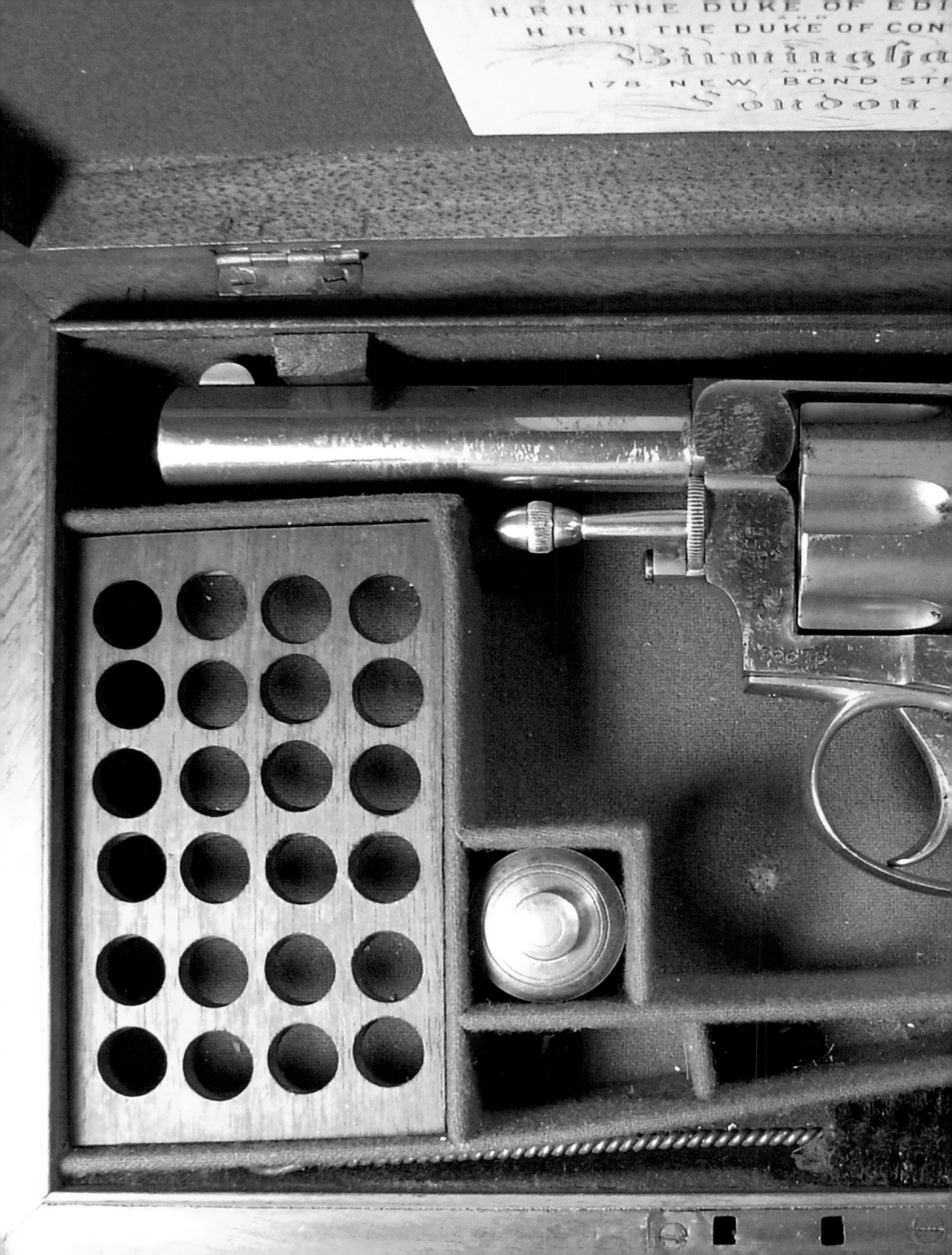
H R H THE DUKE OF
H R H THE DUKE OF
178 NEW BOND
London.